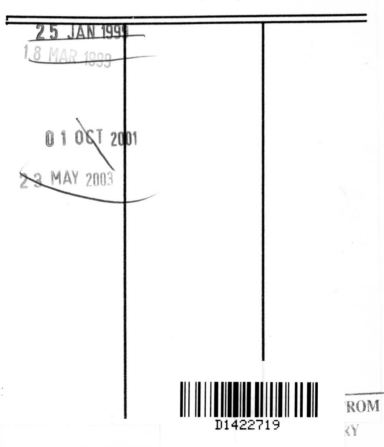

Freedom and the English Revolution

Essays in history and literature

Freedom and the English Revolution

Essays in history and literature

edited by

R. C. RICHARDSON *and* G. M. RIDDEN

King Alfred's College, Winchester

MANCHESTER UNIVERSITY PRESS

Published by Manchester University Press
Oxford Road, Manchester M13 9PL, UK
Wolfeboro, NH 03894-2069, USA

British Library cataloguing in publication data
Freedom and the English revolution:
  essays in history and literature.
  1. Great Britain – Politics and
  government – 1642–1660
  I. Richardson, R.C.   II. Ridden,
  Geoffrey M.
  941.06'2   DA405

Library of congress cataloging in publication data applied for

ISBN 0–7190–1880–3 *cased*

Photoset in Linotron Ehrhardt by
Northern Phototypesetting Co., Bolton
Printed and bound in Great Britain by
Biddles Ltd, Guildford and King's Lynn

Contents

Editors' preface

Collections of essays by a group of different authors, even when concerned with a specific period, are often extremely diverse in approach, highly miscellaneous in character, and only loosely related to each other. This volume, we hope, has greater cohesion and unity.

The idea for the book stems from an interdisciplinary conference on *Freedom and the English Revolution* held at King Alfred's College, Winchester, in the summer of 1984. Four of the essays printed here (those by Christopher Hill, Roger Howell, Warren Chernaik, and Thomas Corns) originated as lectures given on that occasion. The two remaining essays – by Keith Lindley and William Lamont – were subsequently commissioned for the resultant book. We are grateful to all these scholars for agreeing to participate in this venture and for their care and efficiency in producing their contributions. All the essayists address themselves in different ways to the concept of freedom and its implications in the 1640s and, to a lesser extent, in the 1650s, and offer revaluations and new research. Major political and literary figures like Cromwell, Milton and Marvell, are reconsidered here as well as popular freedom movements such as the Levellers and Diggers. The book, therefore, begins at 'the top' as it were and ends with 'history from below'. Together the essays not merely bear witness to the centrality of the idea of freedom both in the turbulent history of the English Revolution itself and in its subsequent interpretation, but underline the range and diversity of its expression. They also warn us to be cautious about accepting contemporary rhetoric and propaganda at face value, urge us to recognise myths, to unscramble terminological confusions, and to be sensitive to form, language and hidden meanings.

July 1985

Introduction

The news of these times are so excellent that he deserves not to breathe this British air who prayeth not God heartily for them . . .For ever be this Parliament renowned for so great achievements, for we dream now of nothing more than a golden age . . . It is the nature of freedom, or the freedom of our own nature, that so pleaseth.[1]

Such was the euphoria of John Bampfield, a puritan squire from Devon, as he contemplated the early triumphs of the Long Parliament in January 1641. A play by Richard Brome, opportunely staged at this same moment when the *ancien régime* in England was being torn down, caught exactly the same spirit of excitement. In what has recently been described as 'the most committed play of the decade', the playwright extolled the 'absolute freedom, such as the very beggars have . . . Liberty. The birds of the air can take no more'. What could one feel but envy, Brome continued, for

> The only Freemen of a commonwealth
> Free above Scot-free; that observe no law,
> Obey no governor, use no religion
> But what they draw from their own ancient custom
> Or constitute themselves, yet are no rebels.[2]

Milton, too, sharing this exhilarating optimism, fervently hoped that the downfall of episcopacy was imminent, and – like Bampfield – had great expectations of the reformation that now seemed possible.[3]

1640–41 was, undoubtedly, a remarkable year that no-one, living through it, would be likely to forget. In the course of it, Prynne, Bastwick and Burton – victims of earlier 'tyranny' – were triumphantly released. The Earl of Strafford, the hated exponent of that tyranny, was impeached, tried, and executed for his crimes. Archbishop Laud – no less hated, and not only by his puritan adversaries – was also impeached and put in prison to await a similar fate. The machinery of absolutism, the detested courts of Star Chamber and High Commission, was abolished. Parliament's presence was guaranteed by the Triennial Act and, more immediately important, the act against dissolution without its own consent. The Grand Remonstrance pressed forward against the isolated and uncomprehending King.[4]

Freedom remained a keynote in the later crises of the 1640s, and indeed in the 1650s, though changing contexts brought changing emphasis and meanings. It was certainly central to the *Agreement of the People*, first issued by the Levellers in November 1647.

> An Agreement of the People, for a firm
> and present Peace, upon grounds of Common-Right
>
> Having by our late labours and hazards made it appear to the world at how high a rate we value our just freedom, and God having so far owned our cause as to deliver the Enemies thereof into our hands: We do now hold ourselves bound in mutual duty to each other to take the best care we can for the future, to avoid both the danger of returning into a slavish condition and the chargeable remedy of another war . . .

It was axiomatic also to the stances taken by Rainborough, Wildman, Sexby and others in the Putney Debates of 1647, and by Winstanley and the Diggers in their attempts at agrarian community building.

> All men have stood for freedom [Winstanley insisted in August 1649 in the aftermath of the King's execution] plenty of petitions and promises thereupon have been made for freedom; and now the common enemy is gone, you are all like men in a mist, seeking for freedom and know not where nor what it is: and those of the richer sort of you that see it are ashamed and afraid to own it, because it comes clothed in a clownish garment . . . For freedom is the man that will turn the world upside down, therefore no wonder he hath enemies.
>
> . . . No true freedom [he went on] can be established for England's peace, or prove you faithful in covenant, but such a one as hath respect to the poor as well as the rich; for if thou consent to freedom to the rich in the City and givest freedom to the freeholders in the country, and to priests and lawyers and lords of manors and impropriators, and yet allowest the poor no freedom, thou art then a declared hypocrite, and all thy prayers, fasts and thanksgivings are and will be proved an abomination to the Lord, and freedom himself will be the poor man's portion when thou shalt lie groaning in bondage.[5]

The world could be, and should be, turned upside down! Nothing ought to hinder the egalitarian social resolution towards which events seemed to be inevitably moving.

> For now['s] the Father's 'pointed time
>   which he did fore-intend
> To set up Freedom, and pull down
>   the man which did offend;
>
> This time, I say, it is now come
>   in which the Lord will make
> All tyrants servants to the Son
>   and he the power will take.

Thus proclaimed some of the verses from a Digger 'hymn' of 1650.[6]

Milton, still an advocate of freedom but far less sure by this point that the 'people' deserved it, wrote more cautiously, and less hopefully. '... None can love freedom heartily but good men: the rest love not freedom but licence; which never hath more scope or more indulgence than under tyrants ...'.[7] Abraham Cowley, Milton's contemporary, thought that social as well as moral considerations inclined men to ideas of liberty.

> Freedom with virtue takes her seat
> Her proper place, her only Scene,
> Is in the Golden Mean,
> She lives not with the Poor nor with the Great.

Thomas Hobbes, profoundly pessimistic in his view of human nature, deplored the misguided puritan and parliamentarian search for liberty, the outbursts of ambition, and the struggle for sovereignty. So did Robert Filmer.[8]

These are examples only. There is no doubt that the evidence of the 1640s expressing, justifying and commenting on notions of political, religious, intellectual and social freedom is impressively large. The breakdown of monarchical and ecclesiastical government at the outset of the decade removed the machinery through which censorship had been exercised. For a time at any rate, before the Parliamentarians erected their own censorship and clamped down on heresy under the Blasphemy Act of 1650, writers were free to speak openly and without fear of retribution; new kinds of radical authors could get into print and could reach a wider audience than ever before. The number of new publications suddenly shot up; 9000 per cent more pamphlets were published in 1642 (giving a grand total of 1966) than in 1640.[9] 'Newspapers' made their first effective appearance in England in the course of the Civil War. The pulpit, too, joined the press in extending its role once the restraining hand of the church courts was removed. Fast sermons were preached before Parliament. During the fighting army chaplains stiffened the resolve of the troops and urged them on to yet more glorious deeds. Privately and in public, orally and in print, politics and religion were hotly debated. 'Teeming freedom' gushed out everywhere, fortified by, and expressed in language reminiscent of, the Bible. 'Puritan Revolution', indeed, in every conceivable sense once seemed the most accurate description of England's mid-century high-principled and decisive re-orientation.

Luxuriating in his nineteenth-century vantage point, Macaulay believed there was no question that 'the Puritans espoused the cause of civil liberty mainly because it was the cause of religion'. They were, perhaps, 'the most remarkable body of men which the world has ever produced'. Faced with the obstinate, ambitious, untrustworthy, and tyrannical Charles I what was left to the Puritans in the end but to defeat him?

For more than ten years the people had seen the rights which were theirs by a double claim, by immemorial inheritance and by recent purchase, infringed by the perfidious king who had recognised them. At length circumstances compelled Charles to summon another parliament: another chance was given to our fathers: were they to throw it away as they had thrown away the former? Were they again to be cozened by *le Roi le veut*? Were they again to advance their money on pledges which had been forfeited over and over again? Were they to lay a second Petition of Right at the foot of the throne, to grant another lavish aid in exchange for another unmeaning ceremony, and then to take their departure, till, after ten years more of fraud and oppression, their prince should again require a supply, and again repay it with a perjury? They were compelled to choose whether they would trust a tyrant or conquer him. We think that they chose wisely and nobly.[10]

S. R. Gardiner, though far more scientific in his historical methods and much less stridently Whig in his approach than Macaulay, fundamentally agreed with these sentiments. Writing later in the nineteenth century it was no less clear to him than it had been to Macaulay that:

The interest of [English] history in the seventeenth century lies in the efforts made to secure a double object – the control of the nation over its own destinies and the liberty of the public expression of thought, without which parliamentary government is only a refined form of tyranny.

England came through in Gardiner's pages as an advanced, progressive nation in whose 'imperishable vitality . . . lay the fundamental laws' of the land. Puritanism and liberty, for Gardiner, went inseparably together.

Above all, it was Puritanism which gave to those whose energies were most self-centred the power which always follows upon submission to law. Puritanism not only formed the strength of the opposition to Charles, but the strength of England itself. Parliamentary liberties, and even parliamentary control, were worth contending for.[11]

The concept of freedom, indeed, was sacred to the historians of this era. Lord Acton projected a full-scale treatment of the subject from ancient to modern times. G. M. Trevelyan, too, whatever his topic – whether it was Wyclif and the late medieval church, or the Italian *Risorgimento* of the nineteenth century, or England under the Stuarts – saw the struggle for liberty as the main issue.

In England [unlike France at the end of the eighteenth century] the revolutionary passions were stirred by no class in its own material interest. Our patriots were prosperous men, enamoured of liberty, or of religion, or of loyalty, each for her own sake, not as the handmaid of class greed. This was the secret of the moral splendour of our Great Rebellion and our Civil War . . .
The puritan patriots, [he went on] secured for ever that monarchy in England should not be a despotism. Our island had been cut free from the political history of the continent. No King should ever triumph here by the sword. When royalty was restored, it was restored by the restoration of Parliament. And because under a parliamentary rule, however intolerant it may be for a while, every religious and political party has hope of asserting sooner or later its place in the national life, there never has been that exodus of freemen from England, that abandonment of the hope of liberty, which must have followed from the armed victory of Charles I.[12]

The seventeenth-century past seemed, undeniably, to have conferred benefits on the present, and offered instructive guidelines for coping with later emergencies that called liberty into question. Such was the conviction which lay behind J. A. R. Marriott's *The Crisis of English Liberty*, which appeared in 1930 at a time when the new Leviathan of state power was increasing its claims over the subject.[13] In a similar kind of way, A. S. P. Woodhouse's *Puritanism and Liberty*, first published in 1938, combined present purposes with scholarly intentions. As well as being an edition of the Putney Debates – those stirring and epoch-making exchanges about first principles between all classes of men – the text was simultaneously a gift 'to all those who wish to be able to give a reason for their democratic faith'. The hope was that the book 'could be read so as to stop the mouths and pens of those who produce facile refutations of the fundamental ideas of democracy. These ideas, liberty, equality and fraternity, if divorced from the religious context in which they belong, become cheap and shallow'.[14] More recently still the American William Haller, in his *Liberty and Reformation in the Puritan Revolution* (New

York, 1955), presented revolutionary Puritanism as 'such a cyclonic shattering storm of the spirit as that by which we have been beset in our own time'.[15]

'Freedom' and 'the English Revolution' thus seemed to become inextricably joined, and their connection, largely undisputed though variously explained, has become one of the commonplaces of historical discourse. But the historian's training and instinct should teach him to beware of orthodoxies, however alluring. This volume, therefore, takes the opportunity to re-assess, and not simply illustrate, the assumed linkages between freedom and the English Revolution. It asks at various points how extensive the evidence is and whether it always means what it seems to be saying? Are there terminological difficulties which need to be confronted and awkward paradoxes to be explained? Was there in fact a unifying and singular concept of freedom in these years, or, if to think in terms of plurals seems more realistic, how central were different and perhaps competing ideas of freedom to the participants in the events of the 1640s and to the literary figures of the time? How can we properly gauge the effects of the removal of censorship? How much abstract theorising about freedom took place at this time? Was Milton an original political thinker? Was Cromwell capable of anything more than pragmatism?[16] Was Cromwell a protagonist of freedom or its great adversary and betrayer?[17] How did literature contribute to and not simply reflect what was happening? What were the consequences for writers, literary genres, and literary style of the revolutionary situation? What were the implications of the upheavals for author–reader relations? Were there changing expectations on both sides?[18] What was the significance of individuals as contrasting as Prynne, Lilburne and Winstanley? What happened in the 1650s? With the King and episcopacy safely removed, with the Levellers and Diggers defeated, with a new censorship in force, and with a centralised, heavy-handed military régime in being, did the debate on freedom suffer an enforced eclipse? Once questions begin they naturally multiply.

The Whig interpretation of this period, it goes without saying, is no longer accepted. We no longer share its assumptions and priorities, and find it deficient in the kind of questions we now deem important. Moreover, we can now see that Whig historians over-simplified their task by restricting their vision; theirs was predominantly constitutional history with Parliament in a hallowed central position. For them, the House of Commons was truly the representative of the people. Freedom and civil liberty were equated. Documents like the Petition of Right and the Grand Remonstrance were accepted at face value as literal truth not as political propaganda, and their contents and principles incorporated into their historical interpretations.

For its most recent historian, the Petition of Right itself was less important than the public response which it provoked.[19] Politics, (in the full sense), he and others now recognise, involved more than Parliament, and Parliament's self-estimate of its significance and role ought not to be unquestioningly accepted. More generally, historians would now agree that the concept of freedom in the 1640s was not unanimously understood, nor was its definition fixed and finite. Neither was it confined to politics or religion. Expressions of economic, social, and sexual freedom now rightly claim the historian's attention in a way which they have never done before. Popular politics, too – as Keith Lindley's chapter on London makes clear – is now accepted as worthy of study not only as a subject in its own right but also for the light which it throws on the gentry's actions.[20] Gerrard Winstanley – unmentioned in Macaulay's *History of England* – appropriately in this volume receives a whole chapter to himself.[21]

For Winstanley, freedom, to be real, had to be total. It is significant, as Christopher Hill reminds us, that Winstanley always thought in terms of *freedom* whereas orthox Parliamentarians were more likely to speak of *liberty* or *liberties*. There was, indeed, a real difference – and not just of semantics – which Whig historians failed to recognise. For Parliamentarians, and this came through unmistakably in the Petition of Right, liberty and property went together. For Winstanley, on the other hand, private property was a sin, an obstacle to, and contradiction of, freedom; as such it ought to be abolished. For Parliamentarians, liberties were tangible and specific; for Winstanley freedom was unrestricted and general. Its enlarged meaning was part of the revolutionary experience.[22] A. F. Pollard long ago insisted on this vital terminological distinction.

Nothing has proved more elusive [he claimed] than liberty, and its endless pursuit has filled the pages of English history . . . To say that a man has achieved liberty is an inaccurate way of stating that some men have achieved some liberty. The problem of liberty, like that of property, is one of distribution, and cannot be divorced from that of equality. [A medieval liberty, he went on, was] . . . almost always a legal monopoly . . . A liberty was in no sense a common right or a popular conception . . . Medieval liberties were large but their recipients were few . . . It was the Tudor despots who emancipated England from its medieval liberties.[23]

With this in mind it becomes easier to understand the paradox that *both* Charles I and the Long Parliament believed that they were defending liberty; both, as Pollard saw, were irresponsibly self-centred. There ceased to be a meeting point between them. Charles I was tried as an enemy to the public interest and to the liberties of his subjects; he died in the firm belief that he was defending the constitution and all it stood for, and that if he, as King, could find no justice, there was no hope that his subjects could expect it. For Clement Walker, as for others, it had become a real question 'whether our laws, liberties, and properties are not now as liable to an invasion from the Legislative power as formerly from the Prerogative. '[For now Parliament's] little finger is heavier than the loins of the King'.[24]

Other paradoxes, too, emerge once the ramifications of 'freedom' in this period are explored. Four further examples must suffice here, three of them historical and the fourth specifically literary: (1) the use made of Magna Carta; (2) the nature of Puritanism; (3) the principles and programme of the Levellers; (4) Free debate: writers and their audience.

(1) *Magna Carta*

It has long been recognised that the 'myth' of Magna Carta was more influential – because more elastic – than its original reality.[25] Parliamentarians appealed to Magna Carta in 1628 and later to justify themselves, to claim history as an ally, and to provide a yardstick against which the erring Charles I could be measured. Coke's influential *Commentaries* on the Charter were strategically published in 1642. Yet later in the 1640s Parliament itself could be accurately accused of contravening many of the Charter's clauses. And Oliver Cromwell, in a well-known episode in 1655, told the irate judges that 'their *Magna Farta* should not control his actions which he knew were for the safety of the commonwealth'.[26] Archbishop Laud was accused at his trial in 1645 of subverting the Charter and conspiring against the law of the land. Yet, such was its flexibility, that it was just as easy to use it in his defence. A defender of Laud could rightly claim that, Magna Carta notwithstanding, the church's freedom had been violated, and the Archbishop himself imprisoned without charge and unlawfully deprived of his lands, jurisdiction and rights.[27]

The Levellers were less than unanimous about the values and significance of Magna Carta. To Lilburne – Freeborn John – it guaranteed 'the Englishman's legal birthright and inheritance'. It was, said another

Leveller sympathiser (probably Henry Marten) 'that brazen wall and impregnable Bulwark that defends the common liberty of England'. Richard Overton, another of the Leveller group, graphically described how he and Magna Carta were forcibly separated on his unhappy journey to Newgate Prison.

I clapped it in my arms [he moaned] and I laid myself upon my belly, but by force they violently turned me upon my back, then Briscoe smote me with his fist to make me let go my hold, whereupon as loud as I could, I cried out murder, murder, murder! And thus, by an assault they got the great Charter of *England's Liberties and Freedoms* from me, which I laboured ever to the utmost of power in me to preserve and defend, and ever to the death shall maintain.

William Walwyn, however, took a very different view. He dismissed the Charter as 'that mess of pottage', a deceitful document, unjustly venerated, which upheld the privileges of the oppressors rather than the freedom of the people. For Walwyn, as for the Diggers, the natural rights of man were more important than anything granted by a mere legal document which had half-heartedly attempted to mitigate the Norman Yoke. The law itself – Magna Carta included – stank of injustice and demanded fundamental reform. God and Nature, not law and history, were the fount of freedom.[28]

(2) *Puritanism*

Puritanism, too, was full of paradoxes and was more ambiguous in its connections with freedom than Macaulay and Gardiner recognised. Warren Chernaik and William Lamont do well to remind us of some of these things in their respective chapters.[29] Christian liberty, as Dr Chernaik shows, was as much restrictive as liberating in its applications; submission to God's will was the necessary precondition, and the unregenerate were denied the benefits. Professor Lamont, too, reminds us that a concern for discipline, not unrestrained liberty, was the hallmark of the mid-1640s, just as earlier Prynne had castigated the Laudians for laxity rather than extolled the virtues of the brave new world of puritan freedom. For Independents, the stress on congregational organisation facilitated closer moral and doctrinal surveillance rather than encouraged unrestricted religious experimentation. Religious toleration was seen not as a glorious ideal to be striven for but was an expression of expediency, a compromise to be lived with.[30] Freedom, Lamont insists, was neither the chief goal nor the main source of inspiration of revolutionary Puritanism; it was a by-product.

R. H. Tawney long ago warned historians about the dangers of oversimplifying Puritanism and of seeing in it only one shared tendency rather than many that were in latent tension or open conflict. In his classic study of *Religion and the Rise of Capitalism* he declared (in characteristic resounding prose),

There was in Puritanism an element which was conservative and traditionalist, and an element which was revolutionary; a collectivism which grasped at an iron discipline, and an individualism which spurned the savourless mess of human ordinances; a sober prudence which would garner the fruits of this world, and a divine recklessness which would make all things new. For long nourished together, their discords concealed, in the furnace of the Civil War they fell apart, and Presbyterian and Independent, aristocrat and Leveller, politician and merchant and utopian, gazed with bewildered eyes on the strange monsters with whom they had walked as friends . . .

"The triumph of Puritanism", it has been said, "swept away all traces of any restriction or guidance in the employment of money". That it swept away the restrictions imposed by the existing machinery is true; neither ecclesiastical courts, nor High Commission, nor Star Chamber, could function after 1640. But if it broke the discipline of the Church of Laud and the State of Strafford, it did so but as a step towards erecting a more rigorous discipline of its own. It would have been scandalised by economic individualism, as much as by religious tolerance, and the broad outlines of its scheme of organisation favoured unrestricted liberty in matters of business as little as in the things of the spirit.[31]

Nearly sixty years of subsequent research on Puritanism and the growing recognition of its complexities have increased rather than reduced the need for caution about all aspects of its history, including its links with freedom.[32]

(3) *The Levellers*

Mention has already been made of one of the paradoxes surrounding the Levellers, that they were inconsistent and disagreed about whether their claims for freedom rested on an appeal to history or to natural rights.[33] *The Agreement of the People* went through three successive versions, each more cautious than the last. No wonder, then, that historians, too, have disagreed about the Levellers and their place in the growth of democracy. Inflated claims were made for their progressive ideas by writers as different as Eduard Bernstein and D. M. Wolfe.[34] They have been variously heralded as the founding fathers of English trade unionism, of Chartism and of American republicanism. Their power and influence have been exaggerated by paying too little attention to the temporary conjunction of favourable circumstances that made these possible. There has been disagreement also about the Levellers' religion and its contribution to their politics. Here, too, the Levellers themselves were less than consistent and united.

There seems much to be said, however, for the case recently advanced by Brian Manning that for the Levellers political liberty was the overriding aim, with religion as the cornerstone of the ideology which equipped them to struggle for it. In a paradoxical way, Levellers – as both Manning and Hill agree – were 'Arminians of the left'; exponents of an essentially practical Christianity expressing social concern and social action. 'The great end wherefore God sent man into the world', declared John Lilburne, 'was that he should do good in his generation, and thereby glorify God in his generation'.

And thus in every age sometimes upon a religious, and sometimes upon a civil account, and very often upon both in one and the same persons: the most faithful servants of Christ in every country where they lived [have been] ever the greatest enemies to tyranny and oppression, and the most zealous maintainers of the known laws and liberties of their country.[35]

This brand of Arminianism, it should be noted, enabled Levellers to harmonise what would otherwise have been a conflict between their religious thought – resting on the notion of God's grace – and their secular thought – which stressed the universal natural rights of man. Grace that was freely available, however, blended with natural rights. The conflict was resolved and left the Levellers free to attack political and social oppression and the disease of poverty which these evils had produced or countenanced.

This did not mean, however, as C. B. Macpherson was at pains to point out, that the Levellers believed in complete freedom and complete equality.[36] Leveller democracy was a democracy of predominantly urban property-owners; the property-less – Rainborough's protestations at Putney notwithstanding – were excluded from the franchise. The Levellers held back from daring schemes of property confiscation and re-distribution. Their political programme offered nothing to women. Moreover, Levellers recognised that in the public interest individual freedom would need to be restricted by the civil power. Government was necessary and might, in certain circumstances, have to enforce obedience from its subjects. Even religious freedom would ultimately have to submit to natural law if it proved socially harmful.[37] For the Levellers, as for Milton, there was a recognisable dividing line between liberty and licence. Cromwell and the army leaders, therefore, may have been unduly alarmed about the anarchical tendencies of the Levellers.

There were distinct limits to their social revolutionary creed. That being so, the Diggers necessarily took great pains to differentiate themselves from their more cautious and conservative brethren and pointedly described themselves as *true* Levellers.

(4) *Free debate: writers and their audience*

Paradoxes of other kinds concerning freedom are found when we turn to the relations between authors and readers in this period. When Milton wrote near the beginning of *Paradise Lost,* Book VII, of the problem of finding a fit audience, he exposed a complex issue which might not have existed for the serious writer before 1640.

> still govern thou my song, Urania, and fit audience find, though few.
> But drive far off the barbarous dissonance
> Of Bacchus and his revellers, the race
> Of that wild rout that tore the Thracian bard
> In Rhodope, where woods and rocks had ears
> To rapture, till the savage clamour drowned
> Both harp and voice; nor could the Muse defend
> Her son.

(30–8)

In acknowledging the problem of a limited serious readership, and the possibility that even the greatest writer risked misinterpretation by the rude multitude, Milton was following established precedents and, in part, alluding to his own earlier description of the fate of Orpheus in 'Lycidas':

> When by the rout that made the hideous roar,
> His gory visage down the stream was sent,
> Down the swift Hebrus to the Lesbian shore.

(61–3)

On the other hand, in the years between 1637 and 1667 Milton had become increasingly aware of, and sensitive to, hostile reaction, 'barbarous noise', from various quarters, and his strategies for dealing with his audience and anticipating likely criticisms are a test-case for the general issue of self-presentation which many writers encountered.

Milton's first three prose tracts appeared anonymously, although there can be no question of an attempt to evade the responsibilities of authorship. His identity was evident enough to draw the personal abuse of his opponents, and thus to mould the strategy of his succeeding tracts. The autobiographical descriptions in *Reason of Church Government* and

An Apology refuted particular attacks by his opponents, but they are testimony also to the fact that a classic choice was now under question. It was no longer universally accepted that the retirement of a poet was of equal status with the engagement of the man of action; it could have the appearance of a life of indolence and self-indulgence.

By the time he published the first tract to bear his name, *Reason of Church Government*, Milton had learned that free debate was unlikely to take place at a uniformly elevated level. It was as likely to involve stylistic objections, personal abuse, and scholastic pedantry as the real engagement with fundamental issues. In *Animadversions* Milton had sought to defend himself from the charge of stylistic scurrility by appealing to 'grave Authors' who sanctioned the propriety of laughter, thus involving himself in that long-running debate best known to his contemporaries from Sidney's *Apology For Poetry* and to ours from Umberto Eco's *The Name of the Rose*. Such disputes were hardly at the centre of the turmoils of the early 1640s, yet their resurrection became part of the strategy to prevent the free play of ideas and to divert a potential audience from the mainstream of controversy into some less troubled backwater.

The reaction to Milton's divorce tracts, and its effect on Milton's reputation, is sufficiently well-charted to need little further comment: the misfortune of being associated with libertines was hardly one which a man of property, associate of Wotton, and a recipient of the patronage of the Countess of Derby and the Earl of Bridgewater, might expect.[38] His response is evident in the arguments of the later divorce tracts which attempted a mutual reinforcement through the assemblage of biblical precedents; it may also be a factor, as Thomas Corns has suggested, in the shaping of *Poems 1645*; it is certainly plain in the title-pages and prefaces to those tracts written between the first edition of *The Doctrine and Discipline* in 1643 and *Tenure* in 1649.

The title-page of the second edition of *The Doctrine and Discipline* acknowledged its author 'J.M.', modified its lengthy title, added an extra biblical quotation, and, perhaps most significantly, addressed a very explicit audience 'To the Parliament of England with the Assembly'.[39] The tract itself was preceded in this second edition by a letter to Parliament, as in *Martin Bucer*, *Tetrachordon*, and *Tenure*. *Areopagitica* has no prefatory letter, and needs none, since the entire pamphlet is cast in the form of an address to Parliament. Thus, all but two of the pamphlets written by Milton in this period are specifically addressed to Parliament and acknowledge his authorship. Those two,

Of Education and *Colasterion*, target their intended audiences even more precisely, each ostensibly addressed to a single individual.

By the time that Milton first raised the question of a limited readership, therefore, in the Preface to *Eikonoklastes*, he had already taken steps to safeguard the readership of his own tracts.

> though it be an irksom labour to write with industrie and judicious paines that which neither waigh'd, nor well read, shall be judg'd without industry or the paines of well judging, by faction and the easy literature of custom and opinion, it shall be ventur'd yet, and the truth not smother'd, but sent abroad . . . to finde out her own readers; few perhaps, but those few, such of value and substantial worth, as truth and wisdom, not respecting numbers and bigg names, have bin ever wont in all ages to be contented with.[40]

In setting out to write a tract which was, unusually for him, not targetted at a specific audience, Milton was well aware that the less readerly among his public would not, in all likelihood, make the effort to grapple with his argument – that, after all, was his experience in writing on divorce – and so he reserved for himself that very particular freedom of expressing a truth which he knew to be held only by a minority.

These four examples or case studies all point to a similar conclusion, that the revisionism which has resulted from the abandonment of the Whig interpretation of the English Revolution has not removed freedom from the picture but has transformed our understanding of it. Whether we are dealing with the Levellers and Diggers or with the questions surrounding freedom of debate, we are being taken in the same general direction. Historians no longer accept at face value the rhetoric, calculated propaganda, or self-delusions of the parliamentarian gentry. They are increasingly unable to see a logical, inexorably linear sequence in the confused and competing tendencies of the 1640s. Macaulay's interpretation of that period, we now recognise, revealed as much, if not more, about the nineteenth than about the seventeenth century. Historians today are more interested in why and how Parliamentarians appealed to Magna Carta than in the mere fact that this is what they did. They are much more interested than Whig historians were in the wider environment of parliamentary politics and in popular initiatives and responses. Like seventeenth-century politics itself, freedom cannot be understood only within the narrow arena of Westminster.

Historians, too, have now learned to insist that Puritanism was a spectrum rather than a monolith, with subtleties, complexities, structural changes, and inconsistencies which affected its links with seventeenth-century perceptions of freedom. It is no longer taken as self-evident that Puritanism and liberty went hand in hand – at least in the way that used to be supposed. Puritan moderates and conservatives, in the light of modern research, seem to have been extremely numerous, and need to be assessed alongside the Ranters, Quakers, Seekers, Fifth Monarchists, Baptists and Muggletonians.[41] As a concept, freedom could as easily divide as unite. It looked different when viewed from different social vantage points. Its most ardent advocates were those to whom it had been most unknown and to whom, therefore, it had most to offer. Freedom had different meanings at different times and in different circumstances. It attracted misconceptions and misunder-standings. Toleration, for example, was for many not a goal but an enforced and unwanted halt. The freedom of the press enjoyed in the 1640s was largely the result of accident rather than a victory for high principles.

Moving out of the charmed circle of parliamentary politics has enabled that aspect itself to be re-interpreted as well as encouraged historians to take stock of popular politics and popular attitudes. The 'new' political history of Conrad Russell, David Underdown, Austin Woolrych and Blair Worden is worlds away from that produced by an earlier school of historians.[42] Here, too, as well as entering completely unexplored territory, some existing landmarks and reputations – that of the Levellers, for instance – have been reappraised. On both these counts Christopher Hill's *The World Turned Upside Down* (London, 1972) constituted a major turning point in English Revolutionary stu-dies. The losers' definition of freedom as well as the winners' insistence on liberties, we now accept, both deserve the attention of historians.

The essays which follow, therefore, express the continuing and varied interests of historians and literary specialists alike in the multiplicity of freedoms aimed at, claimed, discovered, or resisted in the turbulent decades of the 1640s and 1650s. The collection is interdisciplinary – a feature which, presumably, would have appalled those late nineteenth-century scientific historians who, in their uncompromising profes-sionalism, believed that the study of history itself provided all the answers. Literature is present in this volume both in its own right and in the conviction that the writers of this period like Milton and Marvell were not detached observers of the revolutionary scene but participants in its changes and cross-currents. More generally, the literary 'pres-ence' here helps to guarantee that proper attention is given not only to what was said and written in these decades but to the ways in which ideas, opinions and information were expressed and communicated. Style and genre, after all, in the last analysis, deserve to be as important to the historian as they already are to the student of literature.

One such stylistic issue which had a significant bearing upon the reception of writings in this period was the way in which generic constructs came to acquire quite new significances in the light of political and religious change.

John Bampfield's words in the quotation at the outset of this Introduction allude to the coming of 'a golden age': this concept is, of course, a literary and artistic construct of considerable potency which had been particularly popular from the Elizabethan period onwards. Writers of pastoral poetry could refer retrospectively to the image of this glorious time, and hope the freedoms which it had incorporated might one day be recaptured.

> O happy golden age!
> Not for that rivers ran
> With streams of milk, and honey dropped from trees;
> . . . But only for that name –
> That idle name of wind,
> That idol of deceit, that empty sound –
> Called Honour, which became
> The tyrant of the mind,
> . . . Was not yet vainly found,
> . . . Nor were his hard laws known to free-born hearts;
> But golden laws like these,
> Which nature wrote: 'That's lawful which doth Please.'[43]

In this tradition, the meek and the lowly were particularly blessed: free from the cares and strife of the sophisticated, fallen world, they obeyed the natural laws of freedom, and their condition was, therefore, superior to that of contemporary rulers;

> Envy of a foreign tyrant
> Threat'neth kings, not shepherds humble;
> Age makes silly swains delirant,
> Thirst of rule gars great men stumble.
> What to other seemeth sorry,
> Abject state, and humble biding,
> Is our joy and country glory;[44]

Shakespeare's Henry VI found time to muse upon the respective states of kings and shepherds in the middle of the battlefields:

> O God! methinks it were a happy life
> To be no better than a homely swain;
> . . . Ah, what a life were this! how sweet! how lovely!
> Gives not the hawthorn bush a sweeter shade
> To shepherds looking on their silly sheep,
> Than doth a rich embroider'd canopy
> To kings that fear their subjects' treachery?
> O yes, it doth; a thousand-fold it doth.[45]

These views of the idealised shepherds' life were not, of course, composed by shepherds, nor were they intended for a readership of manual workers, and a real difficulty began when this allusion moved from a retrospective literary device to the prospect of political achievement, when the millenium and the Second Coming were at hand: then the rift between image and reality became exposed. Once the monarchy had been challenged, then those in 'humble biding' were far from content to remain aloof from the struggle for power, but, as the contributions in this volume demonstrate, the issue was complicated by disputes over who exactly had 'free-born hearts', and how far laws could be based on the principle of what was pleasurable. Nor did the distinction between those who were care-worn with the wielding of power and those who were free from that burden disappear with the execution of Charles I (although the portrayal of Charles's execution drew explicitly upon the tradition of the care-worn king leaving for the freedom of a care-free heaven).[46] It became the distinction between Cromwell, who had power, and those without it who had looked to him for their own particular versions of freedom.

The success of the image of the golden age was based upon the premises that all men came from a starting point of equality, and that the world was without ambition (and hence without the possibility of factional or divided interests). In reality, however, those working for and writing about freedom in the 1640s did not share common backgrounds, as the contributions below on Milton, Lilburne, Marvell, and Winstanley make clear. They arrived in the same place by very different routes, and their ambitions, and their views of what freedoms could be achieved, were radically separate. The title page of Milton's *Areopagitica* includes a five-line translation from Euripides which encapsulates many of the problems with the concept of 'freedom'.

> This is true liberty when freeborn men
> Having to advise the public may speak free,
> Which he who can, and will, deserv's high praise,

> Who neither can nor will, may hold his peace;
> What can be juster in a State than this?[47]

For Milton, liberty implied the condition when property-holders have the ear of those in power (the variety of petitions to Cromwell in the 1650s from Milton, Marvell, Winstanley, and Harrington, is illustrated in the essays which follow). Those who were not freeborn men, and who wished to advise the public rather differently than he did were roundly condemned by Milton the following year

> this is got by casting pearl to hogs;
> That bawl for freedom in their senseless mood,
> And still revolt when truth would set them free.
> Licence they mean when they cry liberty;[48]

Roger Howell's essay on Cromwell indicates that Milton was not alone in discriminating carefully between liberty and licence – 'that's lawful which doth please' was proving to be a difficult dictum to live up to. Freedom needed to be made distinct from licentious behaviour, but reaching an agreed definition of the dividing line might not prove so easy, although many would follow Milton in making the division a social distinction. The labourer could not, in the view of many writers, be allowed the same freedoms as the squire, and the servants and paupers were, to many, self-evidently still to be enslaved. Keith Lindley illustrates the ways in which excessive or unpalatable revolutionary behaviour was blamed on the lower classes wherever possible, and the kinds of editing which took place in the signatories of petitions to exclude baser hands. This seems a very long way from the idealism of the 'golden age', but it is a practical illustration of a fear which was constantly expressed in literature from the Elizabethan period onwards, the fear of mindless anarchy and the overthrow of all institutions. This is the danger of Vincentio's Vienna in *Measure for Measure:*

> liberty plucks justice by the nose;
> The baby beats the nurse, and quite athwart
> Goes all decorum.[49]

When all decorum had gone, in the mid-1640s, the problem of freedom became, as Christopher Hill points out, partly a linguistic one, perhaps even a problem for the lexicographer. When Lovelace wrote, in 1642, that physical imprisonment was tolerable,

> If I have freedom in my love,
> And in my soul am free;[50]

he cannot have anticipated the extremes to which a belief in 'freedom in love' would be taken within the next decade. He could not have predicted the sexual freedoms of the Ranters, nor that it might be possible to advocate, as Baillie claimed that Milton advocated 'a full liberty for any man to put away his wife, when ever he pleaseth'.[51] Nor can Lovelace have fully realised how vexed the definition of 'freedom of the soul' might become. Thomas Corns illustrates how Milton manipulated the flexibility of this definition by refusing to concede that any right-thinking reader could possibly hold another view: his is a strategy of assumed collaboration rather than of persuasion or even confrontation. Milton might have said what William Warburton, among others, is credited with saying in the next century 'Orthodoxy is my doxy; heterodoxy is another man's doxy'.

Technically, it was impossible to be other than orthodox before the seventeenth century, if only because the word did not exist: 'Orthodoxy' is cited by the *Oxford English Dictionary* as being first used by Prynne in *Anti-Arminianisme* (1630). Once the issue of orthodoxy became debatable, it could no longer be taken for granted that any two groups would be working towards an agreed set of freedoms. The bitterness that might occur between man and man is well illustrated in Milton's comment on his betrayal by Prynne in *Colasterion* (1645):

I stood a while and wonder'd what wee might doe to a mans heart, or what anatomie use, to finde in it sincerity; for all our wonted marks every day fail us, and where wee thought it was, wee see it not.[52]

The absence of 'wonted marks' presumably accounts for the presence of serious tracts explaining the differences between the opinions held by the various sects, as well as royalist lampoons, and the blistering attack of Edwards,

among all these sorts of sects and sectaries, there are hardly now to be found in England . . . any sect that's simple and pure, and not mixt and compounded, that is, any sect (among them all) which holds only the opinions and principles of its own way, without enterfering and mingling with the errours of other sects . . . One and the same society of persons in our times, being both Anabaptisicall, Antinomian, Manifestarian, Libertine, Socinian, Millenary, Independent, Enthusiasticall.[53]

Even allowing for the exaggeration of an aggressive polemicist, there is no doubt that many a man or woman in the 1640s and 1650s would have been hard pressed to have put a name to the brand of freedom which he or she espoused. The frequent references to and developing exposition of Arminianism in the essays in this book are a testament to the common ground shared by many writers and reformers who might not have thought of themselves as having much in common: their own priorities for localised freedoms might have prevented them from seeing what they shared.

The contributions in this book demonstrate that the debate about freedom could operate at the level of rational discussion, of political action, or through the character-assassination of one's opponents: none of these is peculiar to the English Revolution. What, perhaps, is distinctive is the exploitation by all sides of the potent emotional symbols available to them from the Bible. England was, of course, as Keith Lindley reminds us, the new Israel, and even as late as 1660 Milton still saw the restoration of monarchy as a return to Egypt. Charles I and Lilburne were each celebrated as martyrs to their respective causes, at a time when that term had more resonance than it has today, but they were not the only individuals to whom such an image could be applied. The analogy of Christ's temptation on the Pinnacle, 'the thirst of rule' so despised in the pastoral tradition, could be variously deployed by Milton, Marvell, or Spittlehouse on a varied range of targets,[54] and the venom in Milton's description of the portrait of Charles I at his prayers is in itself an indication of his own awareness of the power the image possessed:

to catch the worthles approbation of an inconstant, irrational, and Image-doting rabble; (that like a credulous and hapless herd, begott'n to servility, and inchanted with . . . a new device of the Kings Picture at his praiers, hold out both thir eares with such delight and ravishment to be stigmatiz'd and board through in witness of thir own voluntary and beloved baseness.)[55]

This attitude to the freedom which the people might be allowed to have in receiving such images and judging for themselves, is very far removed from the faith in the 'freedom of the mind' which he had advanced in *Comus* in the 1630s, but then, of course, his representative had been a Lady. By 1649 it seemed that the majority of the people were willing to relinquish the freedom of their intellects, and to opt instead for the enchanted Circean cup of 'image-worship'. In such circumstances, they would have to be abandoned to their own voluntary enslavement,

> by their vices brought to servitude,
> . . . to love bondage more than liberty,
> Bondage with ease rather than strenuous liberty[56]

The debate on freedom took a range of different paths in the 1640s and 1650s but certain issues continued to be raised. Was political freedom inseparable from freedom of worship? How did those freedoms combine with freedom of expression and freedom of the press? Could freedom be safely enjoyed by all? It is around such issues that this book revolves.

Notes

1   Historical Manuscripts Commission, Fifteenth Report, Appendix, pt. VII, p. 64. Quoted in J. T. Cliffe, *The Puritan Gentry. The Great Puritan Families of Early Stuart England*, London, 1984, p. 223.

2   R. Brome, *A Jovial Crew, or the Merry Beggars* (1641). Quoted in M. Butler, *Theatre and Crisis, 1632–1642*, Cambridge, 1984, pp. 273, 279.

3   The anti-prelatical tracts *Of Reformation*, *Of Prelatical Episcopacy*, and *The Reason of Church Government* all belong to 1641.

4   S. R. Gardiner, *History of England 1603–42*, new ed., IX and X, London, 1894, deal with the early 1640s. Modern studies of this critical juncture include A. Fletcher, *The Outbreak of the English Civil War*, London, 1981; R. Ashton, *The English Civil War. Conservatism and Revolution 1603–49*, London, 1978; B. Manning, 'The Aristocracy and the Downfall of Charles I' in Manning (ed.), *Politics, Religion, and the English Civil War*, London, 1973; Sheila Lambert, 'The Opening of the Long Parliament', *Historical Journal*, XXVII, 1984; P. Christianson, 'From Expectation to Militance: Reformers and Babylon in the first two years of the Long Parliament', *Journal of Ecclesiastical History*, XXIV, 1973.

5   G. E. Aylmer (ed.), *The Levellers in the English Revolution*, London, 1975, p. 89. A. S. P. Woodhouse (ed.), *Puritanism and Liberty*, 2nd ed., London, reprinted 1973, contains the text of the Putney Debates. On Winstanley see Hill pp. 151–67, below. C. Hill (ed.), *Winstanley. The Law of Freedom and Other Writings*, Harmondsworth, 1973, pp. 128–9.

6   *The Diggers' Mirth, or Certain Verses composed and fitted to tunes for the delight and recreation of all those who dig or own that work in the commonwealth of England* in Woodhouse, *op. cit.*, p. 386.

7   Milton, *The Tenure of Kings and Magistrates*, CPW, III, p. 190.

8   A. R. Waller (ed.), *Abraham Cowley, Essays, Plays and Sundry Verses*, Cambridge, 1906, II, p. 388. Thomas Hobbes, *Leviathan*, ed. C. B. Macpherson, Harmondsworth, 1968, *passim*; Thomas Hobbes, *Behemoth or the Long Parliament*, ed. F. Tonnies, 2nd ed., London, 1969, *passim*. Robert Filmer, *Patriarcha and Other Works*, ed. P. Laslett, Oxford, 1949, *passim*.

9   C. Hill, *Some Intellectual Consequences of the English Revolution*, London, 1980, p. 49. The breakdown of censorship and its consequences are examined in C. Hill, 'Censorship and English Literature' in the same author's *Writing and Revolution in Seventeenth-Century England*, Brighton, 1985, pp. 32–71, and in Annabel Patterson, *Censorship and Interpretation. The Conditions of Writing and Reading in Early Modern England*, Madison, Wisconsin, 1984.

10   Macaulay, *Critical and Historical Essays*, London, 1852, pp. 24, 22, 17.

11   Gardiner, *The First Two Stuarts and the Puritan Revolution, 1603–1660*, London, 1888, p.v; Gardiner, *History of England 1603–42*, new ed., London 1893–6, VIII, pp. 84–5; Gardiner, *History of the Great Civil War 1642–1649*, London, 1893, I, p. 9.

The changing trends in the historiography of this subject are discussed in R. C. Richardson, *The Debate on the English Revolution*, London, 1977, and in H. Tomlinson (ed.), *Before the English Civil War*, London, 1983, pp. 7–26.

12   Acton never came anywhere near completing it. Glimpses of what might have been, however, can be found in Gertrude Himmelfarb (ed.), *Lord Acton. Essays on Freedom and Power*, London, 1956, and more indirectly in J. Bryce, *Studies in Contemporary Biography*, London, 1913, pp. 396–7. G. M. Trevelyan, *England under the Stuarts*, 12th ed., London, 1925, pp. 196, 270–1.

13   A similar preoccupation – even more crudely expressed – underlies the selection of *Documents of Liberty, from Earliest Times to Universal Suffrage*, ed. H. Marsh, Newton Abbot, 1971.

14   Woodhouse, *op. cit.*, p. 3

15   Haller, *op. cit.*, p. xiv.

16   On the political thought of this period see P. Zagorin, *A History of Political Thought in the English Revolution*, London, 1954; G. R. Cragg, *Freedom and Authority. A Study of English Thought in the Early Seventeenth Century*, Philadelphia, 1975; A. Sharp, *Political Ideas of the English Civil War*, London, 1983; and Z. Pelczynski and J. Cray (eds.), *Concepts of Liberty in Political Philosophy*, London, 1984.

17   Roger Howell's chapter (pp. 25–44) below squarely confronts this and other related questions.

18   Answers to some of the questions rehearsed here have been offered in Joan Webber, *The Eloquent 'I': Style and Self in Seventeenth-Century Prose*, Madison, Wisconsin, 1968; K. W. Stavely, *The Politics of Milton's Prose Style*, New Haven. Con., 1975; A. L. Morton, *The Matter of Britain*, London, 1966; and C. Hill, *Writing and Revolution in Seventeenth-Century England*, Brighton, 1985. H. Erskine-Hill and G. Storey (eds.), *Revolutionary Prose of the English Civil War*, Cambridge, 1983, strangely has little to offer on these aspects.

Dr Corns's chapter, pp. 93–110, below, makes a contribution to the study of author-reader relations and the variety of freedoms of interpretation assumed.

19   C. Russell, *Parliaments and English Politics 1621–1629*, Oxford, 1979, p. 389. See also D. Hirst, *The Representative of the People? Voters and Voting in England under the Early Stuarts*, Cambridge, 1975, and B. Manning, *The English People and the English Revolution*, London, 1976.

20   See Lindley (pp. 111–50) below.

21   See Hill (pp. 151–67) below.

22   See Hill (pp. 152–3) below.

23   A. F. Pollard, *The Evolution of Parliament*, London, 1920, pp. 167, 170, 171.

24   F. Maseres (ed.), *Select Tracts Relating to the Civil Wars in England*, London, 1815, II, p. 349. Quoted in R. Ashton, 'From Cavalier to Roundhead tyranny 1642–9' in J. Morrill (ed.), *Reactions to the English Civil War, 1642–1649*, London, 1982, p. 205.

25   W. S. McKechnie, *Magna Carta*, 2nd ed., Glasgow, 1924; Faith Thompson, *Magna Carta: Its Role in the Making of the English Constitution, 1300–1629*, Minneapolis, 1948; J. G. A. Pocock, *The Ancient Constitution and the Feudal Law*, Cambridge, 1957; H. Butterfield, *Magna Carta in the*

Historiography of the Sixteenth and Seventeenth Centuries, Stenton Lecture, Reading, 1969; Anne Pallister, *Magna Carta. The Heritage of Liberty*, Oxford, 1971.

26 W. D. Macray (ed.), *Clarendon's History of the Rebellion and Civil Wars in England*, Oxford, 1888, VI, p. 93.

27 Pallister, *op. cit.*, pp. 8–9, 11. On Coke see S. D. White, *Sir Edward Coke and the Grievances of the Commonwealth*, Manchester, 1979, and J. D. Eusden, *Puritans, Lawyers and Politics in Early Seventeenth-Century England*, New Haven, Conn., 1958.

28 Pallister, *op. cit.*, 15, 17, 18. C. Hill, 'The Norman Yoke', *Puritanism and Revolution*, London, 1958, pp. 50–122. S. E. Prall, *The Agitation for Law Reform during the Puritan Revolution*, The Hague, 1966. D. Veall, *The Popular Movement for Law Reform 1640–1660*, Oxford, 1970. See also R. Tuck, *Natural Rights Theories. Their Origin and Development*, Cambridge, 1979.

29 See pp. 45–71 and pp. 72–92 below.

30 W. K. Jordan, *The Development of Religious Toleration in England 1640–1660*, London, 1938–40, gives a more conventional view.

31 R. H. Tawney, *Religion and the Rise of Capitalism*, London, 1929, pp. 212–13.

32 The modern historiography of Puritanism is now very voluminous. See, for example, C. Hill, *The Economic Problems of the Church*, Oxford, 1956; C. Hill, *Society and Puritanism in Pre-Revolutionary England*, London, 1964; P. Collinson, *The Elizabethan Puritan Movement*, London, 1967; P. Collinson, *The Religion of Protestants 1559–1625*, Oxford, 1982; M. G. Finlayson, *Historians, Puritanism and the English Revolution*, Toronto, 1984. Local studies include R. C. Richardson, *Puritanism in North-West England*, Manchester, 1972 and W. Hunt, *The Puritan Moment. The Coming of Revolution in an English County*, London, 1983.

33 See pp. 8–9 above.

34 E. Bernstein, *Cromwell and Communism*, London, 1930; D. M. Wolfe (ed.), *Leveller Manifestoes of the Puritan Revolution*, London, 1944. G. E. Aylmer (ed.), *The Levellers in the English Revolution*, London, 1975, provides a balanced assessment of the movement and a convenient collection of sources.

35 J. Lilburne, *An Impeachment of High Treason against Oliver Cromwell*, London, 1649, p. 23 and W. Haller and G. Davies (eds.), *The Leveller Tracts, 1647–1653*, New York, 1944, pp. 405–7, 452–5, quoted in B. Manning, 'The Levellers and religion', in J. F. McGregor and B. Reay (eds.), *Radical Religion in the English Revolution*, Oxford, 1984, pp. 68, 71. See also J. C. Davis, 'The Levellers and Christianity' in B. Manning (ed.), *Politics, Religion and the English Civil War*, London, 1973, pp. 225–50.

36 C. B. Macpherson, *The Political Theory of Possessive Individualism*, Oxford, 1962.

37 Manning, *article cit.*, *passim*.

38 See, for example, T. Corns, 'Milton's quest for respectability', *Modern Language Review*, LXXVII, 1982, pp. 769–79.

39 *CPW*, II, p. 221.

40 *CPW*, III, pp. 339–40.

41 J. Morrill, 'The Church in England 1642–49' in J. Morrill (ed.),

Reactions to the English Civil War, London, 1983, pp. 89–114, offers evidence of religious conservatism. On the radical religious groups see C. Hill, *The World Turned Upside Down*, London, 1972; J. F. MacGregor and B. Reay, *op. cit.*, *passim*; C. Hill, B. Reay, and W. Lamont (eds.), *The World of the Muggletonians*, London, 1983; N. Smith (ed.), *A Collection of Ranter Writings from the Seventeenth Century*, London, 1983; B. Reay, *The Quakers in the English Revolution*, London, 1985.

42   C. Russell, *Parliaments and English Politics 1621–1629*, Oxford, 1979; D. Underdown, *Pride's Purge. Politics in the English Revolution*, Oxford, 1971; A. Woolrych, *Commonwealth to Protectorate*, Oxford, 1982; B. Worden, *The Rump Parliament 1648–1653*, Cambridge, 1974.

43   S. Daniel, 'A pastoral' in G. Hiller (ed.), *Poems of the Elizabethan Age*, London, 1977, p. 247.

44   T. Lodge, 'Old Damon's pastoral', *ibid.*, p. 260.

45   W. Shakespeare, *Henry VI Part III*, Act II scene 5.

46   See the verse accompanying the frontespiece to *Eikon Basilike*, cited in Lois Potter, *A Preface to Milton*, London, 1971, p. 25.

47   *CPW*, II, p. 485.

48   Sonnet XII, in J. Carey and A. Fowler (eds.), *The Poems of John Milton*, London, 1968, p. 295.

49   W. Shakespeare, *Measure for Measure*, Act I scene 3.

50   'To Althea, From Prison'.

51   cited in W. R. Parker, *Milton's Contemporary Reputation*, New York, 1940, p. 75.

52   *CPW*, II, p. 722.

53   T. Edwards, *Gangraena*, London, 1645, p. 16 (reprinted Exeter, 1979). See also Woodhouse, *op. cit.*, pp. 179–81, and W. Lamont and Sybil Oldfield (eds.), *Politics, Religion and Literature in the Seventeenth Century*, London, 1975, p. 70.

54   See Chernaik (p. 56) below and G. M. Ridden, 'Winstanley's allusion to Milton', *Notes and Queries*, XXXI, 1984.

55   *Eikonoklastes*, *CPW*, III, p. 601.

56   *Samson Agonistes*, 269–71, Carey and Fowler, *op. cit.*, p. 356.

Cromwell and English liberty

To remark that the English Revolution constituted a significant stage in the history of freedom and liberty would be to state the obvious. To single out Oliver Cromwell as the most significant political personage in those events might occasion more objection, but would, in the end, also be a relatively unsurprising assertion. To link the two observations, however, by stating that Cromwell played a leading role in the history of English liberty is to enter more controversial territory.[1] Cromwell's attitude towards liberty and his actions in support of it have created a stormy heritage as subseqent generations have sought to absorb and come to terms with the meaning of those tumultuous years in which he strode the land, sword and Bible in hand.

That opinion in his own lifetime and in the years immediately following his death was divided, should occasion no surprise. Opinions were sharply polarized by the events of revolution, and judgement of Cromwell logically followed from the position taken with regard to the civil strife. To a supporter, he was a man who

constantly stood firme and trusty in upholding the established Religion, the Laws of the Land, and Libertyes of his Country, even to the very period of his dayes, and in a most devout profession, and defending of them altogether, with the priviledges of Parliament, of the breach of which, none was more tender and fought more valiantly for their preservation.[2]

To a Royalist, on the contrary, he was a person

wading to the Government of these Nations over head and ears in blood . . . He cares not to spill the blood of his Subjects like water, plenty whereof was shed in our streets, during his short and troublesome Reign, by his oppression, dissimulation, hypocrisies, and cruelty.[3]

That opposite sides differed in their assessment of Cromwell's motives

and actions is not particularly noteworthy; that the debate continued and
still continues is rather more so. In part the continuation of the debate
only reflects the fact that people will find in the past what they want to
find there and will do so in terms of their own contemporary concerns
and perceptions. To eighteenth-century dissenters he remained a hero
in the struggle for religious liberty.[4] To a political writer on the eve of
the American Revolution he breathed the spirit of the Sons of Liberty in
Boston and was offered as a beacon to them.[5] To Carlyle in the
nineteenth-century he was the Hero the age needed, to Gardiner a
Victorian liberal misplaced in another century.[6] And yet, the continuation of the debate, one senses, has deeper roots than this. It is striking,
for example, that Cromwell has been placed not just for or against Liberty,
but, on the contrary, has been portrayed in just about every conceivable
position with respect to it on the continuum between the two polar
positions. To some, his expressions in defence of liberty have seemed
only hypocrisy, covering rather base forms of personal ambition. Few, if
any, would now be content to explain him, as the early historical
tradition did, simply in terms of his being an ambitious hypocrite, but
even those who have recognized greatness and liberality in him have
sensed how uncomfortably close at times he came to hypocrisy,[7] and
certainly few Irish, then or now, have taken at face value his assertion
that he came to that country 'to hold forth and maintain the lustre and
glory of English liberty'.[8] Others have seen him as the actual destroyer of
liberty, and the fact that those who have expressed this view have been
both to the right and to the left of him is suggestive in itself of the
complexity of his own relation to liberty.[9] In any case, making a hero in
the cause of liberty out of a man who rode to power on the back of the
army and maintained power in the same way, who quarrelled with every
parliament with which he had to deal and who dismissed them by both
force and specious legality, who browbeat judges who had the temerity
to raise questions about the basis of his authority, is not a self-evident
action. The sense that there was in him more than a touch of the tyrant
lingers in the popular mind, and not just in Ireland. The *Oxford Mail* in
1960 reported that Wallingford Borough Council had banned the suggestion that a road on a new private estate should be called Cromwell
Gardens; explaining their decision, they commented, 'We have more
than enough benefactors whose names we would like to commemorate
without entertaining a malefactor of his class'.[10]

The complexity of the situation is further underlined by those who
held, at different times, essentially contrasting views of him, who saw

him both as defender of liberty and destroyer of it. The condemnation of Cromwell by Ludlow is well known; here Cromwell appears as the failed hero, the one who had led the republican cause to victory only to abandon it to serve his own ends because, at bottom, he was indeed no more than an ambitious hypocrite, a man who, in Ludlow's words, sacrificed 'all our victories and deliverances to his pride and ambition'.[11] The critiques of Cromwell penned by John Lilburne are equally familiar, but it was the same Lilburne who wrote to Cromwell, 'God hath honoured you . . . and truly my selfe and all others of my mind that I could speak with have looked upon you as the most absolute single hearted great man in England, untainted or unbiased with ends of your owne'.[12] When one individual can be portrayed in such incompatible guises as radical regicide, conservative constitutionalist, reluctant dictator, fascist tyrant, representative of the emergent middle class, and spokeman of the declining gentry, not to mention his characterisation as a textbook case of the manic-depression psychosis or as the realiser of the ultimate Oedipal fantasy – the murder of the father of the country – the dimensions of the problem become apparent.

There is yet a further and obvious element in the problem of assessing Cromwell's role in the struggle for liberty. Cromwell was essentially a practical man, a man of action. Theoretical schemes had little appeal to him, and abstract philosophising about such things as the concept of liberty had no place in his character. His letters and speeches admittedly contain a number of memorable statements about liberty, and these cannot be ignored of liberty must be derived as much or more from his words. And this is not a simple exercise. It is complicated by the fact that his career spanned the whole revolution from moderate to radical and on to conservative reconstruction ging political context, by itself, may well create some differences in his views on liberty. He was also repeatedly faced with complex political decisions in which it is now difficult to liberty or some more immediate political goal was the Later champions of Cromwell have written glowingly of his intercession on behalf of the beleaguered Protestants of the Vaudois as a striking example of the application of the principle of liberty to foreign policy, but it is important to ask whether he was indeed making a statement that England had a duty to be an international defender of liberty, or whether he was simply employing a tactic to gain a diplomatic advantage with France. His intervention in the case of James Nayler provides a similar instance;

when he questioned Parliament's right to try Nayler was he making a fundamental statement about religious liberty or was he concerned with other sorts of constitutional issues such as the practical political problems of the relation of Lord Protector to Parliament and the relation of Parliament to the constitution of the nation? The answers to such questions are not simple, but, by examining carefully Cromwell's actions in conjunction with his words and expressed intentions, some of the apparent contradictions can be resolved and a more balanced assessment of his role in the history of English liberty perhaps achieved.

Given the centrality of religion in Cromwell's character, it is appropriate that it is in the sphere of religious liberty, and by extension freedom of thought, that his contribution is most clear. His advocacy of religious toleration was not unlimited but it stood far in advance of predominant opinion in his time and establishes him as a key figure in the enunciation of a constitutional principle on which Englishmen have rightly placed great stress. There is no need to take seriously the accusations that Cromwell's religion and his advocacy of toleration were simply further manifestations of his ambition and hyprocrisy, that he advocated toleration and championed the position of the Independents simply to sow the seeds of confusion in a distracted state and hence further increase the possibilities of his own rise to the top.[13] Such speculations are the stuff of Royalist myth and propaganda. However fervently they were believed for a century or more after Cromwell's death, there is no more genuine historical evidence for them than there is for the also popular myth that Cromwell had sold his soul to the devil.[14]

The historical record of Cromwell's sincerity and activity in this area is clear. It is not saying too much to argue that one of the main reasons that Cromwell fought in the revolution in the first place was that he was concerned to ensure freedom of conscience and to protect citizens from what he regarded as the tyranny of the Laudian bishops. From his first recorded speech – to the Commons Committee on Religion in February 1629 – in which he complained about how Dr Beard had been 'exceedingly rated' by Bishop Neile,[15] to his actions as Lord Protector, the concern for tender consciences is clear and evident. In 1644, on a rare visit to the House of Commons, he urged on Oliver St. John the wording of a motion that asked 'to endeavour the finding out some way, how far tender consciences, who cannot in all things submit to the common rule which shall be established, may be borne with according to the Word, and as may stand with the public peace'.[16] In the summer of 1646 he wrote to Thomas Knyvett, one of whose tenants was the landlord of a group of poor men living in a hamlet in Norfolk who apparently were in danger of being evicted because of their religious opinions.

The trouble I hear [is that] they are like to suffer for their consciences. And however the world interprets it, I am not ashamed to solicit for such as are anywhere under a pressure of this kind; doing herein as I would be done by. Sir, this is a quarrelsome age; and the anger seems to me to be the worse, where the ground is things of difference in opinion; which to cure, to hurt men in their names, persons or estates, will not be found an apt remedy.[17]

In September 1645, following the reduction of Bristol, he reminded the House of Commons that 'from brethren, in things of the mind we look for no compulsion, but that of light and reason'.[18] In 1656, addressing the second Protectorate parliament, he stressed the reality of toleration.

Our practice since the last Parliament hath been, to let all this Nation see that whatever pretensions to religion would continue quiet, peaceable, they should enjoy conscience and liberty to themselves; – and not make Religion a pretence for arms and blood, truly we have suffered them, and that cheerfully, so to enjoy their own liberties.[19]

His actions on behalf of the Jews are well-known, and Anglicans and Catholics, officially excluded from the toleration established under the Instrument of Government, found their lot under his rule less onerous than the actual legal situation might have seemed to warrant. John Evelyn's memoirs provide detailed accounts of the Anglican use of the Book of Common Prayer in the last years of the Protectorate,[20] and when Cromwell's daughter Mary married Lord Fauconberg the Anglican rite had been followed at the latter's insistence.[21] As far as Catholics were concerned, there was some genuine measure of effective toleration in the years of the Protectorate; the eight priests arrested in Covent Garden in 1657 suffered little more than being made figures of fun.[22] How seriously one should take Cromwell's expressed desire to Mazarin to achieve some form of official toleration for the Catholics is another matter.[23] Given the climate of opinion, there was no realistic chance of his procuring such a provision, and his assurance to Mazarin that he should just trust him in this regard may be taken more as the language of diplomacy than as a statement of conviction and intention. But for those Catholics who did not trouble the state, the legal force of repression was often quietly checked.

The issue of the Catholics points to one of the essential dilemmas for Cromwell in terms of freedom of religious opinion, but indeed the issue was to be met not just here but at every turn. That he believed passionately in the principle of liberty cannot be doubted; it is a recurring theme in his letters and speeches. But like all who have had to grapple with this issue, at either the theoretical or the practical level, he found that the problem of determining the line at which liberty became licence could not be avoided. In general terms Cromwell had no doubt that the distinction between the two could be made and that the one should be tolerated and the other repressed. He had never, he argued, sought for 'licentious liberty under the pretence of obtaining ease for tender consciences'.[24] In practice, drawing the line is infinitely difficult, for the boundary between liberty and licence is more a matter of perspective than it is one of established, unarguable fact. For Cromwell, the line was essentially drawn at the point where liberty of conscience proved to be incompatible with the maintenance of law and order, and yet even here, at an individual level, he found the line at times difficult to discern. This is nowhere more clearly illustrated than in his relations with the Quakers as a sect and in his relations with individual Quakers such as George Fox. Certainly he could not and did not approve of their more extreme actions. If they disrupted church services or abused the minister in the pulpit, they could not, to his mind, be allowed to express their feelings unchecked. And yet at the same time there is abundant evidence that he attempted to understand their position and tried to persuade them that if only they would conduct themselves in a peaceable manner, the government would not disturb them. Whatever he may have felt constrained to do for the promotion of civil order, he did not share the view advanced by some anti-Quaker writers that the sect was in and of itself subversive to the authority of the state.[25] And even when coercion was applied, he was sensitive to the issue of religious liberty as the case of the Quakers of Horsham reveals. They had written directly to Cromwell because they had heard of his declaration 'that none in this nation shall suffer for conscience'; in response, he ordered an enquiry into their case, and they were released.[26] What is to be observed here is that there was indeed for Cromwell a tension between the dictates of conscience and the demands of social order. Perhaps naively but nonetheless genuinely, he hoped that tension could be resolved by discussion and mutual understanding. After the siege of Bristol he wrote to Speaker Lenthall,

Presbyterians, Independents, all had here the same spirit of faith and prayer; the same pretence and answer; they agree here, know no names of difference: pity it is it should be otherwise anywhere. All that believe have the real unity, which is most glorious, because inward and spiritual.[27]

It was in the same spirit that Cromwell remarked to Fox, 'Come again to my house, for if thou and I were but an hour of a day together, we should be nearer one to the other'.[28] It must be admitted that Cromwell did not, in fact, completely resolve the dilemma posed by the challenge of licence to liberty; in choosing to define the dividing line in terms of political order, he ensured that toleration would extend to, but not go beyond those who were not inconvenient to the state. The fact constitutes a real and visible limit to the generality of some of his more famous and sweeping pronouncements about religious liberty. He had no desire to bother men's consciences; his reiterated assertions, that all who would live peaceably in the state would receive his protection, ring true. But if they chose not to live peaceably with each other or with the state, he found himself forced, for the sake of stability, to act contrary to his own first principle of religious freedom. Cromwell was certainly not the first, nor the last statesman to be confronted with the problem of how to tolerate a sincere opposition. In a position of power, he ultimately favoured order over liberty, though there is every sign that he was acutely conscious of the sad irony involved in doing so.

The dilemma of preserving civil order and at the same time advocating freedom of expression was not the only problem posed to Cromwell in this area. In various ways, his capacity to make a solid contribution to liberty was held back by the realities of the climate of opinion. There is a liberality to his dream for a non-coercive public profession of faith, but in practice it foundered because some felt it was too lax, while others saw it as not yet lax enough. He sensed with a particular pain the all too human failing that turns the person once persecuted into a persecutor as soon as he gains the upper hand. He inveighed against it with the sturdy eloquence of which he was capable.

Liberty of conscience is a natural right; and he that would have it, ought to give it . . . Indeed that hath been one of the vanities of our contests. Every sect saith: 'Oh, give me liberty!' but give him it, and to his power he will not yield it to anybody else. Where is our ingenuousness? Truly, that's a thing that ought to be very reciprocal.[29]

On another occasion, he returned to the same theme.

Those that were sound in the faith, how proper was it for them to labour for liberty, for a just liberty, that men should not be trampled upon for their consciences! Had not they laboured, but lately, under the weight of persecutions? And was it fit for them to sit heavy upon others? Is it ingenuous to ask liberty, and not to give it? What greater hypocrisy than for those who were oppressed by the Bishops to become the greatest oppressors themselves, so soon as their yoke was removed. I could wish that they who call for liberty now also had not too much of that spirit, if the power were in their hands![30]

Here as elsewhere rhetoric and persuasion were insufficient. In his vision of liberty, Cromwell stood far in advance of the generality. Given a free choice, most men would not endorse the position that Cromwell felt so strongly about, and that realisation led him to the formulation of a radical solution, that people should be quite literally forced to accept such freedom. To counter illiberality by the application of force is to enter into dangerous waters, but intractable problems require drastic solutions, and Cromwell did not shrink from taking the plunge. In 1647 he had stated that his purpose was 'What's for their good, not what pleases them'.[31] During the brief, unhappy experiment with the Major-Generals, he did not shrink from the idea that liberty might be imposed by essentially tyrannical means, and, however dangerous the precedent he was setting, it remains the case that his military government enforced a larger measure of religious toleration than any 'free' institution in mid seventeenth-century England would have contemplated. His retort to Calamy's objection, 'Tis against the will of the nation, there will be nine in ten against you', was blunt and to the point. 'But what if I should disarm the nine and put a sword in the tenth man's hand. Would not that do the business?'[32] He was speaking on that occasion of political matters, but the same sentiment could be applied to his sense of the religious situation. It is a dangerous doctrine, and certainly not a liberal one, but rather a radical, revolutionary one. Yet liberty is seldom granted without a struggle, and one senses that Cromwell knew that uncomfortable truth. Clearly he would have liked it otherwise, would have preferred that light and reason would suffice, but he felt strongly enough about the principle of liberty to subvert it in one sense in order to achieve it in another.

To claim that Cromwell made significant theoretical contributions to the development of religious liberty or freedom of thought would be misleading. He was not a theorist. Yet it is possible to suggest that his words and actions taken together constitute significant stages in the arguments about these subjects and that in several particulars they added significantly to the force of those arguments. Practical considerations led him to face three extremely difficult questions: to what extent is the state entitled legitimately to interest itself in a person's private opinions? Is the danger of abuse of liberty a sufficient reason for curtailing it? Can one trust that truth will prevail in the battle of ideas? To each of these questions Cromwell returned answers that were resoundingly on the side of liberty. The first is perhaps best illustrated in the well-known case of Cromwell's exchanges with Major General Lawrence Crawford over the issue of insisting on religious conformity among the troops. The Scottish Presbyterian views of Crawford clashed with the more liberal conceptions of Cromwell. Trouble first surfaced in the case of Lieutenant William Packer, a known Baptist, who was arrested by Crawford, apparently on religious grounds; Cromwell rose to his defence, insisting he was a godly man.[33] Far more striking was Cromwell's reaction to Crawford's moves against his own lieutenant-colonel, Henry Warner.

Ay, but the man is an Anabaptist. Are you sure of that? Admit he be, shall that render him incapable to serve the Public? He is indiscreet. It may be so, in some things, we have all human infirmities. I tell you, if you had none but such indiscreet men about you, and would be pleased to use them kindly, you would find as good a fence to you as any you have yet chosen.[34]

To this point, Cromwell has said nothing more remarkable than urging the purely pragmatic point that one should not lightly turn away supporters in the midst of the struggle. But as he continued the letter to Crawford, he extended the individual case into a general statement about the extent to which the state should concern itself about the private opinions of those who sought to work for it.

Sir, the State, in choosing men to serve them, takes no notice of their opinions, if they be willing faithfully to serve them, that satisfies. I advised you formerly to bear with men of different minds from yourself . . . Take heed of being sharp, or too easily sharpened by others, against those to whom you can object little but that they square not with you in every opinion concerning matters of religion.[35]

The point is fundamental; the State may demand many things of its servants, but absolute conformity in matters of belief is not one of them.

Cromwell likewise engaged directly the argument, so frequently used, that freedom should not be extended too far because the people will abuse it. In countering this position, Cromwell never denied the possibility that liberty might indeed be abused; that is to say he never argued for a liberty that was unqualified under any circumstances. But the critical point, to his mind, was the abuse itself, not the mere possibility that abuse might occur.

Your pretended fear lest error should step in, is like the man who would keep all the wine out of the country lest men should be drunk. It will be found an unjust and unwise jealousy, to deny a man the liberty he has by nature upon a supposition he may abuse it. When he doth abuse it, judge.[36]

Here, as in the case of the state's right to be concerned about an individual's opinions, Cromwell defined the limits of acceptable liberty in terms of actual rather than hypothetical behaviour and practice. Liberty could not exist without the possibility that some may indeed abuse it. To limit all because some may offend is unjustified; the proper remedy is to limit none, and chastise those who do exceed the acceptable limits.

The danger, of course, in allowing freedom and only punishing abuses when they occur is that truth may be corrupted by error. The classical liberal answer to that danger is to assert that, in the nature of things, truth will triumph over error and that one cannot be sure of truth unless it is constantly tested in this way. Cromwell, on more than one occasion, came close to advancing this argument, and his actions (one thinks, for example, of his conversations with George Fox) suggest that his words had substantive meaning. To the Governor of Edinburgh he wrote, 'If a man speak foolishly, ye suffer him gladly because ye are wise; if erroneously, the truth more appears by your conviction. Stop such a man's mouth with sound words that cannot be gainsayed'.[37] Where Cromwell falls short of the classical liberal position is in his belief that the truth is what it is, not because it has been tested against error, but because it is God's truth. Nonetheless, in his confidence that it need not be sheltered from error and that, in the confrontation with it, it will not only triumph but be the more evident for its triumph, Cromwell anticipated a fundamental point about freedom of thought.

Liberty in terms of religious thought, then, was fundamental to Cromwell and by itself would assure him a place in the history of English liberty. In a remarkable statement, he summed up his position by announcing, 'I had rather that Mahometanism were permitted amongst us than that one of God's children should be persecuted'.[38]

Cromwell's contribution to political liberty is rather more ambiguous. Opposed as he was to arbitrary government, he was impelled to be arbitrary himself. Devoted as he was to Parliament, he never worked smoothly or successfully with one. Concerned as he was to find a civilian settlement, he could never escape the fact that ultimately his position and power rested on the armed force of the military. But the argument cannot be left at that point. It will not do to assert that though he may have had more liberal aspirations, the force of circumstances made him, in the last analysis, nothing more than a dictator. One way to view this situation is to admit that he was dictatorial, but that this was done with reluctance. Only the most intense anti-Cromwellian would deny the element of reluctance, but this is still not the whole story. His aspirations, even if they were not achieved, need also to be considered carefully and seriously; they too are part of the history of English liberty even if it is more difficult in this case than it was in the case of freedom of religion to square completely actions and words.

On the positive side of the ledger, he clearly saw the importance of a civil settlement; the fruitless search for it is, indeed, the story of the 1650s.[39] In like fashion he sensed the importance of certain kinds of constitutional safeguards; if he did not express himself all that coherently on the point, he clearly was grasping for the concepts of separation of powers and constitutional checks and balances as protective devices against arbitrary government. He realized the importance of the principle of consent, and he hoped in vain that Parliament would act as a vehicle for the expression of it.

On the first of these points – the importance of civil settlement – a few observations need to be made. That Cromwell saw this as the fundamental political problem of the 1650s seems beyond argument. That he tried to emphasize that point, even in unpromising circumstances, is also evident. His formal installation as Lord Protector in December 1653 provides an illustration. In its own way, that ceremony emphasized the very ambiguity with which Cromwell had to contend. The new constitution, after all, was the product of a group of army officers, and it was being forced on the nation by the power of the army they controlled. But it is significant that Cromwell, on the occasion, deliberately chose to wear a plain black coat; it was to emphasize that he accepted this new role as a civilian, not as a military man.[40] Of course it was a futile, if not pathetic gesture; changing one's coat could hardly change political reality. But the sincerity as well as the futility must be acknowledged; to those who assembled for the ceremony, Cromwell pledged to rule not as military dictator but as a constitutional head of state.

I do promise in the presence of God that I will not violate or infringe the matters and things contained therein, but, to my power, observe the same, and cause them to be observed; and shall in all other things, to the best of my understanding, govern these nations according to the laws, statutes, and customs thereof; seeking their peace, and causing justice and law to be equally administered.[41]

If the Instrument was far from being a perfect constitution, it was better than no constitution at all. Between the resignation of Barebones Parliament and the acceptance of the Instrument, Cromwell had been, in a constitutional sense, vested with full, arbitrary power; his comments on that situation leave no doubt that he saw this as the very antithesis of freedom and sound government.

My power again, by this resignation, was a boundless and unlimited as before; all things being subject to arbitrariness and myself a person having power over the three nations, without bound or limit set . . ., all government being dissolved, all civil administration at an end.[42]

Given his outlook on government, Cromwell had everything to gain from the conversion of the constitution from a military one to a parliamentary one. This is why he was favourably inclined to the Humble Petition and Advice at a later date. But, as is well known, when, in the first Protectorate Parliament, the House set about precisely on this task, Cromwell was immediately at odds with them. The reasons for his opposition are central to any understanding of his role in the creation of political liberty. The famous speech on the four fundamentals comes as close as any statement of Cromwell to being a theoretical analysis of the basis of government; if the ideas contained in it are imperfectly articulated and formed, they are, nonetheless, of lasting significance. Of one of the fundamentals, liberty of conscience, no more need be said at this point; it has already been discussed at length. But the other three points touched equally significant constitutional issues. 'The Government by a Single Person and a Parliament is fundamental! It is the *esse*; it is constitutive'.[43] In saying this, Cromwell touched a troublesome feature of the Instrument, namely the rather ill-defined relationship of the executive and legislative branches of the government. If the constitution itself did not sufficiently delineate this relationship, Cromwell appears to have sensed that clarification of the issue by making one dominant over the other was not in the best interests of political liberty. It would be reading too much into his statement here to see behind it a fully developed theory of the separation of powers; what he was defending, after all, was a constitution in which those powers were, in rather ill-defined ways, shared. But it may not be wrong to suggest that he was groping in the right direction. In the second fundamental, he touched more directly and unambiguously on a key point. 'That Parliaments should not make themselves perpetual is a fundamental'.[44] The point is so obvious that it seems almost trivial, but it is not. Cromwell here was indicating that the existence of the institution of Parliament was not, in itself, a guarantee of liberty. It may have seemed so during eleven years when there had been no Parliament. But a body that does not regularly justify itself to those whom it claims to represent is, in the end, as much an expression of tyranny as a despotic king. Admittedly, Cromwell's convictions about the extent of representation did not satisfy radicals then, and they clearly would not now. But the central point he was making about the responsibilities of a representative body to its electorate was indeed just as he identified it, a fundamental. In the last fundamental, the question of the control of the armed forces, Cromwell had an obvious personal stake, but again, the general point, that authority should be shared so that one branch would not have complete control over the military, and hence be in a position to dictate its views by force, was both valid and important. Just as he did not fully articulate a theory of the separation of branches of government, he did not construct a full elaboration of the theory of checks and balances, but he had grasped the central point: 'For, put the absolute power of the militia into one without check, what doth it?'[45]

This quarrel with Parliament was only one of many that Cromwell had. There is no point in denying that Cromwell's relations with Parliament were far from fruitful and that his high hopes for successive meetings of that body were dashed. That realisation has led to various negative judgments on Cromwell that each, in one way or another, reflect on the manner in which one should consider his place in the history of liberty. The most negative judgment, of course, is that he was not at heart a believer in Parliament. There seems no reason to accept that view. The very vehemence with which he denounced the shortcomings of Parliaments suggests not his dislike of the institution but his sorrow that it could not engage in what he felt were constructive ways the task of building a godly England. His failures have also been explained by asserting that he had no positive programme, only a negative one, but this too seems a misinterpretation. The early Protectoral ordinances stand as testimony that he had a positive programme; the problem was not that he did not know where he was going but rather that where he wanted to go, particularly in the area of religious freedom, had little appeal to those he was attempting to lead.[46] It has also been said that he failed in this regard because he did not understand Parliament itself, that with a backbench perspective, he was a poor manager of parliamentary politics.[47] This seems dubious on two grounds. In the first place, his skilful handling of the protracted negotiations over the Humble Petition and Advice, by which he secured much of what he wanted before army intransigence over the issue of the kingship lost everything, suggests he was not all that clumsy at parliamentary politics after all. In the second place, he failed because he conceived of Parliament as ideally an occasion of consensus rather than as an arena of confrontation. In this, his view was intrinsically traditional and conservative, and it was out of touch with reality, for Parliament by the 1650s had become an arena of confrontation; traditional methods of management no longer worked. But there is a deeper point here too. Just because he could not find consensus, Cromwell did not abandon the principle of consent. He was taxed on precisely this point in 1656 by Ludlow, who sharply criticised him for not achieving 'that which we found for, . . . that the nation might be governed by its own consent.' Cromwell's answer was simple: 'I am . . . as much for a government by consent as any man, but where shall we find that consent? Amongst the Prelatical, Presbyterian, Independent, Anabaptist, or Levelling Parties?'[48] Ludlow rather simply retorted that consent was to be found 'amongst those of all sorts who had acted with fidelity and affection to the publick.' It was the language of fantasy, as Cromwell all too sadly knew, but that realisation on his own part did not mean that he had abandoned the principle; he simply could find no way to put it into practice.

If Cromwell then stood for non-arbitrary government, the principle of consent, and a central role for Parliament, there is, nonetheless, a darker side to his role in the story of political liberty. It is obvious that his conception of political liberty was substantially moulded in traditional and conservative practices. Anything approaching democracy in a political form was, to his eye, a manifest absurdity. It could not seem otherwise to him in a world where the godly were mixed with the ungodly. He believed firmly too in a 'natural' magistracy and in a system of ranks and orders. 'I beseech you, for the orders of men and the ranks of men, did not that Levelling principle tend to the reducing all to an equality?'[49] And if need be, he had few qualms about employing force to curb those who would upset that order; the Cromwell who pounded on the Council table and said of the Levellers 'I tell you, Sir, you have no other way to deal with these men but to break them or they will break you'[50] was as real as the Cromwell who spoke of consent in the political process. In the political sphere, even more so than in the area of religion, concern with order tempered his contribution to liberty. Constraints of class and of the time he lived in placed limits on his political vision. In opposing arbitrary government, in advocating consent, he did not stand as far in advance of the generality as he did when he advocated religious toleration. But as much as anything else, it was the practical necessity of ruling which put limits on his contribution to political liberty. He could never escape the ambiguity of ruling by military force. Whatever his personal feelings about arbitrary government (and there seem no grounds to doubt his sincerity in this regard), the necessities of preserving order in a divided society and the desire to bring reform to it, led him in turn to be arbitrary. When that fact was combined with an outlook that was essentially traditional in a social and political sense, and above all pragmatic rather than theoretical in its day-to-day application, the surprising thing is not that the contributions were limited but that they were as significant as they were.

Of Cromwell's contributions to social liberty, there is less to say. His broad and general sympathy with the lot of the oppressed is clear enough, as is his conviction that it was the responsibility of the government to do something about it. 'Relieve the oppressed, hear the groans of poor prisoners in England; be pleased to reform the abuses of all professions; and if there be anyone that makes many poor to make a few rich, that suits not a Commonwealth'.[51] But in this area, constraints imposed by his visions of class, by his concern for a reformation of manners, and by the exigencies of practical politics all combined to condition his activities. As a firm believer in the traditional social order, Cromwell was, by nature, not sympathetic to proposals that would have substantially altered the traditional relationships in the countryside. He talked frequently about reform of the law; in common with many of his contemporaries he found the law complex, its administration arcane, and the practices of lawyers unduly self-serving. Of his Protectoral government he said 'it hath desired to reform the laws . . . to consider how the laws might be made plain and short, and less chargeable to the people; how to lessen expense, for the good of the nation'.[52] To the second Protectorate parliament he declared,

There is one general Grievance in the Nation. It is the Law. Not that the Laws are grievance; but there are Laws that are a grievance; and the great grievance lies in the execution and administration . . . To hang a man for six pence, thirteen pence, I know not what; to hang for a trifle, and pardon murder – is the ministration of the Law, through the ill-framing of it.[53]

Even in voicing these criticisms of the legal system, however, he indicated his limits as a reformer in the area. To his mind, it was the administration of the law, not the content of it that was the major problem. The contrast in his approach to law reform with that taken by the Barebones Parliament is striking; the latter wielded a radical sledgehammer designed to shake the whole edifice of the law; Cromwell's efforts were characterised by a stance of pragmatic conservatism.

Cromwell's abiding concern with reformation of manners was, in his view of things, very much connected with liberty.

It is a thing I am confident our liberty and prosperity depends on . . . Make it a shame to see men bold in sin and prophaneness – and God will bless you . . . Truly these things do respect the souls of men, and the spirits – which are the men. The mind is the man. If that be kept pure, a man signifies somewhat; if not, I would very fain see what difference there is betwixt him and a beast. He hath only some activity to do some more mischief.[54]

Cromwell's efforts in this regard have been much misunderstood in the popular tradition. The image of the dour Puritan curbing the innocent enjoyments of the population and interfering with their little liberties dies hard. It is, of course, a caricature; Cromwell was not an enemy of enjoyment but rather of dissolute and anti-social behaviour. Still, the attempt to enforce a reformation of manners, especially in the period of the Major Generals, involved an element of centralisation that was uncomfortably reminiscent of the tendencies of the Stuart State. Cromwell may have felt that elevation of the spirit of man was an essential ingredient of liberty; one senses that, for much of the population, the efforts simply were an unwelcome intrusion of the central power into local life and were seen, on precisely those grounds, as an infringement of liberty rather than a step towards its realization.

Practical circumstances likewise continued to limit the effectiveness of Cromwell's efforts. The perhaps unlikely case of Ireland and of Cromwell's declaration that he was bringing English liberty to that land affords one such example. That Cromwell would be viewed by the Irish in some other guise than that of a defender of liberty was inherent in the situation. The nature of the Cromwellian conquest with its well-remembered effusion of blood would have seen to that by itself; the nature of the subsequent settlement, permanently associated in the Irish mind with his name although many of its outlines had been dictated before he came to power, only confirmed a picture of a brutal conqueror who far from bringing liberation instead trampled on the most cherished beliefs of the inhabitants. But that is not the whole story of Cromwell in Ireland; one must not only consider what he did but what he hoped to do, for Cromwell had a vision of what Ireland could be. The working out of things left very little scope for the realisation of that vision, yet it suggests that Cromwell came to Ireland not only in the garb of conqueror, but also in part on what he saw as a civilising and liberating mission. That vision should not be dismissed as mere hypocrisy, though it must also be recognised for what it was, a form of paternalistic colonialism. But behind the paternalism and the realities of external control, there was an idealism that spoke to the issue of liberty. Writing to John Sadler in 1649 in an attempt to persuade him to accept the office of Chief Justice of Munster, Cromwell commented,

We have a great opportunity to set up . . . a way of doing justice amongst these poor people, which for the uprightness and cheapness of it, may exceedingly gain upon them, who have been accustomed to as much injustice, tyranny and oppression from their landlords, the great men, and those that should have done them right, as, I believe, any people in that which we call Christendom.[55]

And to Ludlow he remarked that Ireland was 'capable of being governed by such laws as should be found most agreeable to justice; which may be so impartially administered, as to be a good precedent even to England itself'.[56] Cromwell's hopes were not realized, but, Irish historiography notwithstanding, there was more to him than the fanatical English conqueror.

The case of Ireland is closely related to one final area which should be mentioned, if only briefly, the evocation of the concept of liberty in connection with foreign policy. At the height of England's imperial age, this aspect of Cromwell's political role was frequently remarked on with favour. The radical M.P. Joseph Cowen, speaking in 1876, provides a good example of this sort of adulation.[57]

Never was that power wielded with more dignity in the long period of her history as an independent state. The Protestant residents of an Alpine valley were at that time treated as the Bulgarian shepherds had recently been by their Moslem rulers. And what was his action? The memorable message that Cromwell sent to the Catholic powers of Europe to secure protection for those suffering co-religionists was in very different terms, and couched in a very different spirit from the half-hearted and hesitating remonstrances addressed by our present Foreign Secretary to the Sultan. The Tories boasted of their spirited foreign policy. There never was a Tory statesman who manifested the energy, courage, and determination that the Puritan Protector showed.

Despite the enthusiasm of such Victorian opinions, it can in fact be doubted whether Cromwell made any effective contribution to liberty through the exercise of his foreign policy. That doubt stems from two quite different sources. In the first place, analysing Cromwellian foreign policy in terms of a liberating ideological core distorts the historical record. The rhetoric was often there; the reality of power certainly was too. But for all that it was a policy that was coldly pragmatic; if the ideological expressions coincided with the nation's political and commercial interests, they might be acted on, but they were never the mainspring of policy.[58] In the second place, even in the cases where such an ideological dimension was acted on, there should be reservations about the extent to which it represented a genuine contribution to liberty. It may have seemed to be such at the height of Victoria's reign, but even more so than the already ambiguous case of Ireland it cannot be seen that way by a world disillusioned by the imperial experience and the often well-meaning but nonetheless self-serving arrogance that accompanied it. Cloaking the very practical concerns of power politics in the attractive mantle of liberty does not, in and of itself, make them contributions to the history of freedom.

Realising that does not diminish Cromwell's contribution to liberty; it only clarifies the circumstances in which it can be reasonably discussed. Cromwell's career, as has been often observed, bristles with paradoxes. His contribution to the development of liberty is not the least of them. He was not consistent; he could be arbitrary. His actions were circumscribed by practical political concerns and a public mentality less tolerant than his own. One should not expect consistency in a man who was, after all, a pragmatic rather than an ideological revolutionary. And yet, for all the inconsistencies, one must accept the over-riding paradox that this reluctant dictator was a major contributor to the growth of English liberty.

Notes

1   There are innumerable studies of Cromwell, most of which consider, though often not systematically, Cromwell's role in the history of liberty. Among the most useful in this regard are M. Ashley, *The Greatness of Oliver Cromwell*, London, 1957; C. H. Firth, *Oliver Cromwell*, London, 1900; Antonia Fraser, *Cromwell, Our Chief of Men*, London, 1973; C. Hill, *God's Englishman: Oliver Cromwell and the English Revolution*, London, 1970; and R. S. Paul, *The Lord Protector*, London, 1955.

2   *An Exact Character or Narrative of the Late Right Noble and Magnificent Lord Oliver Cromwell*, London, 1658, p. 4.

3   G. Bate, *The Lives, Actions, and Execution of the Prime Actors and Principall Contrivers of That Horrid Murder of Our Late Pious and Sacred Soveraigne*, London, 1661, p. 5.

4   See, for example, I Kimber, *The Life of Oliver Cromwell Lord Protector*, London, 1731; J. Banks, *A Short Critical Review of the Political Life of Oliver Cromwell*, London, 1739; W. Harris, *An Historical and Critical Account of the Life of Oliver Cromwell*, London, 1762. Both Kimber and Harris officiated as non-

conformist clergy, while Banks was certainly schooled in the tradition, having been educated by an anabaptist minister.

5   *The Political Beacon: or the Life and Character of Oliver Cromwell Impartially Illustrated,* London, 1770.

6   T. Carlyle, *On Heroes, Hero-Worship, and the Heroic in History,* [1841], London, 1956, pp. 422–467; S. R. Gardiner, *Oliver Cromwell,* [1899], New York, 1962.

7   See, for example, C. Hill, *Oliver Cromwell 1658–1958,* London, 1958, pp. 7–8.

8   T. Carlyle, *The Letters and Speeches of Oliver Cromwell,* ed. S. C. Lomas, London, 1904, II, p. 21.

9   In this regard, the criticisms of Royalist writers such as Heath are no more vehement about Cromwell than the comments of a republican writer like Mrs. Macaulay.

10   Quoted in A. Smith, 'The image of Cromwell in folklore and tradition', *Folklore,* LXXIX, 1968, p. 17.

11   C. H. Firth (ed.), *The Memoirs of Edmund Ludlow,* Oxford, 1894, I, p. 365.

12   W. Haller and G. Davies (eds.), *The Leveller Tracts 1647–1653,* Gloucester, Mass, 1964, p. 12.

13   A typical example is provided by R. Burton, *The History of Oliver Cromwell,* [1692], London, 1698, pp. 168–169.

14   On Cromwell and the devil, see *A True and Faithful Narrative of Oliver Cromwell's Compact with the Devil for Seven Years,* London, 1720.

15   W. C. Abbott (ed.), *Writings and Speeches of Oliver Cromwell,* Cambridge, Mass., 1937–1947, I, pp. 61–62.

16   Harl. mss 166, f 113 b., quoted in S. R. Gardiner, *History of the Great Civil War 1642–1649,* London, 1893, reprinted London, 1911, II, p. 30.

17   Carlyle, *Letters and Speeches,* 1, p. 237.

18   *Ibid.,* I, p. 218.

19   *Ibid.,* II, p. 535.

20   W. Bray, (ed.), *The Diary and Correspondence of John Evelyn,* London, n.d., pp. 210, 214, 219, 223.

21   Fraser, *Cromwell,* p. 641.

22   C. H. Firth, *The Last Years of the Protectorate 1656–1658,* London, 1909, I, p. 79.

23   Carlyle, *Letters and Speeches,* III, pp. 5–7.

24   Ashley, *The Greatness of Oliver Cromwell,* p. 363.

25   Cf. T. Weld, *et. al., A Further Discovery of that Generation of Men Called Quakers,* Gateshead, 1654, pp. 69, 89.

26   Fraser, *Cromwell,* p. 573.

27   Carlyle, *Letters and Speeches,* I, p. 218.

28   G. Fox, *The Journal of George Fox,* London, 1962, p. 106.

29   Carlyle, *Letters and Speeches,* II, pp. 382–383.

30   *Ibid.,* II, p. 417.

31   C. H. Firth (ed.), *The Clarke Papers,* Camden Society, London, 1891–1901, I, p. 27.

32   Hill, *Oliver Cromwell,* p. 6.

33   Abbott, *Writings and Speeches*, I, p. 227.
34   *Ibid.*, I, p. 278.
35   *Ibid.*
36   Carlyle, *Letters and Speeches*, II, p. 129.
37   *Ibid.*
38   R. Williams, *The Fourth Paper by Major Butler* quoted in Hill, *God's Englishman*, p. 78.
39   R. Howell, *Cromwell*, London, 1977, chaps. 10–11.
40   *Ibid.*, p. 198.
41   *Ibid.*, p. 199.
42   Carlyle, *Letters and Speeches*, II, p. 373.
43   *Ibid.*, II, p. 381.
44   *Ibid.*, II, p. 382.
45   *Ibid.*, II, pp. 383–384.
46   Howell, *Cromwell*, pp. 199–205.
47   The best known statement of this view is H. R. Trevor-Roper, 'Oliver Cromwell and his Parliaments', reprinted in his *Religion, the Reformation, and Social Change*, London, 1967, 2nd ed., 1984, pp. 345–391.
48   Firth, *Ludlow's Memoirs*, II, p. 11.
49   Carlyle, *Letters and Speeches*, II, p. 342.
50   M. A. Gibb, *John Lilburne The Leveller: A Christian Democrat*, London, 1947, p. 258.
51   Carlyle, *Letters and Speeches*, II, p. 108.
52   *Ibid.*, II, pp. 352–353.
53   *Ibid.*, II, p. 541.
54   *Ibid.*, II, pp. 540–541.
55   Abbott, *Writings and Speeches*, II, p. 187.
56   Firth, *Ludlow's Memoirs*, I, p. 247.
57   Tyne and Wear Archives Office, Cowen Papers, B178, p. 12.
58   Hill, *Oliver Cromwell*, p. 8.

Christian liberty in Marvell and Milton

I

The aim in this paper is to restore Marvell and Milton to history – not so much to try to provide a 'true' or objective reading (there are no true readings of literary texts, only more or less satisfactory interpretations) as to provide a conceptual framework on which interpretation can be grounded.[1] Though Marvell and Milton were friends and colleagues, the relationship between the writings of the two men has not received much critical attention. Part of the reason for this is conventional literary categorisation and canon formation, under the influence of Eliot and Leavis: the two are often thought of as representing rival schools of poetry, even as standing on opposite sides of a hypothetical divide (the yawning fissure of a dissociation of sensibility, a San Andreas fault running through the middle of the seventeenth century). A further reason is the dislike of political commitment, or distrust of historical fact as a kind of creeping scientism, common both to literary modernism and the tradition it reacted against, that of Victorian and Edwardian *belles-lettres*. The disciplines of literature and history still normally resemble two armed camps, only rarely permitting messengers and hostages to pass to and fro. There are significant differences between the two authors in their poetic styles and in the personae they characteristically present in their writings, but as this essay will try to show, they were strikingly similar in their response to the political events they lived through and in the ethical problems with which they were concerned.

Both Marvell and Milton wrote a great deal during the period of the English Revolution (Marvell mostly verse, Milton mostly prose), and both were largely formed by the Revolution, the hopes of its success and the growing awareness of its failure, so that their later writings are in a sense predicated on, and serve as commentaries on, the Civil War, the Commonwealth, and the Protectorate. For both writers, religion, politics, and ethics were inseparably interwoven. Both were Arminian Puritans, and this doctrinal allegiance (an unpopular and heterodox belief in their day) led them to place great emphasis in their works on the idea of Christian liberty: both present a world in which moral choice is both imperative and infinitely problematical, since man is both free and hedged round with uncomfortable constraints.[2] The specific religious beliefs and political allegiances of Marvell and Milton are matters for historical investigation – are 'dead ideas', to quote a once influential denigratory comment on Milton – but the ethical issues at the heart of their work are matters of direct contemporary relevance. How does one balance claims of the civil power against those of the individual conscience; what are the limits of conscientious dissent or rebellion; what are the practical consequences of the 'great Charter of Christian Liberty'[3] if we take it not as 'nominal' (to use Swift's term) but as a guide to conduct in our everyday lives?

The main concern in this essay will be the ethical dimension in the writings of Marvell and Milton during this period, taking ethics as that point where psychology and politics meet – axioms of philosophy felt on the pulses. In particular, it will look at the ways in which the two authors treat the ethical problems inherent in the situation of the private individual seeking to 'make impression upon'[4] the relatively inaccessible public domain, and at the tensions created in the work by the felt need to balance the rival, incompatible demands of the sovereign conscience and the sovereign state.

Most of the works that will be discussed – the two partial exceptions are Marvell's 'Horatian Ode' and 'Upon Appleton House' – can be seen as persuasive, as not only reacting to historical events but seeking to change history. In a work written with persuasive intent (leaving aside the immensely difficult question of how we can be sure of the intent of an author or a work), the problem for the interpreter frequently lies in the relationship between 'political beliefs' and 'polemical methods', to quote the title of Barbara Lewalski's excellent essay on Milton's tracts of 1659–60. It is sometimes argued that the literary or aesthetic and the topical, polemical, or political aspects of a work are separable, even that they are inevitably at variance with one another: 'The literary "coherence" of the individual pamphlet interferes with its "correspondence" to political reality, its sense of participation in the currents of actual political and social life.'[5] This view, it would appear, is less a critical principle than a prejudice: it is, arguably, the modern critic who brings about such a divorce, not Marvell or Milton. Keith Stavely's position – and Stavely is cited as representative – depends on a crude glorification of the 'real' or 'actual' (presumably found on the streets and not in books) which is a mirror image of the aestheticism it seeks to reject. As reductive theories often do, it takes the stance of the hanging judge, assuming that an author is guilty unless proved innocent. There is a marked contrast between the Arminian theology of Milton and Marvell, with its concern for clearing a space for human freedom, and the relentless determinism of so many modern critics, who imprison authors in an iron cage of history and ideology (where they do not abolish authors altogether), while arrogating to themselves the arbitrary freedom of the Hobbesian monarch.

But Stavely raises a legitimate point which we need to consider in examining works like *Areopagitica* and the 'Horatian Ode', which seek to unite the topical and the universal: the two warring elements do not always lie down easily side by side, and the unity and coherence an author seeks to impose on his disparate materials may be factitious, agile sleight of hand designed to distract the reader's attention from innate and unresolved contradictions. Recent criticism of Milton's prose has been alert to occasion, genre, and polemical strategy, but has tended to emphasize the strategic or tactical, 'the pursuit of immediate political ends'[6] and the deployment of arguments in the most efficient way to further these ends, to the exclusion of other less immediate concerns. Once again, the critics seem to be reacting against the conventional view of the ivory tower by showing that poets are just as practical as the Henry Kissingers and Michael Heseltines of the world. Yet the suspicion of ideology and of any universalist claims for literature can have the unfortunate effect of imprisoning an author within his circumstances. Authors are products of history, but neither they nor their works are wholly determined by history, even though the new historicism sometimes would like to claim that they are.

There is much to be said, then, for the continued utility of the 'history of ideas' – the approach of Woodhouse and Barker – as a method of approaching the tracts and poems of the Civil War period. Though we should be alert to the deformations of ideology, aware that the unexamined statements, silences, and omissions in an author's work are sometimes as significant as what he does say, we should never fall into the trap of assuming that beliefs are no more than lies and evasions or ignore, suppress, or expunge an author's words in order to lock him firmly into a context. The ideas of Milton, Marvell, Hobbes, and Winstanley are not mere counters, and are worth taking seriously. Rhetorical analysis – 'observing in any given case the available means of persuasion', as Aristotle puts it in the *Rhetoric* – can be invaluable as a tool of critical investigation. But Milton was consistently a Platonist in his subordination of rhetoric, a mere instrument subject to the 'false guile' of skilful and unscrupulous tempters, to dialectic. 'So that how he should be truly eloquent who is not withall a good man, I see not . . . True eloquence I find to be none, but the serious and hearty love of truth.'[7]

It seems a reasonable working assumption that the political, ethical, and religious beliefs of Marvell and Milton remained essentially consistent throughout this period and later, and that local discrepancies are a matter of shifting allegiances and adaptation to particular audiences and historical events. Few critics any longer charge Milton with insincerity or time-serving in his writings during the English Revolution, though the tendency of Marvell criticism is still to treat his poems as intellectual exercises devoid of content. The argument in this essay is that the idea of Christian liberty is as central to Marvell as to Milton and that the dominant concerns in the writings of both are ethical. But the concept of Christian liberty in itself remains problematical. In this doctrine to which both men are dedicated and which both sought to defend, are there inherent inconsistencies, contradictions, or ambiguities which one writer or both were unable to resolve? Can they do any more than paper over the cracks?

II

Both Marvell and Milton habitually set the 'world' against the individual mind or conscience, focussing on the epistemological and ethical problems presented by the contingent reality pressing in on the individual and refusing to leave him alone: 'Two Paradises 'twere in one / To live in Paradise alone'. ('The Garden', lines 63–4). In *The Poet's Time* there is a lengthy commentary on the dialectic of withdrawal and involvement in Marvell's writings during the period of the English Revolution, a debate enacted in such poems as 'An Horatian Ode', 'Upon Appleton House', and 'Tom May's Death', as in the 'autobiographical' passages in Milton's *The Reason of Church Government*, the *Apology*, the *Second Defense*, and the sonnets. The theme of vocation or 'the choice of life' is, of course, a familiar topic in Milton criticism, and it is now generally recognised that Milton habitually uses the first person to explore ethical problems which are of direct concern to him and at the same time universal: the 'I' is both individual and representative.

> How soon hath Time, the subtle thief of youth,
> Stol'n on his wing my three and twentieth year!
> My hasting days fly on with full career,
> But my late spring no bud or blossom show'th.
> Perhaps my semblance might deceive the truth,
> That I to manhood am arriv'd so near,
> And inward ripeness doth much less appear,
> That some more timely-happy spirits endu'th.
>
> (Sonnet VII, 1–8)

The lines powerfully convey a sense of inward frustration and dissatisfaction conveyed by outward signs: as in Coleridge's 'Dejection: an Ode' or Hardy's 'The Darkling Thrush', everything in the outer world is transformed to metaphor, embodiments of – or ammunition for – a psychological state. Anger and resentment here are fuelled by the comparison with the 'more timely-happy spirits', time's favoured children crowned with early success, as well as by the sense of alienation from normal patterns of growth and ripening. Yet the terms of the consolation are already apparent in the evocation of these normal patterns of the natural world and emphasis on 'semblance', the possibility that the speaker's perception of reality, however strongly felt and expressed, might be self-deceived, myopic:

> Yet it be less or more, or soon or slow,
> It shall be still in strictest measure ev'n
> To that same lot, however mean or high,
> Toward which Time leads me, and the will of Heav'n;
> All is, if I have grace to use it so,
> As ever in my great task-Master's eye.
>
> (9–14)

The sudden shift in perspective is stunning: the pagan conception of time hastening on to oblivion, time the deceiver, a capricious and cynical joker, is supplanted or corrected by a slow, sure providential procession in which the god of time is enlisted in the angelic hierarchy as the servant of a just and benevolent God. 'What in me is dark' is suddenly illumined, 'what is low' (*PL*, I, 22–3) raised and supported: Milton's choice of language in the sestet, bare, dignified, chastened, largely unmetaphorical, reflects the change in perspective, and helps to involve the reader in the internal debate.

The theology of the closing lines is Arminian, yet within the overall framework of Puritan belief. God's grace is freely vouchsafed, but his will is sovereign and incomprehensible; man cannot merit salvation by his works, demanding admission to heaven, and must submit himself to God's will, whatever it may be. But man can *use* his time, is granted the opportunity to take advantage of the offered grace and perform whatever tasks are set him by his invisible master. Each natural object may hold within it the seeds of an unanticipated test:

Wherefore did he creat passions within us, pleasures round about us, but that these rightly temper'd are the very ingredients of vertu?

(*Areopagitica, CPW*, II, p. 527).

The beginning of 'An Horatian Ode' is as explicitly secular as Milton's sonnet is religious: the poem's very title suggests an ethos that is fundamentally classical, worldly rather than otherworldly. A second immediate difference is that Marvell eschews the first person, speaks of an anonymous or hypothetical 'forward youth' rather than his own youth and his own ultimate lot. Yet the same sense of a moment charged with significance, the same suggestion that a task is being set or a test is under way, the same awareness of the power over the individual or external forces which cannot be ignored and must be responded to, one way or another, fills both poems. The task-master here, even more than in Milton, is a *deus absconditus* who gives us no clear hints of how we are to act.

> The forward Youth that would appear
> Must now forsake his *Muses* dear,
>   Nor in the Shadows sing
>   His Numbers languishing.
> 'Tis time to leave the Books in dust,
> And oyl th'unused Armours rust:
>   Removing from the Wall
>   The Corslet of the Hall.
> So restless *Cromwel* could not cease
> In the inglorious Arts of Peace,
>   But through adventrous War
>   Urged his active Star.

(1–12)

It is a mistake to read these lines as expressing any kind of determinism: the imperatives are all, as it were, subjunctives, expressing preferences, inclinations, prudential choices rather than iron necessities. The ethical position implicit in the lines is compatible with the

Arminianism both Marvell and Milton professed, in its emphasis on man's responsibility to grasp the offered opportunity. The emphasis on 'now' and ''tis time' throughout the passage suggests that the particular moment (June 1650) poses particular choices, but 'the forward Youth' only *must* act in this way because he *would* (desires to, wishes to), out of ambition, patriotism, or self-interest. Simarly Cromwell *could not* cease because of the restlessness of his character (or the restlessness of all men, axiomatic for Herbert and Traherne as well as for Hobbes) and the natural impulses or 'inward prompting' (*CPW*, I, p. 810) that led him, propelled by the events of that particular time, toward the sphere in which his talents would find the greatest fulfilment. The paradox of 'urged his active Star' expresses the relationship of outward fate, fortune, or providence, the cloudy prophetic book on which human deeds are enrolled, and the realm of choice through which men realise their destinies. Where Cromwell eagerly embraces whatever 'adventrous War' might bring, the preferences of the budding aesthete of the opening lines (and, one suspects, of the poet and of most of his readers, then and now) plainly favour the study or bedchamber more than the battlefield. But rational choice, as both Milton and Marvell show consistently, often involves conquering our inclinations.

The autobiographical digression from *The Reason of Church-Government* expresses a similar ambivalence: an emotional leaning toward the contemplative life, seen as infinitely preferable under ordinary conditions, but a deliberate choice of the active, with all of its problems, as appropriate to the particular moment. The only necessity here is an internal one: man hears the call and may choose to answer it or not.

I trust hereby to make it manifest with what small willingness I endure to interrupt the pursuit of no lesse hopes than these, and leave a calme and pleasing solitarynes fed with cherful and confident thought, to imbark in a troubl'd sea of noises and hoars disputes . . . Let any gentle apprehension that can distinguish learned pains from unlearned drudgery, imagin what pleasure or profoundnesse can be in this, or what honour to deal against such adversaries. But were it the meanest under-service, if God by his Secretary conscience injoyn it, it were sad for me if I should draw back, for me especially, now when all men offer their aid to help ease and lighten the difficult labours of the Church.

(*CPW*, I, pp. 821–2)

Choice in this passage is presented in theological terms absent from the 'Horatian Ode'. The grounds for choice are not the rational calculations of self-interest, but the inward voice of conscience ('And I will place within them as a guide / My Umpire *Conscience*', [*PL*, III, 194–5]), inscribed in man by God as a means of reminding him of his status as a servant. Marvell's opening lines, on the other hand, like most of his poem, can be glossed with reference to Machiavelli, that most secular of political theorists.[8] In Milton, what tips the balance toward voluntary assumption of the yoke is the sense of vocation: the service of God must be willing service, taken on in full awareness that it may entail a descent into smoky darkness instead of 'the bright countenance of truth', pain and 'drudgery' rather than pleasure, so that one finds oneself surrounded by the noises of chaos while dreaming of the radiant stillness of order.

The external force behind the scenes in 'An Horation Ode' is never presented as either just or benevolent. Indeed, that force, identified in the poem as Fate, Fortune, the stars, or history, would appear not only to be indifferent to man's merits, hopes, or desires, but contemptuous of human values.

> Though Justice against Fate complain,
> And plead the antient Rights in vain:
> But these do hold or break
> As men are strong or weak.
>
> (37–40)

The tragic emotions, here as later in the poem, partly depend on suppressing or withholding the possible consolation of an afterlife in which Fate and Justice, 'helpless Right' (62) and power, are no longer seen as deadly enemies, rapist and victim, but as God's servants; there is no epilogue in heaven in the 'Horatian Ode', and the poem ends as it begins, in uncertainty. We know from *The Rehearsal Transpros'd* that Marvell, like Milton, disliked the doctrine of a 'Universal Dictatorship of Necessity over God and Man' (*RT*, II, p. 230), and the lines just quoted suggest that men, as well as being trapped by fate, can make their own fate by responding to circumstances according to their inner natures. Human freedom, as Marvell presents it in the 'Horatian Ode', finds its scope not in answering God's call, but in facing up to those moments where there is no call. All the troubled observer of events has to go on is a series of ambiguous portents, capable of being interpreted in contradictory ways: a 'bleeding Head' can arouse pity for the defeated victim and contempt for the 'bloody hands' of those actively or tacitly responsible for the judicial murder, or it can serve the state as a favourable omen of a 'happy Fate' which may follow ('Horatian Ode', 55–6, 69–72).

'An Horatian Ode' and 'Upon Appleton House' view the events of the Civil War from two different perspectives, appropriate to their central figures, Cromwell and Fairfax, but they share a prevailing tone of tragic irony, a sense of human helplessness before events. Marvell's emphasis throughout his writings is less on the justice of God's ways than on their inscrutability. As Christopher Hill has said, 'it was in defeat that Milton set about justifying the ways of God to men';[9] the same is true of Marvell, who rarely writes of victory. The chastened tone of *The Readie and Easie Way, Samson Agonistes,* and the closing books of *Paradise Lost* is more congenial to Marvell than the exultation of *An Apology, Eikonoklastes,* and the prophetic passages in *Areopagitica.* But the writings of both throughout the period of the English Revolution, and their retrospective comments on the failure of that revolution, return again and again to the same ethical imperatives: 'to ordain wisely as in this world of evill, in the midd'st whereof God hath plact us unavoidably' (*Areopagitica, CPW,* II, p. 526).

III

The difference between Marvell and Milton is partly one of temperament, partly one of chronology of political development. During the Civil War itself and the Commonwealth they sometimes reacted in sharply different ways to the same events: *Eikonoklastes* and the 'Horatian Ode' state opposite views of the King's execution, and while both men happened to be on the Continent when fighting broke out, Marvell's stance was initially far more that of a non-combatant. (Milton says in the *Second Defense,* 'I thought it base that I should travel abroad at my ease for the cultivation of my mind, while my fellow-citizens at home were fighting for liberty' (*CPW,* IV, p. 619); Marvell stayed away until 1646.) But by 1654 they had arrived at the same place, coming from different directions. It is interesting to compare two passages which employ the apocalyptical imagery we normally associate with seventeenth-century Puritanism and suggest that human will, acting freely, can serve as the instrument of the divine will. The differences, arguably, reflect both 'the Times' and 'the Man', and both passages illustrate the difficulties the authors faced in accommodating the demands of rhetoric and of dialectic, the search for adequate means of persuasion and the search for truth. One passage come from *An Apology* (1642), the other from *The First Anniversary* (1655):

And indeed, if we consider the generall concourse of suppliants, the free and ready admittance, the willing and speedy redresse in what is possible, it will not seems much otherwise, then as if some divine commission from heav'n were descended to take into hearing and commiseration the long remedilesse afflictions of this kingdome ... Therefore the more they seeke to humble themselves, the more does God by manifest signes and testimonies visibly honour their proceedings; and sets them as the mediators of this his cov'nant which he offers us to renew. Wicked men daily conspire their hurt, and it comes to nothing, rebellion rages in our Irish Province, but with miraculous and losselesse victories of few against many is daily discomfited and broken; if we neglect not this early pledge of Gods inclining towards us, by the slacknesse of our needfull aids. And whereas at other times we count it ample honour when God voutsafes to make men the instrument and subordinate worker of his gracious will, such acceptation have their prayers found with him, that to them he hath bin pleas'd to make himself the agent, and immediat performer of their desires; dissolving their difficulties when they are thought inexplicable, cutting out wayes for them where no passage could be seene; as who is there so regardlesse of Divine providence, that from late occurrences will not confesse ... Not that we should think they are at the end of their glorious progress, but that they will go on to follow his Almighty leading, who seems to have thus cov'nanted with them, that if the will and the endeavour shall be theirs, the performance and the perfeting shall be his.

(*CPW*, I, pp. 926–8)

All the 'signes and testimonies' here are interpreted in the most favourable possible way: if a modern reader feels a certain resistance to the eloquence of Milton's prose, it is because, once one is removed from the immediate sway of events, the rhetoric can seem manipulative, a rewriting of history with partisan intent. Miraculous and lossless victories, the discomfiture of wicked men, divine commission, difficulties magically dissolved: it is like the *Sun* during the Falklands war. The insistence that certain phenomena can be interpreted in only one manner (who is there ... that from late occurrences will not confesse) is an appeal to the reader of a rather bullying kind to accept just such an interpretation and embrace the Parliamentary cause the author is defending. Here Milton is coming perilously close to arguing from success, the identification of earthly power with divine power which he argues against in so many of his tracts, as in *Samson Agonistes* and *Paradise Regained*.

Theologically his argument is that the 'testimonies' he adduces are evidence of a covenant, like the covenant with Abraham, by which God has chosen the English as 'one peculiar Nation ... select / From all the rest' (*PL*, XI, 111–2). The covenant or supposed national election, like the covenant of grace to the individual believer, is for Milton conditional: man must recognise, accept, and take advantage of the opportunity of the offered grace. His language in the passage therefore is conditional, with three *if*s and one *as if*, and the words not only suggest that man needs to live up to his part of the bargain, but that he may well fail to do so. What is required of man, a free agent endowed with Christian liberty, is 'will and endeavour' ('Though but endeavoured with sincere intent'), (*PL*, III, 192), but neither may be forthcoming. In the peroration of the *Second Defense*, the possibility of failure is brought out even more fully, and the passage combines exhortation with warning:

If after such brave deeds you ignobly fail, if you do aught unworthy of yourselves, be sure that posterity will speak out and pass judgment . . . It will be a source of grief that to such great undertakings, such great virtues, perseverance was lacking. It will seem to posterity that a mighty harvest of glory was at hand, together with the opportunity for doing the greatest deeds, but that to this opportunity men were wanting.

(*CPW*, IV, i, p. 685)

Marvell's *The First Anniversary* is contemporaneous with the *Second Defense*, argues essentially the same political position, and is similarly balanced between the hope of great accomplishments and the fear that men will not be worthy of the moment. Like Milton, Marvell has embraced the puritan cause and writes of defence of the Protectorate government, urging waverers to support it. The apocalyptical fervour here thus has a persuasive end in mind, as with Milton. It is particularly striking, then, that his praise is so carefully hedged round with conditions and qualifications, his approach so coolly analytical, with such prominence given to the ironic consciousness of failure and loss:

Hence oft I think, if in some happy Hour
High Grace should meet in one with highest Pow'r,
And then a seasonable People still
Should bend to his, as he to Heavens will,
What we might hope, what wonderful Effect
From such a wish'd Conjuncture might reflect.
Sure, the mysterious work, where none withstand,
Would forthwith finish under such a Hand:
Fore-shortned Time its useless Course would stay,
And soon precipitate the latest Day.
But a thick Cloud about that Morning lyes,
And intercepts the Beams of Mortal eyes,
That 'tis the most which we determine can,
If these the Times, then this must be the Man.
And well he therefore does, and well has guest,
Who in his Age has always forward prest:

> And knowing not where Heavens choice may light,
> Girds yet his Sword, and ready stands to fight:
> But Men alas, as if they nothing car'd,
> Look on, all unconcern'd, or unprepar'd . . .
> Hence landing Nature to new Seas is tost,
> And good Designs still with their Authors lost.
>
> (*First Anniversary*, 131–158)

There are two sources of uncertainty here. The first lies in providence itself: God simply, in his inaccessible, incomprehensible wisdom, may choose not to reward England with a reign of millenarian wonders or indeed may not even grant the Cromwellian régime a modest success. God may choose to kill Cromwell off (as Marvell suggests a few lines later) or to thwart his good intentions. Secondly, the leader may not have any followers: the unregenerate multitude, sottish and indifferent, may pass up the opportunity God has offered them. The 'Conjuncture' of political or military power with divine election, of the general will, the will of the leader, and the will of God, of the man and the times, may well happen (a mighty harvest of glory was at hand), but it may well not. Cromwell's Christian liberty shows itself in his choice to assume the stance of the warfaring Christian, without ever being able to anticipate what heaven has in store; his fellow Englishmen have a similar responsibility to exercise the will in choice, but the darkness in which they labour, it is suggested, is not only the cloudiness of God's decrees, but a self-imposed ignorance and folly.

There are relatively few passages in Marvell or Milton in which 'highest Pow'r' in earthly rulers and statesmen is treated with such respect. Normally, for both, power is a temptation, and those who hold it or ardently desire it are likely to be rogues, intriguers, or tyrants, filled with 'Pride and worse Ambition' (*PL*, IV, 40), deaf to the voice of conscience:

There have never been wanting among them such as would set the Magistrate upon the Pinnacle of the Temple, and showing him all the Power, Wealth, and Glory of the Kingdoms of the Earth, have proferr'd the Prince all so he would be tempted to fall down and worship them.

(*RT*, II, p. 239)

The affinities of both Marvell and Milton with the radical wing of seventeenth-century Puritanism are most apparent in their strict segregation of the orders of nature and grace (to use Woodhouse's terms).[10] Christian liberty, more often than not, will therefore be exercised in the rejection of power, or in the tempering of power, when it is used in accordance with virtue and justice by one of the rare political leaders who recognize its dangers and its limitations.

> O yet a nobler task awaits thy hand;
>   For what can War, but endless War still breed,
>   Till Truth and Right from Violence be freed,
> And Public Faith clear'd from the shameful brand
> Of Public Fraud. In vain does Valor bleed
>   While Avarice and Rapine share the land.
>
> ('On the Lord General Fairfax', 9–14)

Most passages in Milton addressed to Fairfax, Cromwell, or the Parliament, or in Marvell addressed to Cromwell, Richard Cromwell, or the Parliament (or later to Charles II) take the form of political advice and counsel, usually urging the recipient to do something he does not especially want to do. Praise is usually calculated, and often entails a double appeal to conscience and self-interest, in an attempt to enlist the addressee's support, not simply in favour of one group within the ruling faction against another ('On the proposals of certain ministers of the Committee for Propogation of the Gospel'), but, as Milton and Marvell argue their case, in support of principles of liberty which transcend historical circumstances and tribal loyalties. That is the central argument of *Areopagitica*, of the *Second Defense* (which as well as being a public defence of 'the cause of the English people and . . . of Liberty itself', seeking to justify the Revolution and the Protectorate before an international audience, embodies an appeal to Cromwell and to his 'fellow countrymen', couched in terms of praise and admonition (*CPW*, IV, i, 549, 685), and of Milton's sonnet to Cromwell.

> Cromwell, our chief of men, who through a cloud
>   Not of war only, but detractions rude,
>   Guided by faith and matchless Fortitude,
>   To peace and truth thy glorious way hast plough'd,
> And on the neck of crowned Fortune proud
>   Hast rear'd God's Trophies and his work pursu'd,
>   While Darwen stream with blood of Scots imbru'd,
>   And *Dunbar* field resounds thy praises loud,
> And *Worcester's* laureate wreath; yet much remains
>   To conquer still; peace hath her victories
>   No less renown'd than war, new foes arise
> Threat'ning to bind our souls with secular chains;
>   Help us to save free Conscience from the paw
>   Of hireling wolves whose Gospel is their maw.

The praise of Cromwell in the octave is, as it were, a precondition of the

plea to him to join in an alliance against those who seek to establish a
national church with coercive powers and thus (to quote a poem written
six years earlier) 'force our Consciences that Christ set free'. The
'hireling wolves' would use their new-gained freedom to impose slavery
on others. The language of panegyric is partly intended to predispose
Cromwell, when he reads the poem, to look sympathetically on the
speaker. But the poem is a public statement, not a private letter, and
addresses a wider audience, suggesting that the speaker, Cromwell, and
the party of the virtuous in the England of 1652, as they have made
common cause so far, should continue to do so. On the evidence of
'signs and testimonies' drawn from recent historical events, Cromwell's
victories are interpreted as God's work carried out by a human agent.
The contrast with 'An Horatian Ode', which treats some similar materials, is pronounced: where in Marvell's poem, written two years earlier,
an amoral Fortune appears to rule and Cromwell, child of the moment,
is disquietingly compared to a lightning bolt and a bird of prey, efficient
engines of destruction, here God strides triumphantly over prostrate
Fortune and Cromwell, the Christian hero, bears the shield of faith.
The polemical strategy of Milton's sonnet is to isolate the theocratic
party, those who demand stringent restrictions on liberty of conscience,
as God's enemies: pretending to serve God, like the worldly prelates
before them, they serve only their bellies.

Liberty of conscience, as Milton and Marvell see it, is always under
threat from those who seek to violate it (the sexual metaphor, or the
related metaphor of the wolf in the fold, is always just below the surface,
and sometimes explicit), those who do not understand it, and those who
confound it with the tyranny of their own desires, the slavery of imposed
chains or the slavery of the unregenerate will. In general, Milton's
position and Marvell's are closest in those works in which they satirise
the enemies of freedom or lament men's folly in donning self-imposed
chains. Though the works were written twenty-five years apart, under
different political circumstances, there is no substantive difference
between the position argued in Milton's 'On the New Forcers of
Conscience under the Long Parliament' and Marvell's *The Rehearsal
Transpros'd*. Both are sharp satiric attacks on ambitious, revengeful
clerics, and both explicitly argue that the lust for power as a motive
transcends circumstances and ostensible doctrinal allegiances. The
resemblance of the sonnet 'I did but prompt the age' to Marvell's
writings is subtler and harder to define: the modulations from dignified
apologia to harsh satiric attack on 'barbarous' adversaries to ironic

impasse resemble the shifts in tone characteristic of Marvell, and the final lines have tragic dimensions relatively rare in Milton's works written during the revolutionary period and more common in Marvell's:

> But this is got by casting Pearl to Hogs,
> That bawl for freedom in their senseless mood,
>   And still revolt when truth would set them free.
>   License they mean when they cry liberty;
> For who loves that, must first be wise and good;
>   But from that mark how far they rove we see,
>   For all this waste of wealth and loss of blood.

(8–14)

Hope and despair are finely balanced in these lines, as they are throughout Marvell's 'Upon Appleton House'. Milton's sonnet suggests that the pathway to the bright realm of truth and liberty is clear, but that men in their blind folly turn away, wilfully bringing about their own destruction: 'I form'd them free, and free they must remain, / Till they enthrall themselves' (*PL*, III, 124–5). The contrast between a presumed absolute liberty, wrongly defined to mean 'licence', and Christian liberty under God, as expressed in these lines, lies at the heart both of Milton's thought and of Marvell's. Marvell draws a similar distinction in *The First Anniversary* between 'that sober Liberty which men may have' (289) and the self-delusive craving for absolute, untrammelled liberty ('a Freedom, that where all command' [280]), which simply cloaks the lust to possess and to destroy. In *The First Anniversary* as later in his post-Restoration political writings, he argues for a liberal 'mixed state', a constitutional settlement by which 'stubborn Men' (78), led by enlightened self-interest, enter into a 'willing' (76) contractual agreement protecting the rights of the individual without degenerating into anarchy and licence. The conflict of order and conscience is resolved by a voluntary relinquishing of any claim for absolute freedom – and, in terms of practical politics, by urging acceptance of the Protectorate government as the best possible under the circumstances.[11]

In 'Upon Appleton House', written three years earlier, Marvell could not envision any such reconciliation of earthly power and the tender conscience. The poem's addressee, Fairfax, had retired from public affairs shortly before at the height of his fame, disturbed at the course the Revolution was taking. The Civil War is seen here as a re-enactment of the Fall, and the poem holds out no hope either of millenial transformation or of rational compromise as political ideals capable of realisation. God has ordained not a succession of glorious victories, but only

(to adapt Milton's phrase) 'waste . . . and loss of blood', a landscape of
desolation stretching as far as the eye can see: 'But War all this doth
overgrow: / We Ordnance Plant and Powder sow' (341–2). The conscientious Christian, as exemplified here by Fairfax, exercises his faculty
of rational choice by eschewing the world of political action altogether,
treating the temptation of power rather as Christ does in *Paradise
Regained*:

> And yet there walks one on the Sod
> Who, had it pleased him and *God*,
> Might once have made our Gardens spring
> Fresh as his own and flourishing.
> But he preferr'd to the *Cinque Ports*
> These five imaginary Forts:
> And, in those half-dry Trenches, spann'd
> Pow'r which the Ocean might command.
>
> For he did, with his utmost Skill,
> *Ambition* weed, but *Conscience* till.
> Conscience, that Heaven-nursed Plant,
> Which most our Earthly Gardens want.
> A prickling leaf it bears, and such
> As that which shrinks at ev'ry touch;
> But Flowrs eternal, and divine,
> That in the Crowns of Saints do shine.
>
>   (345–360)

The passage is tragic, not least in the suggestion that the devastation
of the garden-state of England is irreversible, the inevitable result of
God's decrees and man's actions. In both stanzas, Fairfax's free choice
is emphasised, as well as the congruence between his unconstrained will
and the will of God (had it pleased him and *God*). In the first stanza, we
are made aware of potential unfulfilled, hopes unrealised; the world of
action, as the stanza presents it, has already receded into the past. The
idea of free will presupposes that other choices would have been possible in other circumstances, and that another man might have interpreted the voice of conscience differently from Fairfax. But though in
other poems written during this period Marvell can suggest a scope for
conscientious action within the world, here his conclusions are grimly
ascetic, as 'the one just Man' finds himself compelled 'To save himself
and household from amidst – A World devote to universal Rack' (*PL*,
XI, 20–1).

IV

Each of the two contrasting positions on the relationship between conscience and civil power argued under different circumstances by Marvell and Milton – the rejectionist stance, as exemplified by 'Upon Appleton House', and the accommodating position, as exemplified by 'The First Anniversary' – is fully compatible with Arminian notions of Christian liberty. Indeed, if there were a simple formula determining choice in all circumstances (civil power must always be obeyed; civil power must never be obeyed), the gift of freedom would become derisory. Where there are two competing obligations, Marvell argues in *The Rehearsal Transpros'd*, one must take precedence over the other: since men are both 'free' and 'the servants of God', it follows that where obedience to the civil power and the commands of conscience 'come to be contradistinguished, not man but God is to be obey'd' (*RT*, II, p. 248). In *A Treatise of Civil Power*, *The Rehearsal Transpros'd*, and *A Short Historical Essay*, Milton and Marvell are particularly concerned to define Christian liberty as the freedom to practise the religion of one's choice, arguing against the imposition of coercive laws, but the very nature of their arguments precludes any sharp distinction between religious and political liberty, since one entails the other.

Government as Marvell and Milton see it is both a product of the fallen state and a partial remedy for the inconveniences of that state. Unlike Locke and most later contract theorists, they identify the hypothetical state of nature presupposed by such theory with the Garden of Eden, where neither law nor magistrate was required. It is no more possible to separate politics from ethics in the following passage from *The Rehearsal Transpros'd* than in parallel passages from *Areopagitica* and the divorce tracts. But the ironic poignancy of this passage is characteristically Marvellian:

And so also in the Government of the World, it were desirable that man might live in perpetual Peace, in a state of good Nature, without Law or Magistrate, because by the universal equity and recititude of manners they would be superfluous. And had God intended it so, it would have succeeded, and he would have sway'd and temper'd the Minds and Affections of Mankind so that their Innocence should have expressed that of the Angels, and the Tranquility of his Dominion here below should have resembled that in Heaven. But alas! that state of perfection was dissolv'd in the first Instance, and was shorter liv'd than Anarchy, scarce of one days continuance.

(*RT*, II, p. 231)

A recurrent theme in both authors is that the ways of providence, however little they correspond to our desires and preferences, cannot finally be challenged: freedom is possible once we acknowledge God's sovereignty.

The evils that men are forced to endure – physical, psychological, political – Marvell like Milton presents as direct consequences of the Fall. As in *Paradise Lost,* the unleashing of destructive passions, the introduction of inclement weather and of baneful planetary influences, the progression of the seasons (*PL,* X, 651–707) are seen as related phenomena. 'The raging of the Seas' is equivalent to, indeed is the result of, the mutiny of the passions, the 'high Winds worse within' (*PL,* IX, 1122): the macrocosm receives the infection from man. What Marvell, like Milton in his great poem published six years previously, seeks to do in this passage in *The Rehearsal Transpros'd* is to justify God's ways to men, show how a benevolent deity can permit the apparent triumph of evil in the world, allow his servants to rot in misery. The analogies from nature, manifestations of cosmological and terrestrial disorder, are entirely metaphorical: his primary concern is with 'Slaughter and War', tyranny, 'publick Disturbance', the political evils with which men are beset.

And ever since the first Brother Sacrificed the other to Revenge, because his Offering was better accepted, Slaughter and War has made up half the business in the World, and oftentimes upon the same quarrel, and with like success. So that as God has hitherto, instead of an Eternal Spring, a standing Serenity, and perpetual Sun-shine, subjected Mankind to the dismal influence of Comets from above, to Thunder, and Lightning, and Tempests from the middle Region, and from the lower Surface, to the raging of the Seas, and the tottering of Earth quakes, beside all other the innumerable calamities to which humane life is exposed, he has in like manner distinguish'd the Government of the World by the intermitting seasons of Discord, War, and publick Disturbance.

(*ibid.,* pp. 231–2)

Milton uses similar arguments, though not the same natural and celestial analogies, in explaining the existence of tyranny, to him and to Marvell the worst of political abuses. The passage is famous, but is much misunderstood:

> Reason in man obscur'd, or not obeyd,
> Immediatly inordinate desires
> And upstart Passions catch the Government
> From Reason, and to servitude reduce
> Man till then free. Therefore since hee permits
> Within himself unworthie Powers to reign
> Over free Reason, God in Judgement just

Subjects him from without to violent Lords;
Who oft as undesservedly enthrall
His outward freedom: Tyrannie must be
Though to the Tyrant thereby no excuse.

(*PL*, XII, 86–96)

This passage is often taken as expressing a political quietism, a retreat into necessitarian pessimism, and an abandonment of Milton's earlier championing of political and ethical liberty. But despite the apparent resemblance to the Calvinist view that all Adam's descendants as a result of his 'original lapse' (*PL*, XII, 83) have been 'deprived of freedom of choice and bound over to miserable servitude', Milton's position here remains Arminian.[12] Men are enslaved not as a necessary consequence of original sin, but by re-enacting the Fall: when they misuse their freedom of choice, when they 'enthrall themselves' (*PL*, III, 125), they enter a state of servitude. God, who always wills good, permits or suffers the evil of tyranny as a just punishment for and legal consequences of a free agent's erroneous choice. Rather than seeing mankind as helpless prisoners of the sin of Adam and Eve, Milton presents the descendants of Adam and Eve as having the same opportunity of free choice and as able to profit from their example, though he recognises that most men will be deaf to the voice of reason.

The Arminian distinction between foreknowledge and predestination is an attempt to avoid making God the author of sin, reconciling the knowledge that man is likely to err (or, for an omniscient God, the certainty that Adam and millions of his decendants will err: for God, the future is already past) with the conviction that an unconfined 'freedom to choose' (*CPW*, II, p. 527) is essential to the moral life. The strict Calvinist view which 'makes God to have determined Innocent *Adam*'s Will to the choice of eating the fruit that was forbidden him' was repugnant to both men. Marvell like Milton therefore, while accepting the notion of God's prescience as theologically sound and 'agreeable to all rational apprehnsion', inveighs against 'universal Predetermination' as contrary to 'common understanding', 'right Reason', and scriptural revelation.[13] Again like Milton, he sees Adam's fatal act as essentially symbolic and paradigmatic, rather than as binding his descendants. All men and women, endowed like Adam with capacities which make them 'sufficient to have stood, though free to fall' (*PL*, III, 99), must bear the weight of their freedom and suffer appropriate reward or punishment.

The political corollary of this insistence that postlapsarian man remains free and open to the dictates of reason, if only he will listen, can be seen in Milton's recurrent emphasis on the ways in which men throw away and abuse their freedom ('that a nation should be so valorous and courageous to winn thir liberty in the field, and when they have wonn it, should be so heartless and unwise in thir counsels, as not to know how to use it, value it, what to do with it' [*CPW*, VII, p. 428]). Milton does not argue that only the 'wise and good' should be allowed political, domestic, and religious freedom, ruling over the foolish multitude like benevolent Platonic guardians. Instead, he says that true wisdom and virtue consist in the ability to 'distinguish, and . . . prefer that which is truly better' (*CPW*, II, pp. 514–5), resisting the blandishments of the tyrant within and without.

If men within themselves would be gover'd by reason, and not generally give up thir understanding to a double tyrannie, of Custom from without, and blind affections within, they would discerne better, what it is to favour and uphold the Tyrant of a Nation. But being slaves within doors, no wonder that they strive so much to have the public State conformably govern'd to the inward vitious rule, by which they govern themselves. For indeed none can love freedom heartilie, but good men; the rest love not freedom, but license; which never hath more scope or more indulgence than under Tyrants.

(Tenure of Kings and Magistrates, CPW, III, p. 190)

The ability to distinguish liberty from licence, to tell false metal from true, seeing through the surface glitter of 'some faire appearing good' (*PL*, IX, 354) is the test of true virtue, what separates the 'resolved soul' from its many irresolute companions. But the realisation that most men will fail the test does not mean that the opportunity should be withdrawn; the dazzling brightness of 'heavenly radiance' may pain the eyes, but a surrender to the 'noise of timorous and flocking birds, with those . . . that love the twilight' (*Areopagitica CPW*, II, 558) betokens only cowardice. True liberty – religious, domestic and civil – is rare because most men fear to be free.

Although if we consider that just and naturall privileges man neither can rightly seek, nor dare fully claime, unlesse they be ally'd to inward goodnesse, and stedfast knowledge, and that the want of this quells them to a servile sense of their own conscious unworthinesse, it may save the wondring why in this age many are so opposite both to human and to Christian liberty, either while they understand not, or envy others that do.

(Tetrachordon, CPW, II, p. 587)

In the divorce tracts, Milton applies such arguments to domestic life. Once again, social and political evils – war, alienation of property, inequality, tyranny – are seen as the consequences of man's fallen state, 'suffer'd' or permitted by God. 'Had man continu'd perfet', there would be no laws, no kings, no landlords, and 'there needed no divorce' (*CPW*, II, p. 665). In *Tetrachordon* as in its companion tracts, Milton is arguing for the possibility of divorce as a possible 'remedy' for evils arising in domestic life as a result of postlapsarian man's having 'degenerated to imperfection' (*CPW*, II, p. 665). The emphasis here is less on the chastening of expectations, as in the Marvell passage discussed earlier or the last two books of *Paradise Lost*, than on the divine mercy which provides relief from 'intolerable pain':

He suffer'd his owne people to wast and spoyle and slay by warre, to lead captives, to be som maisters, som servants, som to be princes, others to be subjects, he suffer'd propriety to divide all things by severall possession, trade and commerce, not without usury; in his common wealth some to be undeservedly rich, others to be undeservingly poore. All which till hardnesse of heart came in, was most unjust, whenas prime Nature made us all equall, made us equall coheirs by common right and dominion over all creatures. In the same manner, and for the same cause hee suffer'd divorce as well as mariage, our imperfet and degenerat condition of necessity requiring this law among the rest, as a remedy against intolerable wrong and servitude above the patience of man to beare.

                                              (*Tetrachordon, CPW*, II, p. 661)

In the particular terms of the local dispute, and the polemical strategies of theological disputation, Milton's position here is rather shaky. Where normally he upholds the radical Puritan position that the Mosaic Law was abrogated by the coming of Jesus,[14] here he is forced by the exigencies of the case to argue that particular Old Testament passages (the ones he likes and wants to defend) are still morally binding, even though they appear to be contradicted by more restrictive passages in the New Testament. The Biblical proof-texts on the surface would appear to favour his opponents, and Milton's nimble eloquence cannot disguise the gaping hole in his argument. But the interest in the passage lies far less in its ingenuity in argumentation than in the general moral position – applicable to civil as well as domestic life – which Milton under the pressure of events was led to state. The composition of the divorce tracts, as Barker says, 'forced him to define more clearly his essential principles', and these principles transcend the immediate issue with which Milton was concerned.[15]

The basic position he is arguing is that stated later by Marvell in *The Rehearsal Transpros'd*: 'Whatsoever Obligations may be put upon Mankind, they are to be expounded by that great and fundamental Law of Mercy' (*RT*, II, p. 249). The Atonement, by freeing man from the intolerable burden of his own sin, in the Arminian theology of Marvell and Milton allowed all men, whatever their weaknesses and imperfections, the possibility of redemption. 'The supreme dictate of charitie' (*CPW,* II, 250) is seen as overriding any positive law (both the civil law and the Law of Old Testament morality). Insofar as the teachings of the New Testament serve to 'set free' the conscience ('On the new forcers of Conscience',(6), they have precedence; but, Milton argues, to allow the words of Christ to be 'congeal'd into a stony rigor' is to pervert his words into a restrictive legality 'inconsistent both with his doctrine and with his office' (*Doctrine and Discipline of Divorce, CPW,* II, p. 258), and is an attempt by fearful man 'to set straiter limits to obedience, then God has set' (*CPW,* II, p. 228).

The logical consequence of the belief that 'the Gospel enjoyns no new morality, save only the infinit enlargement of charity' (*CPW,* II, p. 331) is largely to exclude private morality from public restraint: the state, Milton therefore argues, has no business attempting to regulate religious worship or liberty of public expression, and marriage and divorce are also essentially matters of private choice, in which neither state nor church can bind man irrevocably. Milton explicitly draws a parallel between the marriage vows and the social contract. Laws and agreements are made for a particular end and if this aim (the 'general good') is not achieved, then the contract no longer has any validity, for citizen or for spouse: 'No ordinance human or from heav'n can binde against the good of man' (*CPW,* II, p. 588). As Marvell writes, it is the utility of a law which keeps it alive: God, he argues, 'could not institute Government to the prejudice of mankind, or exact obedience to Laws that are destructive to the Society' (*RT,* II, p. 251). Neither reason nor feeling will permit a man to endure 'intolerable wrong' when remedy is available.

He who marries, intends as little to conspire his own ruine, as he that swears Allegiance: and as a whole people is in proportion to an ill Government, so is one man to an ill mariage. If they against any authority, Covnant, or Statute, may by the soveraign edict of charity, save not only their lives, but honest liberties from unworthy bondage, as well may he against any private Covnant, which hee never enter'd to his mischief, redeem himself from unsupportable disturbances to honest peace, and just contentment.

(*CPW,* II, p. 229)

The heart of the political and ethical theory of the two authors is thus the right of revolution, applicable both in the personal and the political sphere, the conviction that nothing can bind the individual conscience.

This position is of course a radical one, and grounds the right to dissent (disobedience to laws, the dissolution of an unhappy marriage, the overthrow of a tyrant) not simply on self-preservation but on the divine commandment of 'charity', seen as 'sovereign' beyond all the claims of earthly power. Christian liberty in their view must be interpreted not as countenancing the restriction of man's natural liberties (as argued by Milton's Presbyterian and Marvell's Anglican opponents), but as enlarging them, freeing man from the bondage which, 'misguided and abused', they would impose on themselves (*Readie and Easie Way, CPW,* VII, p. 463). Natural human liberty and Christian liberty, Marvell states firmly, are not contrary, but one: 'Whereas no man hath devested himself of any Natural Liberty as he is a Man, by professing himself a Christian, but one liberty operates within the other more effectually, and strengthen themselves better by that double Title'(*RT,* II, p. 245).

Milton's defence of tyrannicide, *The Tenure of Kings and Magistrates,* is sometimes seen as anomalous, democratic rather than aristocratic in its assumptions, but the contract theory it argues is entirely consistent with the view of Christian liberty developed in *Areopagitica* and the divorce tracts. Man's natural liberty, in this view, is never entirely lost, but his 'lapsed powers' (*PL,* III, 176) are renewed by a God unwilling to 'abolish his own works' and 'unmake' what he has made (*PL,* II, 370; III, 163). If we conflate passages on the incommodities of the postlapsarian state in the divorce tracts and *The Tenure of Kings and Magistrates,* we find two suggested remedies, one essentially secular and within man's power, the other wholly dependent on God's free gift.

No man who knows ought, can be so stupid as to deny that all men naturally were borne free, being the image and resemblance of God himself, and were by privilege above all the creatures, born to command and not to obey; and that they liv'd so. Till from the root of *Adams* transgression, falling among themselves to doe wrong and violence, and foreseeing that such courses must needs tend to the destruction of them all, they agreed by common league to bind each other from mutual injury, and joyntly to defend themselves against any that gave disturbance or opposition to such agreement.

(*Tenure, CPW,* III, pp. 198–9)

Implicit in this account of the origins of government is the conviction that man retains his capacity of reason in the fallen state: 'the secondary law of nature and of nations' grounds all government on 'the imperfection and decay of man from original righteousness' (*Tetrachordon, CPW,* II, p. 661), but government is a product of rational consent, intended as a remedy against 'wrong and violence', not as a scourge for man. Like other contract theorists, Milton argues that government is a revocable trust. 'Laws either fram'd or consented to by all' are attempts to codify reason, designed to 'confine and limit' rulers who, left to their own devices, would be prey to 'injustice and partiality' because of the 'personal errors and frailities' to which all fallen men are subject (*Tenure, CPW*, III, pp. 199–200). But the ultimate appeal is not to law, but to conscience, as a 'natural birthright' (*Tenure, CPW*, III, p. 202) which can never be surrendered.

> It follows lastly, that since the King or Magistrate holds his autoritie of the people, both originally and naturally for their good in the first place, and not his own, then may the people as oft as they shall judge it for the best, either choose him or reject him, retaine him or depose him though no Tyrant, meerly by the liberty and right of free born Men, to be govern'd as seems to them best.
>
> (*Tenure, CPW*, III, p. 206)

In terms of the politics of 1649 or 1659, this ringing statement of popular sovereignty conceals any number of hidden questions: who are 'the people' and how can they be defined, how do they exercise this right, can they ever lose it, what happens when they express their sovereign will by 'chusing them a captain back for *Egypt*' (*Readie and Easie Way, CPW*, VII, p. 463)? But theologically and ethically, Milton's position is that man must be free to err. 'Man shall not quite be lost': by the Atonement, man's power of rational choice, though by a strict interpretation of the law 'forfeit' as a result of Adam's sin, is restored or renewed (*PL*, I, pp. 4–5; III, pp. 173–7), allowing him another chance.

The paradoxes of Christian liberty are many. Insofar as it is liberty for Christians, so that only the regenerate are deemed worthy of liberty, it can become a restrictive rather than a liberating ideal. Insofar as it defines the proper scope of liberty as that delimited by God, it identifies freedom with service, obeying the often arbitrary-seeming demands of a hidden master, in which any casual incident could conceal a test. Its attitude towards earthly power is profoundly ambivalent, and it holds out for the conscientious man the twin dangers of running into the arms of worldly success or fleeing the world of action and events as potentially contagious. Yet it can be argued that in the writings of Marvell and Milton, the ideal of rational choice is not self-deluding or compromised, but provides a workable sanction for moral and political behaviour in a period of revolutionary upheaval. The two writers recognise the great difficulties men and women may face in choosing, but to both the freedom 'to be his own chooser' rather than existing 'under a perpetuall childhood of prescription' (*Areopagitica, CPW*, II, p. 514) was man's most valuable gift.

Notes

1   In my comments on Milton, I am indebted to the following studies: C. Hill, *Milton and the English Revolution*, London, 1977; A. Barker, *Milton and the Puritan Dilemma*, Toronto, 1942; A. S. P. Woodhouse (ed.), *Puritanism and Liberty*, 2nd edition, London, 1950, reprinted 1973; Barbara Lewalski, 'Milton: political beliefs and polemical methods, 1659–60', *PMLA*, 74, 1959, pp. 191–202; and J. S. Hill, *John Milton. Poet, Priest and Prophet*, London, 1979. See also W. L. Chernaik, *The Poet's Time. Politics and Religion in the Work of Andrew Marvell*, Cambridge, 1983.

2   See 'A Note on Arminianism', at the end of this essay.

3   Andrew Marvell, *The Rehearsal Transpros'd* and *The Rehearsal Transpros'd: the Second Part*, ed. D. I. B. Smith, Oxford, 1971, II, p. 246; subsequent references will be to *RT*, I, and *RT*, II.

4   'The unfortunate lover', line 8, in *The Poems and Letters of Andrew Marvell*, ed. H. M. Margoliouth, rev. P. Legouis and E. E. Duncan-Jones, 3rd edn., 2 vols., Oxford, 1972.

5   K. W. Stavely, *The Politics of Milton's Prose Style*, New Haven and London, 1975, p. 2.

6   T. Kranidas, 'Milton's *Of Reformation*: the politics of vision', *ELH*, 49, 1982, p. 498. Interesting essays placing Milton's prose in historical context include T. N. Corns, 'Milton's quest for respectability', *MLR*, 77, 1982, pp. 769–79; E. Sirluck, 'Milton's political thought: the first phase', *MP*, 61, 1964, pp. 209–24; and Lewalski, 'Milton: political beliefs and polemical methods', cited in note 1.

7   Aristotle, *Rhetoric*, 1.2, tr. W. R. Roberts, in *The Basic Works of Aristotle*, ed. R. McKeon, New York, 1941; *Paradise Lost*, III, 92, in *Poetical Works of John Milton*, ed. Helen Darbishire, 2 vols., Oxford, 1965; *An Apology against a Pamphlet*, in *Complete Prose Works of John Milton*, ed. D. M. Wolfe *et al*, 8 vols., New Haven and London, 1953, I, pp. 874, 949. Subsequent references will be to *PL* and *CPW*.

8   See J. Mazzeo, 'Cromwell as Machiavellian prince in Marvell's "An Horatian Ode" ', *Renaissance and Seventeenth-Century Studies*, New York and London, 1964, pp. 166–82.

9   C. Hill, *God's Englishman: Oliver Cromwell and the English Revolution*, Harmondsworth, 1972, p. 234.

10   Woodhouse, *Puritanism and Liberty*, pp. 57–60, 68–9, 84–6.

11   On the 'mixed state', see Zera S. Fink, *The Classical Republicans*, Evanston, 1945, pp. 90–122; on the political context of *The First Anniversary*, see Chernaik, *The Poet's Time*, pp. 42–60.

12   John Calvin, *Institutes of the Christian Religion*, II, ii, ed. J. T. McNeill, tr. F. L. Battles, 2 vols., Philadelphia, 1960, I, p. 225, quoted in Milton, *CPW*, VI, p. 77. The lines immediately preceding those quoted could be given a harshly Calvinist reading: 'Yet know withall, / Since thy original lapse, true Libertie / Is

lost, which always with right reason dwells / Twinned, and from her hath no dividual being' (*PL*, XII, 82–5). Yet the emphasis here is on the identification of liberty with reason, and Milton never suggests that the capacity for reason in man is obliterated through Adam's sin. As the poem's opening lines suggest (*PL*, I, 4–5), what is lost initially through the Fall is restored through the Atonement.

13   *Remarks upon a late disingenuous Discourse*, London, 1677, pp. 76–7, 125; cf. *PL*, III, pp. 114–123; and *Christian Doctrine*, I, iii and iv, *CPW*, VI, pp. 156–66, 181–3.
14   Woodhouse, *Puritanism and Liberty*, pp. 65–7.
15   Barker, *Milton and the Puritan Dilemma*, p. 98.

A Note on Arminianism

Christopher Hill has used the term 'radical Arminianism' to refer to the doctrinal position on free will and redemption maintained by Milton, John Goodwin, and other puritan dissenters from Calvinist orthodoxy. The label 'Arminianism' can be confusing, since it was customarily used in Milton's day, with pejorative associations, to refer to the Laudians, as 'a nickname given by the Puritan party to any ecclesiastic who showed no enthusiasm for Calvinist orthodoxy and turned his face back toward the discarded rites and dogmas of Rome'. (A. W. Harrison, *Arminianism*, London, 1937, p. 128). Neither Marvell nor Milton called himself an Arminian (see *RT*, I, pp. 132–3, *Doctrine and Discipline of Divorce*, *CPW*, II, p. 293; and *Areopagitica*, ibid., pp. 519–20), but the tenets of both corresponded with the distinctive doctrines developed in the Netherlands by the Remonstrants, Arminius and his followers, condemned as heretical by the Synod of Dort in 1619.

The major Arminian tenets may be summarised as follows:
1. God's decrees of election are not absolute, but conditional: God 'predestines man not *to* belief, but on *condition* of belief' (*CD*, *CPW*, VI, p. 84, editor's introduction, pp. 176–180, 188–9).
2. God's foreknowledge in no way infringes on man's free will, and is to be distinguished from any form of determinism (*CD*, I, iv, *CPW*, VI, p. 183; *PL*, III, pp. 117–19).
3. Christ died for all men: God's grace is therefore freely available to all, though only the repentant believer will be saved (*PL*, III, 185–202).
4. The idea of total depravity of postlapsarian man is rejected, but man cannot lead a virtuous life without regeneration by the Holy Spirit.
5. The grace of God is indispensable in every step of the spiritual life, but it is not irresistible.
6. Perserverance in grace is not always possible; spiritual vigilance is therefore necessary at all times.

Arminian theology thus seeks to reconcile the ideas of providence and freedom of the will: it sees man as wholly dependent on God's grace, but 'the elect are those who of their own accord use their restored freedom of the will [restored to them by the Atonement] to obey God's will and persist in righteousness' (*CD*, *CPW*, VI, p. 84, editor's introduction).

Christian Doctrine, I, iii and iv ('Of Divine Decree' and 'Of Predestination'), are Arminian in their theology, and Marvell's most explicit statement of similar beliefs can be found in his last work, *Remarks upon a late Disingenuous Discourse* (1678). It is sometimes argued that Milton initially held orthodox Calvinist views and only embraced Arminianism during the 1650's, but there is no evidence from his earlier writings that he accepted Calvinist doctrine on predestination and total depravity; as Maurice Kelley and Christopher Hill point out, nothing in *Areopagitica* or the divorce tracts is incompatible with the position he worked out in greater detail in his later writings (*CPW*, VI, p. 82; *Milton and the English Revolution*, pp. 275–6). The fullest discussion of Milton's Arminianism is D. Danielson, *Milton's Good God. A Study in Literary Theodicy*, Cambridge, 1982; for an excellent brief discussion, see M. Kelley's introduction, *CPW*, VI, pp. 74–86.

Pamphleteering, the Protestant consensus and the English Revolution

Nearly twenty years ago C. H. George wrote an enjoyably bad-tempered article on the nature of English revolutionary Puritanism. He savaged, in the process, nearly all past historians who had written on the subject. In his view, they had perpetrated three major errors. First, they had been guilty of 'manic abstractionism'. He instanced the ease with which they related 'the undefined abstract "Puritanism" ' to such 'undefined or non-historical abstracts' as "individualism", "liberty" or "democracy" '. Second, they failed to recognise a 'a real consensus in religious ideology' in the pre-revolutionary period, which had little to do with any of these concepts. Third, they copied the 'alchemistic tricks' of scholars like Woodhouse and Haller, 'which transmute the base stuff of puritan piety into the gold of egalitarianism, individual liberty and tolerance'.[1]

The intention, in this essay, is to borrow C. H. George's insights and apply them to the pamphlet literature of the 1640s. The study will focus on three important crises in the English Revolution. In the first – between 1640 and 1641 – men were debating whether bishops were worth saving, or whether they should be abolished 'root and branch'. In the second – between 1644 and 1646 – the argument had shifted to the form of government which would replace them. In the third – between 1648 and 1649 – Levellers debated with their opponents on the future constitution. It will be argued here that, on the first two occasions, all sides displayed, as C. H. George had maintained, a fidelity to consensus. When Milton memorably complains that 'new presbyter is but old priest writ large' in 1645, he is telling us more about his own developing Arminianism in the later period, than he is about the earlier mood of himself and his fellow countrymen, when freedom was dismissed as the special pleading of the libertine. Although 'new presbyter' was to be denounced in turn by Independents and Erastians in the middle years of the 1640s, it will be found to be on grounds other than those advanced by Milton. Independents and Erastians were not worried then by the fear that Presbyterians were intent on setting up Popes in every parish. Milton had put that particular straw man up in 1641 only to knock it down again. If he had changed his mind by the time he came to write *Areopagitica* in 1644, his former allies had not: this generalisation holds good, whether we are talking of men who, by the later date, were Presbyterians, Independents or indeed Erastians. It would not be until 1649 that Milton would seem less eccentric in his concern for personal freedom. Once this change in the intellectual climate has been registered, the familiar story of the quarrel between Cromwell and his officers and their Leveller opponents needs to be retold. It is sometimes presumed that, however real their other differences, Cromwellians and Levellers were at one in their quest for religious freedom. This is not so. By 1649 the consensus had been shattered, for reasons which will be advanced in the rest of this essay.

We must start with an acknowledgement of the weakness of our source material. Pamphlets are to the historian of this period what Peruvian silver was to the sixteenth-century economy. It is not simply that there is too much of the stuff, but also that it floods the market at one particular time. Censorship ends; Thomason begins his collection. How can the historian, flattered by the illusion of wealth, avoid the fate of the spoilt *hidalgo*, familiar to all examiners of Decline-of-Spain scripts? There can be no question but that this particular form of wealth is indeed illusory. Conrad Russell tells us why. First, the profusion of printed material in the 1640s must be set against 'the great dearth of archives (extending even to private estate documents)'. Second, the originality of its content has to be measured against the enforced silence of the preceding period, when ideas were not encouraged to surface. Third, the sweep of the literature – 'where Hobbes and Milton rub shoulders with doggerel' – makes it difficult for the historian to handle.[2] These three problems come together in the career of William Prynne: the pamphleteer, whom C. H. George came to see as pivotal to his argument.[3] First, the ratio of printed to unprinted material which has survived, works out, in Prynne's case, extravagantly in favour of the former. This can hardly be said not to matter, when recently we have been made to think afresh about the early career of Prynne's fellow pamphleteer, John Bastwick, precisely because of discoveries based on his personal papers in the Essex Record Office.[4] Second, the apparent novelty of Prynne's radicalism in 1641 must be set against the forces which made for concealment earlier. Third, there is the depressing matter of his popularity, 'depressing' because his writings do seem to have closer affinity with doggerel than they were ever to have with Hobbes and Milton.

The last point, though, is important for understanding the *status* of the pamphleteer. Prynne was popular at two levels: he was Parliament's official apologist for its cause (and later for the trial of Laud); his pamphlets enjoyed a wide readership. It might be thought that these two points were interconnected. But shadows hang over his reputation as official publicist. He called his defence of Parliament, *The Sovereigne Powers of Parliaments*. The text shows that he had read Bodin, and knew what was meant by sovereignty.[5] This did not prevent him from making a hash of it; he proved to be no Henry Parker or Philip Hunton. The work becomes a tedious 'scissors and paste' job, self-contradictory in the places which mattered. At least it can be said that the different parts of the work did come out in time. Not even that, however, can be claimed for his record of Laud's trial. He blamed its publication delays on an exceptionally cold winter.[6] When the work did come out, it travestied the actual proceedings, as the recovery of John Browne's papers have now conclusively demonstrated.[7] Still, those who commissioned him knew what they were getting. Prynne could read the popular mood: this was as much conceded by enemies as urged by friends. In vain for Milton to lament the gout and dropsy of a big margin, overlaid with crude and huddled quotations. Marchamont Nedham – himself no slouch in the circulation race – believed that the secret of Prynne's success was in 'feeding the Phantasie with such Feares and Jealousies, as the weaker sort of men (fruitful enough in these times) create unto themselves out of what they read rather than any Satisfaction to the more solid part of the world'. There were other less grudging tributes to his success. 'I heard it not in Print cry'd up and downe the streets', said one, 'a privilege which any thing, or everything of Mr. Prins enjoyes peculiarly'. Another said of him:

his name only has rendered his subitane Apprehensions, in deed and truth such, to seem good and solid Reasons, and so to passe through the City, as having Truth and Reason in them . . . the weakest and sleightest as ever came from so solid a man upon so weighty a business as is Church Government, yet they take with the people.

We may dismiss as pre-publication hype the feverish claims of *Mercurius Civicus* to 'the great expectation' among 'many well-affected persons' at the imminent fourth part of *The Sovereigne Powers of Parliaments*, or we may blush for a later Parliamentary apologist who claimed, following Prynne, that it was like writing 'Iliads after Homer'; the readiness of Parliament to commission Prynne is, however, the most solid recognition that his words did indeed 'take with the people'.[8]

How Prynne could be simultaneously influential and banal is as good an introduction as any to the nature of the consensus of the early 1640s. For there are ruder ways of describing that consensus: Conrad Russell speaks about 'mediocrity'; Anthony Fletcher calls it 'intellectual poverty'.[9] Prynne was the authentic spokesman for both. What Prynne had to say – at wearisome length – about unity, balance and the Great Chain of Being was said, if more crisply, by Pym *and* Strafford; what he had to say in favour of discipline, the Unity of Jerusalem and intolerance was itself an echo of Calvin *and* Laud. The roots of consensus were in the absence of theological debate. This is a strange claim, at first sight, to make about the pamphleteering of the early 1640s. There was no lack of complaint about the tyrannous imposition of 'Arminian' ideology in the preceding decade. But the imposition had been achieved more by the throttling of debate than by its one-sided transmission. 'Arminianism', as a concept in 1640–1, was more reviled than understood; reviled in part *because* it was not understood. This was the force behind Richard Baxter's retrospective claim that, before the Civil War, 'all my reverenced acquaintance (save one) cryed down Arminianism as the Pelagian Heresie, and the Enemy of Grace'.[10] There was no flood of Arminian apologetics in the 1630s to educate Baxter and his reverenced acquaintance out of these prejudices in 1641.[11] There was, on the contrary, a host of actions (bowing at the name of Jesus, imposing the tax of Ship Money, cutting off the ears of opponents) which were construed as Arminianism-in-practice, and which only tended to reinforce these prejudices. To be against such practices in 1641 was to be, therefore, 'anti-Arminian'. This happy position was thus reached by many members of the Church of England, even bishops at that date, with the minimum of cerebral activity. It was too quick by half for one suspicious Scottish commentator, who suspected the good faith of carpetbaggers, 'who yesterday did rage like Lyons and today take upon them, the skin of the meekest lambs'.[12] But the very comprehensiveness of Laud's defeat in 1640 determined the shape of the debates that followed. The only pamphleteer of note to defend Laud was Joseph Hall.[13] And what he defended was not Laud's Arminian doctrine (actually repugnant to Hall) but his theory of the divine right of bishops. The latter became the focus of the debates between Hall and, respectively, Milton and the

Smectymnuans.[14] Their disagreement was about the nature of bishops then, and not about the nature of man. If even Laud's champion was not prepared to challenge the doctrinal consensus in 1640, it was still less likely that the majority of episcopalians – who were prepared to save their Church by ditching Laud – would develop the case for Arminian theology. That case in the early 1640s was to be made, not by episcopalians, but by Protestants who were themselves not in the mainstream: General Baptists, or the followers of the maverick Independent, John Goodwin. The Independent minister, whose pamphleteering (in particular, his *Protestation Protested*) seemed most to challenge consensus politics in 1641, was not in fact John Goodwin, but Henry Burton; and this, not for his doctrinal lapses (which *were* non-existent), but for his separatist tendencies (which were not).[15]

The pamphlets of 1640 and 1641 expressed disagreements, therefore, but disagreements which were explored within a consensus. Those who wanted bishops destroyed 'root and branch', and those who merely wanted their wings clipped – which was the great divide of those years – were agreed on one thing: on the need for a godly discipline. Liberty was not an issue because that had been secured, so it was thought, by the removal of the unloved Laudians. But which alternative form of control was most suited to the English genius? Those who wanted a 'reduced episcopacy' eschewed Hall's divine right claims for bishops. As Falkland put it, however, to disbelieve in *iure divino* bishops did not mean belief in *injuria humano* bishops.[16] They thought that past guilt clung to persons, not office: a claim which was not countenanced by the Scottish Commissioners in their case against Laud of 14 December 1640.[17] When John Hacket would look back, much later, on the fallacies of 1641, he gave pride of place to the 'rooters'' rejection of the Protestant martyrs.[18] Yet they had no alternative but to rewrite Foxe's history, and to demolish the reputations of Cranmer, Latimer and Ridley, as was demonstrated in Prynne's *The Antipathie*, Milton's *Of Reformation*, Smectymnuus's replies to Hall, the published Commons' speeches of Nathaniel Fiennes and William Thomas, and many other 'root and branch' pamphlets of that time.[19] Once concede virtue to the martyrs, and the case for extirpating an irredeemably corrupt episcopate would fall to the ground. Falkland wanted opinions weighed, not heads counted. He appealed to 'the numberlesse number of those of a different sense who cry not so loud'.[20] But the eighth reason given by the Commons for excluding bishops from the Lords (on 4 June 1641) was precisely because 'multitudes in England and Ireland' *had* petitioned for it.[21] Petitioning went with zeal: a quality celebrated by 'root and branchers' in contrast to the lukewarmness of their opponents, which was identified with that of Laodicea in the Book of Revelation.[22] All these divisions of opinion mattered in 1640 and 1641; but they had nothing to do with the issue of freedom.

The situation would seem to alter radically if we move forward in time, to review the years between 1644 and 1646. The Protestant consensus had surely, by then, irretrievably broken down. Independents challenged Presbyterians, and Erastians challenged both. Presbyterians' 'tyranny' features as a recurrent cliché in the pamphlets of their opponents; liberty would seem, at least, in this way, to have forced itself to the centre of attention. A closer study of the pamphlets corrects this impression. The disagreements are expressed, Milton excepted, not in terms of discipline versus liberty, but in terms of which discipline is the most effective. Take the Independent, Burton. He defends his beliefs on the grounds that all worthwhile disciplinary reform must be both anti-popular in its aim and narrow in its structure. The discipline to be coveted was one which refused 'indulgence to such manners, as cannot easily be brought to enter in at the strait gate and narrow way, that leads into Christs Kingdome'.[23] His Presbyterian colleague, Bastwick, agreed with him. The primary aim of all discipline, he argued, was the exclusion of the impure. The necessary 'reformation in mens lives and manners' could only come from greater stringency in the admission of communicants to the Lord's Supper. He saw how this linked himself with Burton, Presbyterian with Independent: 'The Brethren on both sides agree about the rule in deciding of this controversie and make the written word the rule. They agree also about the materials, both acknowledge a Presbytery, the difference between them is only about the mould and manner of the offering'.[24]

The claim seems impertinent when measured against the Assembly debates and pamphlet skirmishes which were taken up at inordinate length with precisely the question of 'the mould and manner of the offering'. But Bastwick was right to stress the principles which bound them together. It was the Presbyterian, Thomas Edwards, who wrote the classic defence of intolerance: *Gangraena*. But his main adversary there was the sects, not the Independents. And in their two famous testaments, *The Apologeticall Narration* of 1644 and their Savoy Declaration of 1658, Independents themselves would show as much antipathy to the sects as their Presbyterian brethren had done. Their minority position in the Westminster Assembly flattered them, and indeed gave them fleetingly the status of freedom fighters. But freedom, as the Independent Burton saw, was only another word for laxity: 'whither shall the poore soules goe, which live under a prophane Presbyter, or one that admits all sorts rag tag to the Lords Table, with whom godly soules can no more converse, than with Heathens'.[25] The impulse to form Independent congregations was, at root, disciplinarian in its nature, not libertarian: to create, not asylums from tyranny, but superior vehicles for godliness. The Independents came to toleration as a second best. Unmixed communion was the ideal. For want of a Geneva, the least bad alternative was a toleration which would be sufficient in its breadth to allow that ideal to be put into practice on a smaller scale, at the level of the congregation. Burton's pamphlet of 1645 grasped the alternatives.

Good Brother, either provide the people of the Lord an honest godly Presbytery, that may be as many Angels to gather out of Christs Kingdome every thing that offends: or else let there be a tender care of tender consciences, and some provision made for them, that they may not be scandalised, by being forced to be the companion of the scandalous.[26]

Burton was not asking for the moon with his first recommendation. What was this but a restatement of the old Calvinist dream, of a holy commonwealth which separated the precious from the vile? When the leading Presbyterian pamphleteers, George Gillespie and John Ley, argued that if only the Presbyterian ministers would exercise a more rigorous control of admission of candidates to the Lord's Supper, this would – at a stroke – terminate Independent interest in toleration, they had a surer grasp of what their opponents were about than later historians of toleration have shown.[27]

Since the Presbyterian Bastwick and the Independent Burton came together in a defence of clerical discipline against the Erastian arguments of Prynne, can we at least yoke Erastianism to the cause of freedom? Not really: Prynne showed as much eagerness as Bastwick and Burton to exclude the scandalous *impenitent* from the Sacraments. What bothered him was the fate of the scandalous *externally penitent*.[28] Such a concern could not be peripheral to a Calvinist. It touched a critical nerve. How *can* the minister distinguish Elect from Reprobate? The answer he gave in one of his earliest pamphlets, in 1630, showed his awareness of the social consequences of premature selection: 'If God should cull out his Elect from among the reprobate, making an open division or separation from them here, by preaching the Gospel unto them alone; all Reprobates must needes presently despaire of his grace and runne into some desperate course'. It is to avoid such a breakdown of order that 'Reprobates are intermixed and mingled with the Elect, as the weedes, the tares are with the corn and grasse'. Prynne saw no reason to modify his Calvinist answer of 1630 to fit the altered circumstances of 1645.[29]

Here lies the fascination of the pamphlet warfare on clerical suspension and excommunication between 1644 and 1646: we are talking about nothing less than a Calvinist civil war. The idea of freedom had never stirred Prynne, Bastwick and Burton; not even in the 1630s, when opposition to Laudian coercive policies could make all three appear to be defenders of liberty. On the contrary, they offered at that time a Calvinist *critique* of what was seen as years of laxity. This was still the theme which was developed in the 'root and branch' agitation of the early 1640s: the promise that stirred the puritan imagination was a stricter godly control. If that promise was patently unfulfilled in the mid-1640s, that was because (said Presbyterians, like Bastwick) a presbyterian classical system had not yet been put into operation; that was because (said Independents, like Burton) it could only work by devolution; and that was because (said Erastians, like Prynne) 'reall speedy reformation' – which remained, of course, the ideal for all three men – could not come from the 'strict discipline, which really reforms very few or none'.[30]

Is it possible to speak of 'Erastians like Prynne', or is he a law unto himself? Research in the last twenty years has done much to clear past misconceptions about Erastians, and in the process has made Prynne a representative figure of a broad tradition of Protestant thought.[31] There was deliberate obfuscation at work, and the principal villains here were the Scottish Presbyterians. The more we know of their vulnerability at home, the more we can admire their audacity abroad.[32] Baillie, Rutherford and Gillespie: these were the men who came to London to sell a theocratic ideal which had never been properly realised in a Scottish setting. See how Samuel Rutherford *invents* the Erastian myth for his own purposes in his *Divine Right of Church-Government and Excommunication*. He actually recognises that Erastus himself has little to say about the civil magistrate's powers. He notes that Erastus is most concerned with opposing the clergymen's claims to exercise disciplinary powers. The sleight of hand comes with the imputation of motive. Erastus's grievance, according to Rutherford, *must be*, however, not that the clergy were taking on improper functions, but that 'the Christian magistrate doth it not'. Erastus *must*, on this view, be opposed, not to the discipline, but to the persons who were exercising it. The stage is then set for Rutherford's ritual denunciation of the civil magistrate: 'But I pray you, doth one Pastor or the Christian Magistrate know the hearte; but a Presbytery cannot do it, because a Presbytery knoweth not the hearte: Is not this too partiall Logick?'[33]

The partiality of the logic lay elsewhere. It lay in the assumption that Erastus's end was to advance the civil magistrate, and that knocking the clergy was only a means to that end. But the end for Erastus, and for his English followers (Prynne, Coleman, Hussey, D'Ewes, Lightfoot, Parker, Norwood, Mayne, Bacon and Cartwright[34]), was moral reformation. The case which Prynne mounted against the presbyterian attempt at discipline was that 'it really reforms very few or none', not that it got in the way of personal liberties. Religion was too important to be left to clergymen, not a matter of indifference to be consigned to the magistrate. The Scottish divines had no illusions about the real foe that encountered them in 1646. They knew about the old English lay prejudices. They were happy, as we have seen, to project that image on to their new Erastian enemy. But in private they beavered away at procuring translations of Erastus's writings and of his scholastic controversies.[35] W. K. Jordan missed this dimension when, in his comprehensive four-volume work on religious toleration, he despatched the Erastians as part of one group, 'The Laymen and the Moderates', of whom Bacon, Cotton and Selden were treated as representative figures.[36] How Rutherford would have chortled! In reality he, Baillie and Gillespie were straining every nerve to counter the telling propaganda of Erastians like Thomas Coleman. Gillespie and Baillie agreed that he was the man who had put paid to their theocratic hopes.[37] In 1643 he had delivered a celebrated sermon on taking the Covenant: it compliments in rapturous terms some of the leading clerics of the day,[38] and would receive rapturous compliments in turn from them.[39] Three years on, he has not lost his hunger for discipline, but like Prynne, he has come to recognise that what the clergy actually have to offer is 'not a very effectual sin-censuring and Church-refining government'.[40] For the Erastian, the ethical objection is ultimately decisive.

We can summarise the argument of the essay so far. In the early and middle years of the English Revolution, a study of the pamphlets suggests that freedom is an over-blown issue. C. H. George's objections to the 'alchemistic tricks' perpetrated by historians like Woodhouse, Haller and Jordan seem thus far to be warranted. But what of the last years? C. H. George's secondary point was that freedom *did* emerge as an ideology in the course of the English Revolution. This possibility has not been allowed by historians to intrude as a factor in the quarrel between Cromwellians and Levellers. There are several reasons for this.

One is that historians have tended to make Putney not Burford, 1647 not 1649, the focus of their analyses of the Leveller movement. This is as true of historians who have disagreed with C. B. Macpherson's claim that 'possessive individualism' was common to both sides of the franchise dispute, as those who have agreed with it.[41] Second, whatever other differences emerged, religious freedom was seemingly not one of them. Cromwellians and Levellers subscribed with equal conviction to the ideal of religious toleration. Why then did the pursuit of *religious* freedom not extend to the *social* and *political* spheres? David Underdown diagnoses a kind of schizophrenia in a man like Cromwell. He gives full weight to the sincerity of his religious convictions, but sees him as a puritan revolutionary with only one half of his mind. The other half is that of the country squire, conditioned by 'the old-boy network' of Inns of Court and Parliament.[42]

We may wonder if this is right? Cromwell was a religious Independent, a Calvinist, of the kind we have already encountered in the shape of Henry Burton. Burton and Cromwell were both sincere advocates of religious toleration, and were no less sincere because it was for them a second-best. Best, for both men, was a holy commonwealth where the vile and the precious were kept apart; second-best, a toleration which allowed a small-scale exercise of that godly discipline. How far a Calvinist could go, in pursuit of the second-best, is illustrated by Roger William's *Bloudy Tenent of Persecution* of 1644. His second-best took the argument for religious toleration actually further than any non-Calvinist did at that time (Milton included), *without ceasing to be a second-best.* From the depth of his Arminian convictions, Milton, in *Areopagitica*, challenged a crude division of mankind into wheat and tares, and developed the classical philosophical defence of freedom. Williams went further, though, than Milton in extending freedom even to Papists, although ironically freedom was never in fact his primary goal. Williams, as a good Calvinist, accepted that mankind was divided into wheat and tares (as did Cromwell). Nor did he shrink from the prospect of the destruction of those tares. The good Book of Revelation offered this mouth-watering prospect of revenge:

When the world is ripe in sin, in the sins of Antichristianism (as the Lord spoke of the sins of the Amorites) then those holy and mighty officers and executioners, the angels, with their sharp and cutting sickles of eternal vengeance, shall down with them, and bundle them up for the everlasting burnings. Then shall that man of sin (2 Thess 2) be consumed by the breath of the mouth of the Lord Jesus; and all that worship the Beast and his picture, and receive his mark with their forehead or their hands, *shall drink of the wine of the wrath of God; which is poured out without mixture into the cup of his indignation, and he shall be tormented with fire and brimstone in the presence of the holy angels, and in the presence of the Lamb. And the smoake of their torment shall ascend up for ever and ever* (Rev 14, 10, 11).[43]

The first reaction on reading such a passage, as a critical part of the argument *for* religious toleration, is a keen desire to hear what the arguments *against* would sound like. The second is, like C. H. George, to feel a renewed impatience with the 'alchemistic tricks' perpetrated by historians who have domesticated Williams into a gentle liberalism. The third is, nevertheless, to insist on the genuineness of Williams's commitment to the principle of religious toleration, even though his view of mankind and of its potentialities is that of Prynne (who was against religious toleration) rather than that of Milton (who was for it).

For Williams, and for Prynne – indeed for all Calvinists – there were two sorts of men: the wheat and the tares. Prynne, as we saw, would not let the minister at the Lord's Table make visible that discrimination. Williams, more logical, would not let the civil magistrate do so either. But neither had any illusions about human capacities nor did they question a dispensation, which divided mankind into two sorts of person: freedom was not an ideal to pursue, because the task of any government was to police the depraved instincts of the majority. What was offensive about the act of discrimination was, therefore, not philosophical but tactical. The wheat *must* be separated from the tares, but not yet. To men like Williams and Prynne, impregnated with millenarian assumptions, the imminence of that heavenly discrimination was their supreme comfort. Surrogate earthly claims were gratuitous and, in the final analysis, blasphemous.

It may be that Blair Worden will begin to do for Cromwell what Perry Miller has done already for Williams:[44] that is to say, to put the commitment of both men to religious toleration in a context which is free from associations with Miltonic concepts of freedom and the perfectibility of mankind. Cromwell, like Williams, would not let go that crucial distinction of the precious from the vile. Cromwell, like Williams, thirsted for the forthcoming millennium when that distinction would be given its permanent endorsement. Cromwell, like Williams, treated interim earthly claims to make such distinctions with a profound scepticism.

The Cromwell who is presented here does not need to be treated as a schizophrenic. He can be seen to be quite as inegalitarian in spiritual matters as he is in secular ones (and a hypocrite in neither); he is of a piece. He can tell Colonel Walton that his dead son had been 'exceedingly beloved in the Army, of all that knew him', and than add: 'but few knew him'.[45] They were not feigned words to comfort him: both men knew that the *rationing* of the gift was what made it precious. Cromwell disliked the Levellers, because they broke down all these necessary inequalities, *in spiritual as well as in political matters.* How far has he here misjudged the Levellers' case against him?

Leveller pamphlets are a source which have not been ignored by historians in recent years, but the interest has tended to be lopsided. Their political and social ideas have seemed more interesting than their religious ones. This was a characteristic which Haller and Davies had commented on as early as 1944 when, in an introduction to their edition of Levellers' tracts, they drew attention to the neglect of 'the religious background from which they sprang and by which they continued to be deeply coloured'.[46] That neglect has been repaired by two recent notable contributions. J. C. Davis has demonstrated the importance of equity in Leveller writings. Lilburne thought it a concept which 'God had ingraved by nature in the soul of men' and is 'universally given to all men and women, rich and poor, without any exception'. In similar vein, Walwyn argued that, through practical Christianity, 'feeding the hungry, clothing the naked, visiting and comforting the sick, relieving the aged, meeke and impotent', we thereby manifest 'our universal love to all mankind, without respect of persons, Opinions, Societies or Churches'.[47] Murray Tolmie has come up with valuable findings on the sectarian roots of Leveller organisation. Lilburne's initial base was the Particular Baptist church of Rosier and Kiffin, Walwyn's the Independent church of John Goodwin in Coleman Street, Overton's the General Baptist church, also in Coleman Street, of Thomas Lambe.[48] Lilburne's early prominence in the movement has encouraged the association in historians' minds of the Levellers with Calvinism. A reading of his 1639 tract, *Come out of her My People*, would support this view: it is a notable separatist plea for God's Elect, who are identified as the poor of the world. The pamphlet bears the mark of its Particular Baptist inspiration. What has not been emphasised by historians enough is that no later Lilburne pamphlets carry a similar Calvinist ring of confidence. Instead we have the distinctly unCalvinist emphasis on equity and universal salvation, which Davis correctly reads into the later Leveller pamphlets particularly (although perhaps even he did not make enough of the challenge which this posed to orthodox Calvinist beliefs). We do not know when or why Lilburne changed his doctrinal views; certainly, the later move to Quakerism was anticipated in his spiritual development in the mid-1640s, but for evidence that he had come under the thumb of the Arminian, Walwyn and the General Baptist, Overton we have to rely on nothing more solid than the gibes of opponents.

The problem for students of the pamphlets of the period is that theological terms are bandied about, which convey a delusive air of precision and even science about them. Take the terms 'Baptists', 'Independent' and 'Antinomian'. 'Baptists' were men and women who argued for believers' baptism, but lumped together in this category were the 'General Baptists' (who believed in universal salvation) and 'Particular Baptists' (who did not). Opponents compounded the confusion by calling either group 'Anabaptists', and thus they injected pejorative Munster associations into the English religious scene. 'Independents' seemed a more cohesive grouping, but the doctrinal beliefs within that category embraced John Goodwin's Arminianism as well as Henry Burton's Calvinism.[49] 'Antinomian' poses greater problems still. 'Christ's love', said Walwyn, 'is so exceeding towards us that even when we were enemies Christ died for us.' That was the belief which sustained Ranters, and indeed all Calvinists who revelled in the saint's special mission on earth. But Walwyn has this crucial addition to make, absent from their pronouncements: 'the same Jesus whom the Jewes crucified, was Lord and Christ: That he is the propitiator for our sins, and not only for ours, but for the sins of the whole world'.[50] The addition marks the difference between Free Grace and Universal Grace: a distinction which A. L. Morton failed to make in *The World of the Ranters.*[51] Contemporaries were not better in observing these distinctions. Thus Thomas Edwards says of the General Baptist, Henry Denne, that 'the usuall theam that he is upon, is Christs dying for all, for John as well as Peter', but this makes him in Edwards's book *simultaneously* 'a great Antinomian, a desperate Arminian'.[52] This is at least an enemy's description. But what of Walwyn's *self-description* of a man who 'through God's goodnesse, had long before been established in that part of doctrine (called then Antinomian) of free justification by Christ alone'?[53]

The historian hacks through this linguistic jungle to find for himself a clearing in 1649. After the Army grandees' purge and regicide it is clear that two different world-views are in collision. Lilburne, Walwyn, Overton and Prince were arrested in March 1649 for their *Second Part of Englands New Chains*. They were repudiated by Particular Baptist ministers in a petition to Parliament which called for 'the making and due execution of sufficient laws against whoredome, drunkenness, cheating, and all such like abominations'.[54] Tolmie has shown the significant overlap in membership of the General Council of the Army and of the Calvinistic Independent and Baptist Churches. A month before Burford, the Calvinist members were preaching apocalyptic revenge in *language* which recalls Roger Williams' *Bloudy Tenent*, even if their *conclusion* does not:

hence it is, that the Antichrist Whore is filled with fears that you are the men commission'd by God to execute upon her the Judgment written, to stain her glory and spoil her beauty, to dash her bastards brains against the stones, and to give her blood for blood to drink, to burn her flesh with fire.[55]

Kiffin, Price and Rosier were among the co-authors of *Walwyn's Wiles*. This pamphlet may not be the ideal source for understanding Walwyn's views, but it is *for understanding his Calvinist opponents' perception of what these views were*. In four ways Walwyn seems to challenge the most precious beliefs of the saints. First, he shows a disregard for Fast Days:

Having once upon a Fast Day gone from place to place, hearing here a little and there a little what the Ministers said, making it the subject matter of his prophane scorning and jeering.

Second, he is sceptical about Hell:

At another time speaking of hell, and everlasting fire, and eternal torments, and words to that purpose, Pish, do you think, can it enter into your heart to conceive that God should cast a man into everlasting burnings, where he shall be tormented for ever without end, for a little time of sinning in the world.

Third, he scorns prayer:

What a silly thing it is for a man to drop down upon his knees, and hold up his hands, and lift up his eyes, to mumble over a few words for half an hour, or an hour together, when all this while he might have been doing that which is good in itself, relieving the poor and oppressed.

Fourth, he is lacking in awe of the Almighty's terror:

> most prophanely and lightly replyed, Yea, I hope God is a merry old man, and will make a good Companion when I am dead.[56]

To understand the Calvinists' sensitivity on these particular four points, it is necessary to appreciate how much the world of the Ranters intruded into the politics of 1649. The rise of Antinomianism and Arminianism were interrelated phenomena: excesses in one direction inspired reaction in the other.[57] Cromwell and his officers wanted no truck with Ranters. But in truth they had much in common. They shared a belief in predestinarian élitism, in the conviction that they were the instruments of God's Will, and in the refusal to bind themselves to man-made laws. Where then did they divide? Essentially, in those who were not Ranters, in their refusal to make *rushed* judgments about the identification of God's Purpose. This made for caution and delay, but not for *endless* caution and delay. On the contrary, those who believed in an imminent millennium could afford to wait. Roger Williams did not shrink, as we have seen, from the prospect of 'everlasting burnings'; their postponement was for him a form of deferred gratification, rather than a putting off of evil. In the interim period, however, it behoved the saints to wait. This was not the passive process that the word seems to connote to us: by strenuous prayer sessions, the strict observance of Fast Days, consciousness of the perils of damnation, and humility before an All-Knowing God, the saints tested Providence.[58] And in so doing they cut themselves off decisively from their Ranter associates. *Walwyn's Wiles* fascinates us as an attack upon a *perceived* state of mind, which allows no such distinctions to emerge between Ranter and Calvinist. The Walwyn figure of that pamphlet derides those very activities which are most precious to an *anti-Ranter* Calvinist.

Brian Manning has claimed that 'the egalitarianism of the Leveller leaders was limited by their puritan backgrounds and preconceptions ... the most convenient doctrine for them was not the democracy towards which the radicals were tending but the rule of the saints'.[59] If historians continue to focus on Putney and the franchise debates of 1647 the argument has much to commend it. If, however, they shift the focus forward to the pamphleteering war of 1649 the argument loses its plausibility. It is the Calvinist conquerors of Burford – the Axtells, Prides, Okeys, Iretons and Cromwells – and not their Leveller victims, who were looking forward then to a 'rule of the saints'.[60]

We end where we began: with C. H. George's analysis of revolutionary Puritanism. From even this brief impressionistic survey of a vast pamphlet literature, certain conclusions may be drawn. First, that C. H. George was right to scorn the 'alchemistic tricks' of an older generation of scholars, who transmuted puritan piety into the gold of freedom. G. K. Chesterton knew better than the alchemists when he called the nonconformity of his own day a weak and lukewarm torrent, 'melting down much of that mountainous ice which sparkled in the seventeenth century, bleak indeed but blazing'. Roger Williams and Oliver Cromwell are men of this stamp, 'bleak indeed but blazing'. They are not interested in such wishy-washy nineteenth-century concerns as personal freedoms and equality. Their goal is discipline, not liberty; their inspiration is the Book of Revelation, not the Petition of Right. A concern for liberty is not prominent in pamphlet speculations, either about the fate of the Church of England at the beginning of the 1640s, or about the nature of its successor-rivals in the middle. But the position is not a static one. It is the second strength of C. H. George's article that it refers us to 'the greater importance of humanistic and secular perceptions' in 'the emerging ideology of liberalism' in the late 1640s. This should affect our view of the Levellers more than it has done hitherto. Lilburne's *Come out of her My People* in 1639 has little to say about the ideal of freedom; ten years on, the picture has changed completely. The question often asked is: how could Calvinists, believing in their élitist mission, *permit* false flowers to bloom? Brian Manning gave one answer. The Levellers, because they were Calvinists, were not very good egalitarians. An alternative suggestion is that the Levellers, because they were egalitarians, were not very good Calvinists.

The time is ripe for a reconsideration of the rise of Arminianism. One unsatisfactory aspect of a recent attempt to do so is that the author's search terminates in 1629.[61] But the best of that story was yet to come. It is true that, between that date and 1640, Arminianism became Court doctrine. The feature of that triumph was, however, the attempt to stifle dissidence rather than to propagate orthodoxy. When Arminianism was overthrown, an imposed consensus was replaced by an assumed consensus. It would be as late as 1649 that a mainstream Protestant, Richard Baxter, would challenge the Calvinist assumptions behind that consensus.[62] Baxter was not able, even if he had wanted to, to draw upon Arminian apologetics in the 1630s to make his case. He went back behind that decade to Thomas Hooker, Bolton, Rogers, Hildersham and Fenner: to what he called the 'practical divinity' of the 1620s.[63]

Ironically the bishop to whom he was most indebted, Davenant, was the same man who in 1631 had got into trouble simply for mentioning the word election in a court sermon. Like so many of his fellow puritans, Baxter abhorred before the Civil War the Arminianism which he never understood. The Laudian censor struck at the Calvinist enemy, but perhaps his most wounding blows were ultimately struck at men who were deprived of the opportunity of becoming non-Calvinist friends. When Baxter discovered Davenant in 1649, and with him the insight that Arminianism was not merely Pelagianism writ large, it was by means of a theological do-it-yourself kit. When he did so, the relief felt was palpable. 'How the doctrine of good workes hath hung in our protestant divinity (before your Aphorismes put some reason in it)', said one Presbyterian, who spoke for many.[64] But Baxter, in making this self-discovery, was himself a beneficiary of the growth of those 'humanistic and secular perceptions' which C. H. George detected in the 1640s. The 1650s – not the 1640s – would be the decade in which the issues of freedom and equality were related to Protestant doctrine in a way which had not been allowed to happen since the 1620s. Baxter, and those who followed him in the 1650s, made a crucial double distinction. They separated what they disliked about the Laudians from the theological doctrine of Arminianism with which they had become associated. It was the reverse of Hall's position in 1641 who had wanted to defend Laud but not his doctrines, and different in its turn from Hall's opponents then, who had lumped the two together. But Baxter and his followers would not separate what they disliked about the Ranters from the theological doctrine of Antinomianism with which *they* were associated. Antinomianism begat the Ranters: Coppe was the unpleasant face of Calvinism. These divisions are apparent already, as we have seen, in the Leveller disputes with the Independents and Particular Baptists in Cromwell's Army in 1649. In 1650 George Fox would draw inspiration from his General Baptist roots and help to create, in Quakerism, the most telling challenge to the central theological beliefs of Calvinism. It is more than coincidental that Lilburne and Winstanley, himself smarting from his Ranter disputes in 1649, should end up as Quakers. E. P. Thompson even argues, for a later period, that more attention needs to be paid to the grip of Particular Baptist's ideology on the development of the English working classes.[65] Their defeat of the rival tradition of the General Baptists had been a victory for non-evangelistic élitism: it took Wesley's Arminianism to loosen that grip.[66]

This observation takes us well forward in time from the pamphlets of the English Revolution, but reinforces the lesson which we may draw from this brief survey of them. The pursuit of freedom may have been an unintended consequence of the activities of revolutionary Puritans; it was neither their cause not their inspiration.[67]

Notes

1   C. H. George, 'Puritanism as history and historiography',', *Past and Present*, xli, 1968, pp. 97, 102. His particular targets for attack were: – A. S. P. Woodhouse, 'Religion and some foundations of English democracy', *The Philosophical Review*, lxi, 1952, pp. 503–31; W. Haller, *The Rise of Puritanism*, New York, 1938 and *Liberty and Reformation in the Puritan Revolution*, New York, 1955; M. Walzer, *The Revolution of the Saints*, London, 1966.
The best synthesis of more recent research on the (dubious) relationship between Calvinist theology and revolutionary politics is to be found in Quentin Skinner, *The Foundations of Modern Political Thought*, II, Cambridge, 1978, pp. 189–360. Although I endorse C. H. George's general line of argument in the following pages, I dissented from some of his views in my reply to his article in *Past and Present*, xliv, 1969, pp. 133–146.

2   C. Russell, 'Losers', *London Review of Books*, vi, 18, 1984, pp. 20–2; a review of: C. Hill, *The Experience of Defeat. Milton and Some Contemporaries*, London, 1984.

3   George, 'Puritanism as history', p. 87.

4   Frances Condick, 'The Life and Works of Dr. John Bastwick, 1595–1654', unpublished University of London Ph.D. thesis, 1983, especially chapters 1 and 2.

5   William Prynne, *The Sovereigne Powers of Parliaments*, London, 1643, ii, p. 45.

6   Prynne, *Canterburies Doome*, London, 1646, didicatory epistle.

7   (House of Lords Record Office) Braye MSS: *Proceedings Against Strafford and Laud.*

8   Milton, *Colasterion*, London, 1645, p. 2; Marchamont Nedham, *The Lawyer of Lincolnes-Inn Reformed*, London, 1647, p. 1; Henry Robinson, *The Falsehood of Mr. William Pryn's Truth Triumphing*, London, 1645, p. 23; Hezekiah Woodward, *Inquiries into the Causes of our Miseries*, London, 1645, p. 23; *Mercurius Civicus*, xii, 11–17 August 1643; Anon., *A New and True Echo from Old and Bold Authors*, London, 1648, p. 4.

9   Russell, 'Losers', p. 21.

10   Richard Baxter, *Catholick Theologie*, London, 1675, 1, i, preface.

11   Though Peter White characteristically overstates the even-handed nature of the truce in his 'The rise of Arminianism reconsidered', *Past and Present*, ci, 1983, pp. 34–54. For a more balanced view, see: N. Tyacke, 'Arminianism and English culture', in A. C. Duke and C. A. Tamse (eds.), *Britain and the Netherlands*, vii, The Hague, 1981, p. 104; D. D. Wallace, Jnr., *Puritans and Predestination: Grace in English Protestant Theology 1525–1695*, Chapel Hill, North Carolina, 1982, pp. 83–104.

12   Robert Baillie, *The Unlawfulnesse and Danger of a Limited Episcopacie*,

London, 1641, p. 2.

13   Peter Heylyn, *The Historie of Episcopacie*, London, 1642, preface, suggested that other episcopalians held back in order not to steal Hall's thunder.

14   Joseph Hall, *Episcopacy of Divine Right*, London, 1640, *passim; An Humble Remonstrance*, London, 1640, p. 28; *A Defence of the Humble Remonstrance*, London, 1641, p. 81; Milton, *Of Reformation*, London, 1641, p. 47; Smectymnuus, *An Answer to a Booke entitled, An Humble Remonstrance*, London, 1641, p. 63.

15   Henry Burton, *The Protestation Protested*, London, 1641, no pagination. The work had the distinction of offending simultaneously a moderate episcopalian, a High Church bishop, a moderate presbyterian and a non-separating congregationalist: – respectively (British Library) Stowe MSS 184, f. 43; Hall, *A Survey of that Foolish, Seditious, Scandalous, Prophane Libell, The Protestation Protested*, London, 1641, p. 6; John Geree, *Vindiciae Voti*, London, 1641, no pagination; Thomas Edwards, *Gangraena*, London, 1646, (reprinted Exeter, 1979), iii, p. 243.

16   Falkland, *Speech*, London, 1641, p. 14.

17   Prynne, *Canterburies Doome*, p. 37.

18   John Hacket, *Scrinia Reserata*, London, 1692, p. 196.

19   Prynne, *The Antipathie*, London, 1641, i, p. 147; Milton, *Of Reformation*, pp. 8, 11, 12; Smectymnuus, *An Answer*, p. 103; Fiennes, *Speech*, London, 1641, p. 6; Thomas, *Speech*, London, 1641, p. 19.

20   Falkland, *A Discourse of Infallibility*, London, 1660, p. 4.

21   *An Abstract of those Answers*, London, 1641, p. 5.

22   Milton, *Of Reformation*, pp. 13, 73; Cornelius Burges, *The First Sermon*, London, 1641, dedicatory epistle; Henry Wilkinson, *A Sermon against Lukewarmnesse in Religion*, London, 1640, *passim*.

23   Henry Burton, *A Vindication of Churches Commonly Called Independent*, London, 1644, p. 13.

24   John Bastwick, *Independency Not Gods Ordinance*, London, 1645, p. 7.

25   Burton, *Vindiciae Veritatis*, London, 1645, p. 6.

26   *Ibid.*, p. 7.

27   George Gillespie, *A Sermon*, London, 1645, p. 33; John Ley, *The New Querie*, London, 1645, p. 65.

28   Prynne, *A Vindication of Four Serious Questions*, London, p. 31.

29   Prynne, *God No Imposter Nor Deluder*, London, 1630, pp. 16–7.

30   Prynne, *A Vindication*, pp. 57–8.

31   J. N. Figgis, 'Erastus and Erastianism', *Journal of Theological Studies*, ii, 1900, especially pp. 73–81. Figgis's essay is truly remarkable: for something like half a century his revaluation of Erastianism was largely ignored.

32   W. Makey, *The Church of the Covenant 1637–1651*, Edinburgh, 1979, is the best statement of the Scottish Presbyterians' dilemma in their relationship with the English Revolution.

33   Samuel Rutherford, *The Divine Right of Church-Government and Excommunication*, London, 1646, p. 256.

34   Prynne, *Twelve Considerable Serious Questions Touching Church Government*, London, 1644; Thomas Coleman, *Maledicis*, London, 1646; William Hussey, *A Plea for Christian Magistracie*, London, 1645; Simonds

D'Ewes, *Autobiography and Correspondence*, ed. J. O. Halliwell, London, 1845, ii, p. 116; John Lightfoot, *Works*, London, 1923–4, xiii, p. 11; Henry Parker, *A Discourse Concerning Puritans*, London, 1641; Richard Norwood, *Considerations Tending to Remove the Present Differences*, London, 1646; Jasper Mayne, *The Difference About Church Government Ended*, London, 1646; Robert Bacon, *The Spirit of Prelacie Yet Working*, London, 1646; Christopher Cartwright, *The Magistrates Authority in Matters of Religion*, London, 1647.

35   Robert Baillie, *Letters and Journals*, ed. D. Laing, Edinburgh, 1841–2, ii, pp. 265, 365.

36   W. K. Jordan, *The Development of Religious Toleration in England*, London, 1938, ii, pp. 315–491.

37   Gillespie, *A Sermon*, p. 33; Baillie, *Letter and Journals*, ii, p. 360.

38   Coleman, *The Hearts Ingagement*, London, 1643, p. 19: White, Nye, Henderson and Gouge are the clergymen who win his admiration.

39   Thomas Case, *The Quarrel of the Covenant*, London, 1643, p. 53; Daniel Featley, *The League Illegal*, London, 1643, p. 17. See also the respectful reference to Coleman in the dedicatory epistle of Edwards's *Gangraena*.

40   Coleman, *Maledicis*, p. 20.

41   C. B. Macpherson, *The Political Theory of Possessive Individualism*, Oxford, 1962, pp. 107–59. K. Thomas, 'The Levellers and the franchise', in G. E. Aylmer (ed.), *The Interregnum*, London, 1972, p. 177, correctly argues against Macpherson both for a Leveller 'faith in human equality and natural right', and for a recognition that this faith is itself modified 'by traditional patriarchal assumptions' in the actual franchise disputes of 1647.

42   D. Underdown, *Pride's Purge*, Oxford, 1971, p. 8.

43   A. S. P. Woodhouse (ed.), *Puritanism and Liberty*, London, 1973, p. 271.

44   P. Miller, *Roger Williams: His Contribution to the American Tradition*, New York, 1962; B. Worden, 'Toleration and the Cromwellian Protectorate', *Studies in Church History*, ed. W. J. Sheils, 21, 1984, pp. 199–233.

45   T. Carlyle (ed.), *Oliver Cromwell's Letters and Speeches*, London, 1897, i, pp. 188–9.

46   W. Haller and G. Davies (eds.), *The Leveller Tracts 1647–1653*, New York, 1944.

47   J. C. Davis, 'The Levellers and Christianity', in B. Manning (ed.), *Politics, Religion and the English Civil War*, London, 1973, pp. 229, 234.

48   M. Tolmie, *The Triumph of the Saints*, Cambridge, 1977, pp. 66, 146, 151.

49   Edwards, *Gangraena*, i, p. 128, claimed that Burton played down Goodwin's doctrinal heresies deliberately in order to sustain the myth that Independency was monolithic.

50   Davis, 'The Levellers and Christianity', p. 231.

51   A. L. Morton, *The World of the Ranters*, London, 1970, pp. 50, 98, 117. D. D. Wallace Jr., *Puritans and Predestination*, p. 226, carries a shrewd criticism of Morton on this point.

52   Edwards, *Gangraena*, i, pp. 76–7.

53   Haller and Davies, *The Leveller Tracts*, p. 361.

54   Tolmie, *The Triumph of the Saints*, p. 182.

55   Haller and Davies, *The Leveller Tracts*, p. 287.

56   *Ibid.*, pp. 236–7.

57   Richard Baxter, *The Reduction of a Digresser*, London, 1654, p. 13.

58   The best discussion on this is in: C. Hill, *God's Englishman*, London, 1970, pp. 219–50.

59   B. Manning, *The English People and the English Revolution*, London, 1976, pp. 315–6. This view is not modified in a more recent contribution; despite the title which he gives to his essay, he does not develop the doctrinal argument there as far as J. C. Davis had already taken it: – Manning, 'The Levellers and religion', in J. F. McGregor and B. Reay (eds.), *Radical Religion in the English Revolution*, Oxford, 1984, pp. 65–90.

60   Tolmie, *The Triumph of the Saints*, pp. 188–9.

61   P. White, 'The rise of Arminianism reconsidered', *Past and Present*, ci, 1983, pp. 34–54.

62   Baxter, *Aphorismes of Justification*, London, 1649.

63   Baxter, *Apology*, London, 1654, dedicatory epistle.

64   (Dr Williams's Library) Baxter MSS, iv, f. 6v.

65   E. P. Thompson, *The Making of the English Working Class*, London, 1963, pp. 34–5.

66   B. Semmel, *The Methodist Revolution*, New York, 1973, is the most ambitious attempt yet to relate that revolution to its inspiration in Arminian doctrine.

67   Since writing this essay I have been working through thirty-four volumes of sermon notes of John Pointer (rector of Alkerton, Oxfordshire, 1663–1710) located in the Folger Library, Washington, which will be the basis of a future study. His annotations for 11 May 1690 argue – as this essay does – for the incompatibility of freedom with what he calls 'restraining grace' (Folger Library, Pointer MSS, V.a 29). Although he seems to exempt the few on whom is bestowed 'renewing grace' – 'this new nature unties a man, sets him at liberty, makes him a free man' – he quickly adds the rider, 'not altogether I confess but yet so far as he is renewed and spiritual, so far it makes him free'. The 'not altogether' and 'so far' separate even the Highest of High Calvinists (as Pointer and his spiritual mentor, John Owen, were) from the antinomianism which both men abhorred.

The freedom of reader-response. Milton's *Of Reformation* and Lilburne's *The Christian Mans Triall*

This essay extends the notion of liberty in a direction rather different from that taken elsewhere in the collection. The concern here is not with the freedoms of political choice and action, nor with freedom of speech, nor with freedom from legal and economic restraint. Rather, it is a more intimate freedom which will be explored, the freedom of interpretation and construction which the text permits its reader, the freedom of reader-response.

In a sense, it is the most elusive liberty to restrain. Even a captive audience is free to doubt, disbelieve, dislike and reject what is said to it. An Elizabethan Puritan or crypto-Catholic could be pressurised into attending the services of the Church of England, but he or she remained free, silently, to despise the liturgy or dispute the homily. A prisoner in the dock might be pinioned and gagged to hear the judge's comments, but he or she remained free to doubt their fairness, their pertinence, even their eloquence. Kings and parliaments could command proclamations to be read in every market place, but they could not command that they be believed. This essay is concerned with prose writing of an openly polemical nature, published in an era of crisis and confusion, in the interests of a movement, the broad puritan opposition to prelacy, which had not yet so captured the apparatus of the state that it could command, nationwide, even this last sort of enforced attention. Not only could Lilburne and Milton not require, through external compulsion, belief or agreement: they could not secure an audience save by the inherent interest of what they wrote.

So what, then, is this freedom – or restraint – of response to political prose? It is a subtle, but not illusory, thing, best conceived as a spectrum. The constraining text targets its readership, while simultaneously, with some 'Procul, o procul este, profani' motif expelling those whose assent is not sought, perhaps because it is perceived as beyond achievement. A single voice is to be heard, guiding and cajoling the chosen reader towards the intended belief or action. Alternative or dissenting voices are excluded. Imagery and information that may conflict with the dominant thesis are controlled or omitted.

At the other end of the spectrum, the unconstraining text is not exclusive in the readership it requires. Nor does it eliminate all alternative or dissenting voices from the discourse. Information and argument are presented in ways which permit a variety of construction, and imagery may subvert the predominant thesis. The unconstrained or free text is open to a multiplicity of responses from a multiplicity of readers. The constrained or unfree text requires a unanimity of response from a readership which it purges of dissenters. It is closed to subversive reading.

The purpose of this essay is the demonstration and validation of these concepts in the interpretation of prose polemic of the English Civil War, and to this end two situationally analogous items have been selected which represent positions close to the opposite extremes of the spectrum which has been defined, John Milton's *Of Reformation* and John Lilburne's *The Christian Mans Triall*.

Milton's earliest antiprelatical pamphlet, *Of Reformation*, raises a set of familiar questions about the libertarian or repressive nature of the militant version of Presbyterianism it expounds. As an attack on Laudianism, it rejects interdiction against the preaching ministry and requires that the debate about further reformation of the English church begin. But it also anticipates with enthusiasm a puritan victory that would include the trial and removal of bishops. That, presumably is what Milton means by the immediate fate he envisages for them, 'a shamefull end in this *Life* (which *God* grant them)'.[1] Implicitly, his sympathies are, as they will remain, with the active suppression of worship on the Laudian model, with the smashing of icons and figurative windows, altar rails and organ pipes, and with the ejection and silencing of those who favour a ceremonial and liturgical style of worship; peaceful coexistence with fellow christians who would retain them is no part of his programme.

The libertarian status of the thesis of *Of Reformation* remains controversial, and Milton's inclusion on the side of the angels of progress is problematic. But, as has been explained, the concerns in this essay are with a rather different aspect of freedom, freedom of reader-response. It will be contended here that this pamphlet is an *unfree text* in that it excludes from its potential readership all who are not already broadly in agreement with its puritanical assumptions, it feeds its readers with information and argument so organised as to prohibit questioning and the exploration of alternatives, and it demands of them an unqualified assent to its conclusions.

Of Reformation was published in May 1641 as a contribution to the broad puritan attack on prelacy. The arguments it rehearses have been interpreted as an extension of the history of prelacy fixed as a postscript to the *Answer to a Booke Entituled, An Humble Remonstrance,* written by Smectymnuus, a writing consortium of presbyterian divines. This appendix has sometimes been attributed to Milton.[2] *Of Reformation* is the first of a series of pamphlets in which Milton more or less directly endorses the Smectymnuan attack on prelacy in general and Bishop Joseph Hall in particular. Its historical moment is that buoyant, puritan ascendancy of the very early 1640s, an ascendancy confirmed by early and important victories such as the release in triumph of Prynne, Bastwick and Burton and, shortly before the publication of *Of Reformation,* the impeachment of Laud and Strafford. The pamphlet proceeds on assumptions of unity of purpose and the certainty of success, culminating in an ecstatic prayer:

O how much more glorious will those former Deliverances appeare, when we shall know them not onely to have sav'd us from greatest miseries past, but to have reserv'd us for greatest happiness to come. Hitherto thou hast but freed us, and that not fully, from the unjust and Tyrannous Claime of thy Foes, now unite us intirely, and appropriate us to thy selfe, tie us everlastingly in willing Homage to the *Prerogative* of thy eternall *Throne*.[3]

Unusually within the Milton prose *oeuvre,* the pamphlet simulates the form of correspondence, as the title page states, 'TWO BOOKS, Written to a FREIND.' The epistolary stance, so lightly and improbably assumed, may suggest the tentativeness of the neophyte pamphleteer who may seem to have taken too literally a Smectymnuan request that he write something for them. But, whatever the motivation, the posture is important to the polemical strategy of the pamphlet.

In this 'friend' Milton produces within the discourse a figure, almost a character, which fills the space the real reader should occupy. The 'you' created is persistently invoked, as friend, as comrade, as revered equal (Milton calls him 'Sir'), as co-worker in the proposed completion of the reformation in England. The reader–friend is invited to cooperate with the author in reviewing the evidence against prelacy: 'Mark Sir here how the Pope came by S. *Peters* Patrymony, as he feigns it, not the donation of

Constantine, but idolatry and rebellion got it him. Yee need but read *Sigonius . . .'*.[4] He is urged to consider recondite evidence which Milton, rather flatteringly, assumes he is already familiar with: 'You know Sir what was the judgement of *Padre Paolo* the great Venetian Antagonist of the *Pope . . .'*.[5] As the reader is produced, so, too, is the author. Milton offers himself as friend and aid, furnishing the data for the process of co-discovery: 'Hitherto Sir you have heard how the *Prelates* have weaken'd and withdrawne the externall Accomplishments of Kingly prosperity . . . now heare how they strike at the very heart, and vitals'.[6] Milton is constructing within the text an image of the author as disinterested servant of truth. On occasion, this is done through explicit, and perhaps rather strident, declamation:

> wherever I have in this BOOKE plainely and roundly (though worthily and truly) laid open the faults and blemishes of *Fathers, Martyrs,* or Christian *Emperors*; or have otherwise inveighed against Error and Superstition with vehement Expressions: I have done it, neither out of malice, nor list to speak evill, nor any vaine-glory; but of meere necessity to vindicate the spotlesse *Truth* from an ignominious bondage.[7]

But this is relatively crude. Pervasively and much more subtly, seeming performatives function to construct a writer dedicated to the service of his friend-reader, abbreviating documentation: 'I will not run into a paroxysm of citations again in this point, only instance *Anthanasius . . .'*;[8] presenting a translation: '*Dante* in his 19. *Canto* of *Inferno* hath thus, as I will render it you in English blank verse';[9] and anticipating objections with a timely tendered citation: 'Now lest it should bee thought that somthing else might ayle this Author thus to hamper the Bishops of those dayes; I will bring you the opinion of . . .'.[10] The text thus assembles a comfortable relationship between the author and reader it produces, and, besides this 'I' of the author and 'you' of the reader–friend, Milton offers, somewhat ambiguously, the pronoun 'we'.

This often stands for author and reader in their collaborative enquiry into the destructive role of prelacy in the English Reformation. 'We' are frequently involved in reviewing evidence and agreeing conclusions:

> But since hee [Constantine] must needs bee the Load-starre of *Reformation* as some men clatter, it will be good to see further his knowledge of *Religion* what it was, and by that we may likewise guesse at the sincerity of his Times . . . .[11]
> Lastly, we all know by Examples, that exact *Reformation* is not perfited at the first push . . . .[12]
> Now certaine if Church-government be taught in the Gospel, as the Bishops dare not deny, we may well conclude of what late standing . . . .[13]

Yet the pronominalisation cannot always be thus interpreted. The 'we' offered must sometimes embrace agents outside the simple duality of author and reader. The term widens to include all decent, Protestant Englishmen, groaning under the prelates' tyranny and struggling to be free:

> yet me thinkes the *Precedencie* which GOD gave this *Iland*, to be the first *Restorer* of *buried Truth*, should have beene followed with more happy successe, and sooner attain'd Perfection; in which, as yet we are amongst the last . . . . Certainly it would be worth the while therefore and the paines, to enquire more particularly, what, and how many the chiefe causes have been, that have still hindred our *Uniforme Consent* to the rest of the *Churches* abroad, (at this time especially) when the *Kingdome* is in a good *propensity* thereto; and all men in Prayers, in Hopes, or in Disputes, either for or against it.[14]

This passage is deeply suggestive of the reception Milton requires, and of the authorial and readerly locations his tract has established. The 'we' that must still perfect reformation must include all England while the national church remains deviant from the continental reforms. This 'we' surely includes Milton and his reader–friend, but it includes, too, all his sounder countrymen. Seemingly, if I may adopt the rhetoric of a more recent crisis, Milton speaks for England; and he represents himself as trying to incorporate into this 'we' all but a few: 'the *Kingdome*', he tells us, 'is in a good *propensity*' towards the puritan perfection of reformation.

Those few excepted from this 'we' of author-plus-reader or author-plus-sound Englishmen are the chief enemies of the nation, the bishops and their supporters. These are persistently referred to in the third person and pronominalised as 'they' and 'them' (though on one occasion Milton does apostrophise them[15]):

> And as for the *Bishops*, they were so far from any such worthy Attempts, as that they suffer'd themselvs to be the common stales to countenance with their prostituted *Gravities* every Politick Fetch that was then on foot, as oft as the Potent *Statists* pleas'd to employ them. Never do we read that they made use of their Authority and high Place of accesse, to bring the jarring Nobility of *Christian peace* . . . .[16]

A comfortable polarity develops between 'they' and 'we' and 'them' and 'us':

> Having fitted us only for peace, and that a servile peace, by lessening our numbers, dreining our estates, enfeebling our bodies, cowing our free spirits by those wayes as you have heard, their impotent actions cannot sustaine

themselves the least moment, unlesse they rouze us up to a *Warre* fit for *Cain* to be the leader of . . . .[17]

The configuration offers an implacable and unresolvable opposition of Milton and the godly united against the bishops, who are represented as a limited and removable enemy:

if we will now resolve to settle affairs either according to pure Religion, or sound Policy, we must first of all begin roundly to cashier, and cut away from the publick body the noysom, and diseased tumor of Prelacie.[18]

The surgical procedure sounds unpleasant but straightforward.

This is the appropriate point at which to introduce a thesis developed by Stanley Fish in his account of a slightly later anti-prelatical pamphlet by Milton, *The Reason of Church Government* (1642). Fish, surely correctly, notes a similar author–reader relationship in this tract, though it is a little simpler: Milton does not locate a surrogate 'reader–friend' within the text as fixed recipient of address. What Fish has to say is creatively provocative. He notes that the tract seemingly offers a *reason* for church government, but, instead of a rationally developed exposition, Milton presents a reiterated assertion of the unresolvable polarity between divinely legitimised Presbyterianism and the obscenity of episcopal church government. Milton's perception of his audience is of central significance. Fish writes

The assumptions that dictate the strategy of *The Reason of Church Government* entail the futility of the entire enterprise. There are only two kinds of readers in Milton's audience, those for whom the reasons imply themselves, and those so unregenerate that no reason, of man or God, will convince them. . . . Milton stands alone, or with those of his audience who, like him, are 'eye-brightened', and the prose continues to pressure the reader to enroll himself in that number. . . . [*The Reason of Church Government*] does not provoke the self of the reader to change, merely to acknowledge his position in the polarities it continually uncovers. The tract does not persuade or convert; rather it bullies . . . .[19]

Fish's account of the later tract obviously accords in some respects with the interpretation being developed here of *Of Reformation*. But arguably, if we understand correctly the historical moment of that pamphlet, what is noteworthy about it is not the 'futility' of the 'enterprise', but its purposefulness and cunning. Fish's book carries the subtitle *The Experience of Seventeenth-Century Literature*. What it offers, for the most part, is a twentieth-century experience of that literature. That is not objectionable at the level of theory, but it is a rather different response from that which may, with difficulty and no doubt only partially, be reconstructed of likely seventeenth-century responses. Milton has a capacity to manipulate that is inadequately represented by Fish's notion of his 'jumping up and down in one place.'[20] Let us return to *Of Reformation* to consider the ideological determinants of its original reception.

The spring of 1641 was a period of buoyant optimism for the broad puritan movement, that puritan opposition which had now captured important political institutions, pre-eminently, of course, Parliament itself, and which had released its martyrs, imprisoned Laud, and, even as Milton was publishing *Of Reformation*, was completing the trial and execution of Strafford. But such moments of victory are often characterised by anxiety and hesitation. Retrospectively, we can discern how unstable a coalition of ideologically diverse groups that broad puritan movement constituted. On the ground, in spring 1641, the debate within the movement focussed on how rigorously episcopacy should be treated. Should it be extirpated? Or could it be reformed? In December 1640 the London Petition, signed by 15,000 citizens, was presented to the Commons. This advocated root-and-branch extirpation and thus embodied the hard line on episcopacy.[21] But in the moment of victory some Puritans were checked by fears of provoking a reaction or of destabilising the larger social structure by so radical a change. This generated a search for a new consensus, and found expression in opposition to root-and-branchism within the Commons and among Puritan divines. A petition of seven or eight hundred ministers, among them two of the Smectymnuans, was presented to the Commons as a compromise formula. In March, maybe eight or ten weeks before the appearance of *Of Reformation*, the Commons passed resolutions to strip bishops of temporal power and undermine their position economically. Root-and-branchism, however, had run into the sand.[22]

Meanwhile, the public face of episcopacy was transformed. Laud was in jail, where he would remain till his execution. John Williams, Bishop of Lincoln, emerged in early 1641 as politically the most influential of the bishops. He had a long record of very public antagonism to Laud, who had conducted a vendetta against him. His prominence in a re-arranged prelatical configuration is indicated by his appointment to the archbishopric of York late in the same year. Joseph Hall, who as bishop of Exeter had assumed a conciliatory attitude to his own puritan ministers, took over the role of leading press apologist for prelacy, and, as a mark of his new importance, he was translated to the more prestigious see of Norwich in the autumn. James Ussher, Archbishop of Armagh, seconded his efforts, publishing a learned defence of episcopacy actually in the same month as *Of Reformation* was published, followed by several others. Ussher, besides being widely acknowledged as the only scholar writing in English to rival Selden's standing, was widely known to have opposed concessions to Catholicism in Ireland. None of them were Arminians, and together they entered into formal negotiations with moderate puritan divines, including three of the Smectymnuans.[23] By late spring 1641, more amenable Puritans could well have felt confident that the Laudian model of Arminianism, popish ritual and authoritarianism had gone for ever.

In this context, the purposefulness of Milton's strategy for reader-response manipulation emerges. Milton's own position is not in any doubt. Whatever compromises his Smectymnuan associates were prepared to entertain, Milton stood among the most militant advocates of the root-and-branch extirpation of prelacy. *Of Reformation* ends with a foam-flecked section in which, as I have said, he seems to advocate the execution of bishops. Nor is he satisfied with their mere death. In a flourish of vindictive eschatology, he offers a vision in which his enemies are

> thrown downe eternally into the *darkest* and *deepest Gulfe* of HELL, where under the *despightfull controule,* the trample and spurne of all the other *Damned,* that in the anguish of their *Torture* shall have no other ease then to exercise a *Raving* and *Bestiall Tyranny* over them as their *Slaves* and *Negro's,* they shall remaine in that plight for ever, the *basest,* the *lowermost,* the *most dejected,* most *underfoot* and *downe-trodden Vassals* of *Perdition.*[24]

The work of *Of Reformation* is to incorporate the broad puritan front into this most uncompromising perception of prelacy.

That work is largely performed through the manipulation of the polarity of, on one side, author and reader ('you-me-us') and, on the other, the 'them' of the ungodly bishops.

The logic of *Of Reformation* contains a *lacuna* which had been present in the analogous postscript to the Smectymnuan *Answer. Of Reformation* offers a historical rhapsody in which English Protestant bishops are equated with pre-Reformation ones and indeed with the bishops of Constantine's day. Distinctions of period and denomination are tacitly suppressed. All represent the same perversion in the same way. Those who are English and Protestant are inserted into the same category as Catholics and foreigners, a category which is separate in every way from the godly. Discontinuities are ignored, and the discreteness of the categories reinforced by Milton's insistence that we, the godly, should regard them as creatures apart. Their alienness is pronounced in terms that at times set them not only outside the ranks of the godly, but outside the human species. They are grotesque ingestion machines, with 'many-benefice-gaping' mouths and 'canary-sucking' and 'swan-eating' palates.[25] Wolfe's comment that Milton does not give credit to 'such an admirable man in private life as Ussher or Hall'[26] is an understatement. Thus, Milton sweeps away the middle ground, leaving the compromisers to build their new consensus over an abyss.

His pamphlet is not designed to work at all if the reader is not already a Puritan. Milton creates a location for the reader to occupy, but an opponent of Puritanism would find it untenable. Its full title signals that this is no text for the non-partisan: *Of Reformation Touching Church-Discipline in England: And the CAUSES that hitherto have hindered it*. A supporter of prelacy would not have accepted that the English Reformation was less than complete, that England remained behind the rest of Protestant Europe in its church settlement. Throughout, the text assumes, though never proves, that the Church of England is corrupt and perverse – assumes, though never proves, because the 'you', the reader Milton addresses, shares those assumptions. For the non-Puritan, the image of bishops is unrecognisable, unreal, and the author's insistence on comradeship is denied: he knows Milton is no friend of his or he of Milton, and he turns away from the text in shock or contempt. Indeed, we have some evidence of such contemporary responses in the comments of Thomas Fuller, a conciliatory episcopalian, that 'One lately hath traduced them [English, Reformed bishops] with such language, as neither beseemed his parts (whosoever he was) that spake it, nor their piety of whom it was spoken',[27] and of John Bramhall, Ussher's eventual successor in the see of Armagh, who remarked, 'With what indignation doe all good Protestants see those blessed Men, now stiled in Print by a young novice, *halting and time-serving Prelates*.... It was truely said by *Seneca*, that the most contemptible Persons ever have the loosest tongues'.[28] But the puritan reader is secured, addressed as friend and comrade, and inserted, alongside the author, in the category of the godly. The charges of ignorance, corruption, brutality and papistical leanings, inherent in Milton's vision, had been commonplaces of antiprelatical writing since the Elizabethan period.[29] Even puritan compromisers were weaned upon them, and, as the tract does its work, they are obliged to accept the polarisation that it postulates. Compromise with prelacy is taken off the agenda, but the friendship Milton offers more than compensates for this constraint: for all the godly, he defines the prospect of celestial triumph when they 'shall clasp inseparable Hands with *joy*, and *blisse* in over measure for ever'.[30]

In its manipulation of the reader, *Of Reformation*, then, is emphatically not libertarian. Only one voice is permitted to be heard, the voice of hard-line Presbyterianism. But, it may be asked, is not this in the nature of propaganda? It is not. Many of the contributions made to the debate about prelacy appear to permit a freer, more active role for the reader in the assembly and evaluation of evidence. There is, for example, a sharp contrast between Milton's pamphlet and John Lilburne's account of his experiences at the hands of bishops and their agents, *The Christian Mans Triall*.

Scholars as diverse and talented as William Haller and Joan Webber have been drawn to consider the connections and distinctions between Milton and Lilburne, 'the one so remarkably famous in his own day and now almost unknown, the other now firmly established as England's greatest non-dramatic poet'.[31] Perhaps, since the thesis advanced here depends so much on distinctions in their literary practice in 1641, some further observations may usefully be added.

There are, clearly, acute dangers in overstating political and social differences between them in the early 1640s. Both were from prosperous families and both had some connection with the higher reaches of the Stuart establishment. Milton had produced *Arcades* (1633?), '*an Entertainment presented to the Countess Dowager of Darby at Harefield*', as it is subtitled, and *Comus* (1634), the masque for the grand state occasion of the Earl of Bridgewater's installation as President of the Council of Wales. Lilburne's aristocratic affiliations were through his parents: his father was in service to the Earl of Northumberland and his mother was daughter of a functionary of the royal court at Greenwich, where Lilburne had spent part of his childhood.[32] Webber alludes, as if to distinguish him from Lilburne, to Milton's 'respectable middle-class circumstances',[33] but Lilburne, too, had wealthy relations. Brailsford's 'guess' that he failed to enter his trade at the end of his apprenticeship because he could not raise the entrance fee of £100,[34] is difficult to reconcile with his later success as a brewer, which was founded on his uncle's injection of £1000 of investment capital.[35] More significant, surely, are distinctions in culture, in age and in political opportunity. Milton not only came from a background which valued higher education, but also, as the elder son, was in some ways insulated from the economic pressures of supporting himself – as Lilburne and Milton's own younger brother, Christopher, a lawyer, were not. Secondly, since he was seven years older than Lilburne, he had spent his adolescence and early manhood in the less abrasively anti-puritan days before Laud became Archbishop of Canterbury. The ideological orientation of his earliest poetry has, in recent years, occasioned considerable debate among Miltonists.[36] Certainly, not until 'Lycidas', written in 1637, is he clearly a militant Puritan. Milton's political associations in the late 1630s and very early 1640s were much less dissident and disruptive than Lilburne's. Though some of the five Smectymnuan divines had come to the attention of Laud and his agents, all survived the 1630s without punishment and with some continuity of employment. In contrast, Lilburne's earliest political *confrères* were dangerous activists. As an apprentice, he was introduced by his master to leading figures of the London puritan underground, including the already incarcerated John Bastwick, whom he met shortly before the latter was to be pilloried and mutilated in company with Prynne and Burton.[37] Milton's personal and political life was in the late 1630s private and withdrawn: Lilburne's had led him into the company of the vanguard of extreme Puritanism. Moreover, by 1638 Lilburne had emerged, as we shall see in spectacular circumstances, as a puritan martyr of the first rank.

These distinctions are of central importance for the reading of the two texts with which we are here concerned. It has been demonstrated how Milton in *Of Reformation* carefully produces an image of himself. It is, emphatically, a construction. Milton's three earliest antiprelatical tracts are entirely anonymous, and when his third comes under attack clearly his confuter either knows almost nothing about him or else confidently assumes his readers know almost nothing about him.[38] In a sense, Milton is free to create *ex nihilo* his self-image, and he can do it with unity of purpose which is unhampered by the need to accommodate inconvenient facts. In sharp contrast, Lilburne is a familiar figure and his whole polemical strategy is to describe his already well-known misfortunes, altogether with his perception of them.

Webber, expanding an insight of Haller, observes with great perception that 'structurally, Lilburne's tracts may be considered . . . as dramatic performances'.[39] Here it will be argued that it is in their dramatic character that much of their openness resides. In a sense, all that Lilburne does is to write up his role as puritan hero and insert it into its setting, in court, in prison, under torture. But in producing the setting, he must write, too, the parts of the minor characters, and this admits alternative voices into the discourse. Moreover, there emerges a curious friction between, not exactly 'art' and 'life', but rather between the stereotypical role of the heroic religious martyr and the uncomfortable and sometimes conflicting recollection of what actually happened.

The tract chosen, *The Christian Mans Triall*, appeared in its second edition in December 1641, over a year after the Long Parliament had released him and other puritan martyrs from prison. It reproduces the first edition of 1638 together with *A Worke of the Beast* (1638). The former was an account of his arrest and trial before Star Chamber, the latter narrates his subsequent whipping, pillorying and incarceration. The case against him was that he had, while in the Netherlands, arranged the production and importation of certain seditious works, most significantly John Bastwick's *Letany* (1637). His modern biographer assumes he was guilty as charged,[40] though, as we shall see, his own position was more complex.

Webber is surely right to perceive the strong influence of Foxe's *Book of Martyrs*.[41] It is present both as an element of the intertextual framework and as an influential model shaping the actual conduct of Lilburne at the hands of his tormentors. We see it strongly in the depiction of the most horrific episode, Lilburne's chastisement with a three-corded whip while led at the cart's tail from the Fleet to Westminster. As puritan martyr, he knew how to behave: as martyrologist, he knew how to describe that behaviour:

The Cart being ready to goe forward, I spake to the Executioner (when I saw him pull his Corded whip out of his pocket) after this manner; Well, my friend, doe thy office . . . . [I said], I know my God hath not onely enabled me to believe in his Name, but also to suffer for his sake. So the Carman drove forward his Cart, and I laboured with my God for strength to submit my backe with cheerfulnesse unto the smiter, and he heard my desire, and granted my request; for when the first stripe was given, I felt not the least paine, but said, *Blessed by they Name, O Lord my God, that hast counted mee worthy to suffer thy glorious Names sake,* and at the giving of the second, I cryed out with a loud voyce, *Hallelujah, Hallelujah, Glory, Honour and Praise be given to thee, O Lord, for ever, and to the Lambe that sits upon the Throne.* So wee went up to *Fleetstreet,* the Lord enabling me to endure the stripes with such patience and cheerfulnesse, that I did not in the least manner shew the least discontent at them, for my God hardened my backe and steeled my reynes, and tooke away the smart and paine of the stripes from mee.[42]

Yet this heroic performance is juxtaposed with admissions of grave discomfort. He recalls he was troubled by the dust of the road, and, though God seemingly had providentially hardened his body, he was curiously unwilling to moderate the sun (though it was only April) that 'shined very hot upon mee'.[43] By the time he was pilloried, far from being the beneficiary of an exceptional providence, he chiefly recalled the agony, 'my backe . . . being very sore, and the Sunne shining so exceeding hot'.[44] The narrative cracks open. We are left to make what we can of the two perspectives – that of the puritan martyrologist defining (his own) heroic martyrdom, and that of the tortured young man whose shoulders, in the words of an eye-witness, 'swelled almost as big as a penny loafe with the bruses of the knotted Cords'.[45] It is part of the abiding fascination of the tract that both voices are permitted to speak: it would have been easy enough to edit out the affecting recollection of the poor victim or to drown it with rhetorical flourishes of puritan polemic.

We have spoken of the dramatic structuring of the text. The acts and speeches of the hero require a supporting cast, some sympathetic, others villains. Even the latter, in Lilburne's discourse, retain a voice. The hangman who whips him is given a line which makes him strangely likeable: 'I have whipt many a Rogue, but now I shall whip an honest man, but be not discouraged . . . it will be soone over'.[46] Milton in *Of Reformation* spoke of the officers of the ecclesiastical and Star Chamber courts in such a way as to metamorphose them into savage animals, into mastiffs at the prelates' call: the bishops 'pray us that it would please us to let them still hale us, and worrey us with their band-dogs and Pursivants'.[47] His single perspective reduces all human experience to a binary opposition of good and pure evil. Lilburne, however, as he describes his own arrest, allows the pursuivant to retain his human credibility. He takes his prisoner to a public house, offers him a cup of wine, and observes to him, affably if sarcastically, 'Mr. *Lilburne*, I am glad with all my heart that wee are met for you are the man that I have much desired for a long time to see'. He adds, self-deprecatorily, 'Come . . . be not sad, you are but fallen into knaves hands'. They banter each other. Lilburne responds, 'I am not sad in the least, and for my falling into knaves hands, I verily beleeve without any questioning, that which you have said'. The pursuivant 'swore another Oath, and said it was true enough'.[48] Surely this exchange, in its introduction of an element of verbal play, trivialises the issues in a way which endangers the reader's perception of the supposed high seriousness of the puritan under-ground and its work.

Lilburne even permits his enemies to have their say at the most crucial phase of the proceedings against him. He and John Wharton, his aged co-defendant, are brought before Star Chamber and confronted with the demand that they take the oath *ex officio* to answer all questions, even though they may in so doing incriminate themselves or their comrades. Lilburne and Wharton stoutly refuse. Lilburne replies, 'I finde no warrant in the Word Of God, for an Oath of inquiry'. Brave stuff, but he adds, 'when I named the Word of God, the Court began to laugh, as though they had nothing to doe with it'. Wharton responds with a long account 'against the Bishops':

but the Lords wondering to heare the *Old Man* begin to talke after this manner, commanded him to hold his peace, and to answer them, whether he would take the Oath or no? To which he replied, and desired them to let him talke a little, and he would tell them by and by. At which all the Court burst out laughing.[49]

Lilburne is locating at the heart of the narrative a devastating alternative perspective. In terms of puritan martyrology and from a puritan standpoint, Lilburne and Wharton, ridiculed by their adversaries, present an *imitatio Christi*, reliving Christ's mockery at the hands of his captors. Yet to a non-puritan reader, another construction is offered by the conduct of the members of the Star Chamber, who plainly regard as absurd both Lilburne's adolescent posturing and the octogenarian Wharton's splenetic loquacity. As Webber observes, Lilburne 'often risks personal absurdity without a second thought'.[50] Laud or his supporters could have read *The Christian Mans Triall* with a hearty perverse pleasure.

There is a further area in which Lilburne leaves his readers with problems of interpretation, the question of his guilt. Milner, writing about a later dispute, the issues raised by the execution of the King, has perceptively noted that Lilburne is much concerned with the notion of legality, and he identifies this as a recurrent motif in Leveller ideology.[51] In a rudimentary form, there is a similar concern in *The Christian Mans Triall*, and it produces a curious near-contradiction. The Laudian régime is represented as a tyranny, and its institutions are the apparatus of authoritarian repression. Their laws are not binding on honest Christian men. Indeed, Lilburne plainly represents himself as engaged in the dissemination of subversive and interdicted literature. In his speech from the pillory, he guides his auditors' seditious reading: 'If you please to reade the second and third parts of Doctor *Bastwicks Letany* . . . .'[52] A little later he reaches into his breeches' pocket for concealed copies of Bastwick's books, which he throws into the crowd.[53] Evidently, Lilburne is thoroughly implicated in the puritan underground and in the circulation of its propaganda. Moreover, he is proud to be identified as an enemy of the (Laudian) state and to stand on the scaffold where 'those living martyrs of the Lord',[54] Burton, Bastwick and Prynne, had stood not long before. Yet, while he accepts the 'guilt' of his involvement with the clandestine opposition and while he denies the moral ascendancy of his enemies, he is, nevertheless, obsessed with asseverating that he is not guilty as charged. Even after he has been whipped, he reiterates that he is innocent of the specific charge, namely that he and Wharton had printed at Rotterdam Bastwick's 'Answer and his Letany with divers other scandalous Bookes', and in the pillory he declares:

Now here againe I speake it in the presence of God, and all you that heare mee, that Master *Wharton* and I never joyned together in printing either these, or any other Bookes whatsoever, neither did I receive any money from him toward the printing any.[55]

Obviously, whoever performed the printing and importation was, in Lilburne's view, a hero. Equally obviously, his own writing, the very text which he produced to describe his suffering, is as seditious as any of Bastwick's writings, and it proclaims his involvement with the underground press. Yet the 'injustice' of the oppressors is represented as rankling deeply. He describes himself as welcoming the punishment and applauding the crime while strenuously and indignantly asserting his innocence in this particular. He leaves his readers with a complex near-contradiction. A hostile reader is left to conclude that, even if he did not perpetrate the seditious act for which he was punished, he was scarcely an innocent victim. A puritan reader is left to puzzle why he is so surprised and indignant at the malice of the prelates, and to reconcile the differing voices of Lilburne the puritan dissident and Lilburne the meticulously legalistic defender of himself. Thus the text embodies some of the ambiguities, uncertainties and anxieties present in even radical Puritanism in the 1630s and very early 1640s, when the movement, though clear in its wishes to obliterate prelacy, still declined to engage the whole system of which prelacy was but a part and hesitated to adopt a thoroughly revolutionary stance. The ideological conflict relates to the problem of how to oppose bishops and the other agents of the King without taking the seditious step of opposing the King himself. Lilburne, in his concern with the promotion of militant Puritanism and the assertion of his innocence, dramatises the problem, but he leaves it to the individual puritan reader to resolve, both in evaluating Lilburne's conduct and determining his own, the problems of accommodating the conflicting imperatives of legality and religion.

It might be objected that this essay is an illiberal attempt to inhibit and frustrate the *jouissance* of free play, imposing restrictions upon the boundless infinitude of reader response. For that reason, it might be useful, as a conclusion, to make explicit two theoretical assumptions on which this essay is premissed.

First, reader response is historically determined, and relates to the point of insertion of the individual reader into the larger ideological complex. There is no evident theoretical reason to exclude a late-twentieth-century response to earlier literature which utterly disregards the ways of thought and perception which were current when the literature was produced, although such an approach seems intellectually impoverishing. All late-twentieth-century approaches are informed by the issues, values, techniques, and preoccupations of our own day, and among that range of techniques and preoccupations is the tradition of historical scholarship which informs this essay: a tradition which essays reconstruction by an archaeological process of the ideological configurations of previous ages, an operation which in turn makes it possible to define some of the ways of understanding open to the original readers.

Secondly, operators within the text may function to limit the range of reader response. In some texts, the pieces are laid out and the reader invited to play them as he or she wishes. In others, some players/readers are excluded and the rest obliged to play by strict rules. We have a spectrum of freedom of response, a spectrum quite neatly illustrated by the contrasting practices of *The Christian Mans Triall* and *Of Reformation*. The former, the freer text, admits a plurality of voices, a juxtaposition of ideologically disparate perspectives, and permits alternative constructions by the reader. Milton's text begins by excluding, by its very title, readers who are opposed to Puritanism, and continues by cajoling and manipulating compromisers and moderates into alignment with its root-and-branchism, and it does so with vigour and assiduity.

Notes

1 *Of Reformation, CPW,* I, p. 616. The following publications deal with *Of Reformation* in ways which have some pertinence to my argument in this chapter: D. Masson, *The Life of John Milton,* 6 vols., London, 1859–94; T. Kranidas, ' "Decorum" and the style of Milton's Antiprelatical Tracts', *Studies in Philology,* LXII, 1965, pp. 176–87, reprinted in S. Fish (ed.), *Seventeenth-Century Prose. Modern Essays in Criticism,* New York, 1971, pp. 475–88; Joan Webber, *The Eloquent 'I'. Style and Self in Seventeenth-Century Prose,* Madison, Wisconsin, and London, 1968; S. E. Fish, *Self-Consuming Artifacts,* Berkeley, Los Angeles and London, 1972; M. Lieb, 'Milton's *Of Reformation* and the dynamics of controversy', in M. Lieb and J. T. Shawcross (eds.), *Achievements of the Left Hand. Essays on the Prose of John Milton,* Amherst, Mass., 1974, pp. 53–82; K. W.

Stavely, *The Politics of Milton's Prose Style*, New Haven, Conn., 1975; C. Hill, *Milton and the English Revolution*, London, 1977.

2 D. M. Wolfe reviews and augments the case for a Miltonic attribution, *CPW*, I, pp. 961–65.

3 *Of Reformation, CPW*, I, p. 615.

4 *Ibid.*, p. 578.

5 *Ibid.*, p. 581.

6 *Ibid.*, p. 592.

7 *Ibid.*, p. 535.

8 *Ibid.*, p. 566.

9 *Ibid.*, p. 558.

10 *Ibid.*, p. 558.

11 *Ibid.*, p. 555.

12 *Ibid.*, p. 536.

13 *Ibid.*, p. 574.

14 *Ibid.*, p. 526–27.

15 *Ibid.*, p. 551.

16 *Ibid.*, pp. 530–31.

17 *Ibid.*, pp. 595–96.

18 *Ibid.*, p. 598.

19 Fish, *Self-Consuming Artifacts*, pp. 300–302.

20 *Ibid.*, p. 290.

21 *CPW*, I, p. 63.

22 *Ibid.*, pp. 69–70.

23 *Ibid.*, p. 1031.

24 *Of Reformation, CPW*, I, pp. 616–17.

25 *Ibid.*, p. 549.

26 *CPW*, I, p. 113.

27 Thomas Fuller, *The Holy State*, London, 1642, pp. 291–92; quoted by J. M. French, *The Life Records of John Milton*, New Brunswick, 1949–58, II, pp. 52–53.

28 John Bramhall, *The Serpents Salve, Or, A Remedie For the Biting of an Aspe*, London, 1643, p. 212; quoted by French, *Life Records*, II, p. 83.

29 Comparison with the Marprelate tracts has often been made. See, for example, my 'Obscenity, slang and indecorum in Milton's English prose', *Prose Studies*, III, 1980, pp. 7–8.

30 *Of Reformation, CPW*, I, p. 616.

31 Webber, *The Eloquent 'I'*, p. 53.

32 Pauline Gregg, *Free-born John. A Biography of John Lilburne*, London, 1961, pp. 12–20.

33 Webber, *The Eloquent 'I'*, p. 53.

34 H. N. Brailsford, *The Levellers and the English Revolution*, ed. C. Hill, London, 1961, p. 80.

35 Gregg, *Free-born John*, p. 88.

36 For a recent, brief review of the controversy, see D. Norbrook, *Poetry and Politics in the English Renaissance*, London, 1985, pp. 237–38: for my own position, see my 'Milton's quest for respectability', *Modern Language Review*, LXXVII, 1982, pp. 769–79.

37   Gregg, *Free-born John*, pp. 33–51.
38   Anon., *A Modest Confutation of a Slanderous and Scurrilous Libell, Entituled, Animadversions*, London, 1642, passim.
39   Webber, *The Eloquent 'I'*, p. 68.
40   Gregg, *Free-born John*, pp. 48–49.
41   Webber, *The Eloquent 'I'*, pp. 68–79.
42   John Lilburne, *The Christian Mans Triall*, second edition, London, 1641, p. 19.
43   *Ibid.*, p. 20.
44   *Ibid.*, p. 22.
45   Quoted by Gregg, *Free-born John*, p. 65.
46   *The Christian Mans Triall*, p. 19.
47   *Of Reformation*, *CPW*, I, p. 612.
48   *The Christian Mans Triall*, pp. 1, 2.
49   *Ibid.*, pp. 13, 14.
50   Webber, *The Eloquent 'I'*, p. 63.
51   A. Milner, *John Milton and the English Revolution*, London, 1981, pp. 55–56.
52   *The Christian Mans Triall*, p. 27.
53   *Ibid.*, p. 31.
54   *Ibid.*, p. 26.
55   *Ibid.*, p. 23.

London and popular freedom
in the 1640s

The collapse of Charles I's government and the momentous events of the 1640s permitted all levels of English society to enjoy an unprecedented degree of freedom of thought, expression and action. This freedom made a dramatic impact upon the middle and lower orders of society which were freed from much of their earlier supervision, coercion and control. For a decade those who formerly had had little, if any, voice or influence in matters of church or state made inroads into these once exclusive preserves of the political élite and came to challenge the very assumptions which underpinned traditional authority in both these spheres. This essay examines the ways in which this novel popular freedom manifested itself at the very centre of events, in the capital and its immediate vicinity, as both press and pulpit were thrown open for the expression of divergent opinions among a relatively literate, articulate and sophisticated population, and the way was cleared for the resurgence of religious and political radicalism on a popular basis.[1] Yet although the focus is upon those who took advantage of a new-found freedom to challenge the *status quo*, it would be a gross distortion to view radicalism as the inevitable outcome of popular freedom and ignore a strong and enduring popular conservatism. The advocates of fundamental change did not only provoke alarm and hostility among the ranks of the ruling élite but encountered similar reactions at a popular level.

A consistent theme in royalist explanations of the origins and violent direction of events in the 1640s is the crucial role of an unregulated press and pulpit, poisoning people's minds, and parliamentary endorsed demonstrations and petitions which brought the kingdom to the brink of anarchy.[2] Prior to 1640, the press had been subject to stringent controls by the crown acting principally through the church and the Stationers'

Company, but the silencing of dissident domestic presses failed to halt the dissemination of seditious literature in the late 1630s. The printers of Holland helped fill the gap and men like John Lilburne were prepared to take the risk of dispersing such literature. After the outbreak of war with Scotland, pamphlets stating the Scottish case were also in circulation in England.[3]

By the time the Long Parliament met, the government was already losing its grip on the press. The subsequent abolition of the prerogative courts, coupled with divisions within the Stationers' Company, gave domestic presses an unprecedented degree of freedom at precisely the time when the appetite for political news and comment was becoming insatiable. The resulting publishing explosion enlisted the talents of those who had previously been excluded from the world of writing and who were less inhibited about catering for a wide social spectrum.[4] Initially, a free and informed press was encouraged by parliamentary leaders who appreciated the importance of printed propaganda, although the House of Lords was less permissive in its attitude to the press than the Commons. With or without the author's consent, speeches made by MPs in the House were printed and circulated, thereby violating the convention that parliamentary proceedings should not be publicised, yet very few complaints of breaches of privilege ensued. Furthermore, Pym and other leaders apparently did not scruple to leak important information for publication when it suited them. Such leaders had to tread cautiously, as the sharpness of the debate in the Commons over publication of the Grand Remonstrance demonstrated, when members expressed anxieties about the dangerous novelty of publishing direct appeals to the people about matters of state. Yet in the wake of the Militia Ordinance, parliament sanctioned the publication of increasingly polemical declarations which were later to provide grist to the mill for Leveller polemics.[5]

At no stage, of course, did parliament espouse the principle of press freedom; on the contrary, at the earliest opportunity it attempted to reassert control over the presses, effectively substituting parliamentary for royal restraint. Parliament first turned to the Stationers' Company for assistance and, when that proved ineffective, used its own committees and their pursuivants to track down illicit printers. Its first major attempt to regulate printing, the ordinance of the 14 June 1643, failed to stem the tide of unlicensed publications produced on hidden presses and not until the end of the decade did it encounter any real success. In the intervening years, there were periodic, if not always successful, attempts to enforce censorship with the help of persistent searchers for illicit presses, like Joseph Hunscot. Hunscot and rival searchers became the scourge of the nascent Leveller leadership in London, forcing them to move their presses around the City and out into the suburbs.[6] The Levellers were to make a principled stand upon the freedom of the press as a concomitant of a liberated mind and conscience.[7]

From the comparatively unregulated presses of the 1640s issued forth a rich profusion of pamphlets, newsbooks, ballads and other ephemera, appealing to an exceptionally wide variety of tastes and interests. Unlicensed pamphlets, obliquely undermining the king's authority or defaming the church and its bishops, caused particular scandal in the early days of the Long Parliament. Some unlicensed works were seized, along with their printers, yet very few failed to reach the eyes of the public as it proved much more difficult to trace the occasional pamphlet to its source than the regular newsbook.[8]

One notable exception was the apparently total suppression of Henry Walker's *To your tents, O Israel,* one of the three seditious pamphlets singled out for mention by the King in March 1642. Walker was one of the new breed of London pamphleteers and publicists, men who immediately took advantage of the breakdown of controls over press and pulpit in the early 1640s to turn their hands to writing, publishing and expounding scripture. Having exchanged his earlier troubled trade of ironmonger for that of bookseller, he became one of the most prolific printers and composers of unlicensed pamphlets, with Archbishop Laud and other persecuting prelates as favourite targets. Walker was brought before the Lords on the 12 March 1641 with two other illicit printers and committed to the Fleet from where he was released after only one night. In no way chastened, he continued to publish anti-prelatical diatribes. Yet the most audacious chapter in Walker's career began with his pamphlet *To your tents, O Israel,* composed on the night following the attempted arrest of the five members and intended for distribution the following day. Borrowing a Bible from his printer's wife, Walker chose I Kings 12: 16, with its allusion to wicked kings and the deposition of Rehoboam, as the textual basis for his pamphlet and by working through the night had printed copies ready for distribution the next day. As Charles returned from dining with one of the London sheriffs, Walker threw a copy of the pamphlet into or near the royal coach. Both Walker and the printer were arrested and committed to the King's Bench prison but, in the process of being transferred to Newgate a week later in time for the sessions, they were rescued at Blackfriars by a

sympathetic crowd. For a time Walker managed to evade re-arrest by
flitting about the City and suburbs, sheltered by associates (including
'another usurping pamphleteer, one Fisher a Barber'), and on one
occasion he was again rescued from capture by a group of journeyman
shoemakers. Disguised as a minister, he even managed to preach a
controversial sermon from the pulpit of St Mary Magdalen, Bermond-
sey. Three months after the offence, Walker was eventually committed
to the Tower and later tried and convicted for trespass and misdemea-
nour at the Old Bailey. The King's decision to proceed against him on
this lesser charge (rather than that of treason) may have owed less to
royal clemency than to a recognition that a London jury may have
baulked at the idea of consigning to a traitor's death a man regarded in
some quarters as a popular hero – as John Lilburne was later to discover
in his own case. Walker was fined and imprisoned at the king's pleasure
but by March 1643 he was at liberty pursuing his former trade of
publishing scandalous pamplets, until the Lords committed him to the
Fleet for nine months. From 1644 onwards he devoted his energies
increasingly to journalism and the careerist in him triumphed over the
radical to the extent that he was advocating strict parliamentary
censorship by 1648.[9]

The first English newsbook dealing with domestic news (which
pre-1640 newsbooks studiously avoided) reached the streets of London
in November 1641 and was quickly joined by an increasing number of
competitors until a brief parliamentary clamp-down in March 1642.[10]
This, and later parliamentary attempts to regulate the press, had a
minimal effect upon newsbooks until 1649 when there was a return of
effective censorship and the London weeklies were silenced. The jour-
nalistic high-point was reached in 1645 when there were sixteen separate newsbooks in existence. Despite the numbers, however, if one
discounts the royalist weeklies, there were decided limits to the variety
and quality of newscoverage. Most newsbooks were launched and
maintained to make a profit; they tended to use the same sources and
borrow from one another; and they were generally anxious to keep on
the right side of the law, and avoid offending the authorities, by subjec-
ting themselves to a form of self-censorship. Newsbooks were, after all,
more vulnerable than pamphlets to the searcher with their distinctive
print, their regularity and the ever-present possibility that a vendor
might betray his supplier. The capital, with its potential mass
readership, was of paramount importance in the rise and survival of
newsbooks, and as the vast majority were addressed to Londoners, one

or two decided to appeal to a less sophisticated London readership. Yet although a few earlier newsbooks exhibited occasional radical tendencies, a consistently radical weekly did not appear on the scene until 1648, with the launching of *The Moderate*, which for ten months extensively publicised the Leveller cause.

Ballads were printed in enormous numbers during the years 1642–47 as the profits to be made from feeding a seemingly insatiable appetite for news and satire swelled the ranks of ballad writers. As with pamphlets and newsbooks, attempts at suppression before the end of the decade had little effect upon a flourishing trade which was only diminished by the superior coverage of newsbooks and the drift of ballad writers into journalism.[11] Most surviving ballads are pro-Royalist in sentiment, but one 1641 ballad scandalously celebrated the Queen Mother's departure; another published in 1642 gloated over the imprisonment of the twelve bishops; and yet another rejoiced over the achievements of the Long Parliament and made a veiled attack upon the King. Later ballads attacked the royal family or the Assembly of Divines, or denounced pious hypocricy from a Ranter viewpoint.[12]

The contents of a ballad written to be sung were perhaps more readily transmittable to the generality of people than other products of the printing-press. However, illiterates were read to, and there is some tentative evidence of impressively high rates of literacy in mid-seventeenth-century London, and higher rates than the national average in neighbouring counties, especially Middlesex and Essex. The vast majority of the craftsmen and tradesmen of London and suburban Middlesex would evidently have been able to read any of the literature that came into their hands in the 1640s, and their servants and apprentices were also extraordinarily literate. Even the less-skilled workers of the metropolitan area were more literate than their provincial and rural counterparts, but massive female illiteracy was the rule in London as elsewhere.[13] Barriers to communication were also reduced by supplementing the printed word with striking woodcuts, either as title-page illustrations or as a pictorial series.[14]

The volume of material printed for circulation varied enormously. Pamphlets aimed at a wide readership normally ran to 1,000 to 1,500 copies, but they could go as high as 10,000, and 20,000 copies of a 1646 petition were reportedly printed. Most newsbooks in the 1640s probably had an average circulation of 500 copies; 200 copies was the minimum, and 3,000 the maximum circulation. There are no precise estimates of the runs of ballads but they were probably extensive.[15] Copies of a publication could be produced at great speed – over-night if necessary, as we have seen in Walker's case, – and this contributed greatly to the problems of authorities anxious to silence movements like the Levellers.[16]

From the presses printed material reached the public via the shops of booksellers themselves (or, more surreptitiously, from shops selling other wares); they were hawked on the streets or in taverns by a growing army of women and other Londoners supplementing their means of livelihood, or the destitute from surrounding counties; and they were sold by the book-women of Westminster Hall, under the very noses of parliament. Hawkers of unlicensed publications were liable to be committed as vagrants, yet some had respectable trades or occupations, like the London tallow-chandler who sold pamphlets alongside his customery wares. Occasionally provocative political literature was scattered about the streets at night, thrown among holidaying apprentices in Moorfields, fixed to a post in Cheapside, or distributed by sympathetic sectarian congregations.[17] The handbill and placard became familiar features of the political scene in London. They were posted up in public places, including the entrance to Parliament itself, drumming up support either for or against religious or political radicalism.[18]

The levying of heavy fines upon hawkers signalled the return of press regulation at the close of the decade, the effect of which was to interrupt the free access to printed news, comment and opinion to which many literate Londoners had become accustomed. Yet the existence of a comparatively free press during years of crisis and great change had helped raise the level of popular political consciousness. It had made available to a mass readership a hitherto inconceivably wide choice of alternative views about politics, religion and society.[19]

A liberated pulpit partnered a free press in opening up new vistas for the populace. The Long Parliament lost no time in encouraging some of Laud's more vociferous clerical critics to climb into City pulpits or to preach before them. The Commons established two committees, one for religion and the other for grievances, which gave a sympathetic hearing to complaints against 'scandalous ministers' and set in motion a gradual purge of parish clergy. By 1649 about 81 per cent of the 108 City parishes had been affected by clerical ejections, losing either the incumbent or the curate. This purge, coupled with the Commons' sanctioning of lectureships if parishes so desired, permitted London Puritans, and especially Presbyterians, to seize control of parish pulpits.[20]

Opening pulpits to the more zealously protestant clergy was one thing, but allowing laymen, often of relatively humble social status and with little, if any, formal education, to preach was quite another, and MPs shared in the sense of outrage felt in the upper reaches of society at the outburst of lay preaching in London in 1641. The first man to attract attention was Roger Quatermayne, a Southwark solicitor notorious for his lay preaching and labelled a separatist, although he actually remained in regular communion with the Church of England. With the Long Parliament in session, lay preachers became increasingly bold and less secretive. Some laymen, like the 'buttonmaker' at St Anne's, Aldersgate, in August, or the 'cobbler' at St George's, Southwark, in December 1641, were said to have preached from parish pulpits. Others continued the practice of preaching to more or less secret gatherings in private houses rather than risk popular hostility. The anarchic spectacle of the tub-preacher, drawing crowds in the open spaces that surrounded the City, or in alleys or suburbs, caused the greatest stir. However, lay preaching in public virtually ceased in 1642 in the interests of anti-epi-scopal unity.[21]

The obsessive attacks launched upon lay preachers and their activi-ties by sworn enemies like John Taylor, the water-poet, Thomas Edwards and others have made an accurate historical assessment diffi-cult. Particular emphasis was placed upon the low social origins of the preachers, commonly described as tradesmen or 'mechanic persons' hovering on the very margins of literacy. Such men were not content to observe their station in life but trespassed into the domain of the university-educated preacher, rejecting sound religious principles derived from a conventional education in favour of wild fantasies born of spiritual inspiration. Adding to the chaos, even some women had defied God and nature by preaching.[22] Craftsmen and tradesmen do appear to have had a predominant place in the ranks of lay preachers, alongside men of more substance like Roger Quatermayne. As has been noted, most of the those dwelling in London and the suburbs would have been at least able to read scripture and make some sense of the increasing volume of religious literature, and were more probably self-educated rather than ignorant about the fundamentals of religion. Parliament made several attempts to suppress lay preaching but achieved little beyond harassing a few individuals. Self-restraint removed the public scandal of lay preaching in 1642, but it apparently flourished in private and was barely affected by the ordinance of 26 April 1645. When put to the test by the Lord Mayor of London, it proved totally ineffective, and subsequent Commons' measures all failed to deal with the problem.[23]

The pulpit does appear to have played a key role in London in alienating popular opinion from the King. Puritan clergy and the clerical leaders of separatist congregations were undoubtedly influential in rallying popular support for the parliamentary cause, and the printing-press brought their sermons to a wide audience.[24] But so far as most puritan divines were concerned that support was to be for strictly limited ends, as they were acutely aware of the dangers of popular confusion in church and state under the guise of liberty.[25] A degree of social and political radicalism might be implicit in sermons attacking episcopacy, but a direct recognition of social ills, like that of Simeon Ashe in March 1642 was exceptional in sermons of this kind.[26] It was left to lay preachers to recall how Christ had chosen poor and uneducated fisher-men and other simple folk, not the Jewish élite, to convey his message, and to announce that God was still addressing the world through his humble servants.[27] Later in the decade, some of these lay preachers and their followers were to occupy prominent positions in the Leveller movement or in radical City politics. In 1649, however, London separa-tists traded religious toleration for a withdrawal from radical politics, and freedom of expression from the pulpit was qualified by a parlia-mentary prohibition upon preachers meddling in politics.[28]

Popular political intervention in the form of riots and demonstrations, or mass petitioning, accompanied the relaxation of controls over press and pulpit. Popular disorder in London and its suburbs in the 1640s was not in itself a new phenomenon for the streets and recreational areas had been intermittently disturbed by riots in the early seventeenth century. However, popular political disorders were comparatively rare events prior to 1640 – the most notable being the mobbing of Dr John Lambe, an essentially anti-Buckingham demonstration.[29] The public mutilation of the three puritan martyrs and the flogging and pilloring of Lilburne in the late 1630s drew sympathetic crowds,[30] but not until after the dissolution of the Short Parliament was there a period of popular political mobilisation, on an unprecedented scale, ushered in by the riotous assault on Lambeth Palace and its sequel.

The disorders of the period 1640–2, reaching a crescendo with the King's departure from his capital, stretched the limited civil and military resources available in the London area for the maintenance of order to breaking point, and reduced Charles's government to an angry impotence. Although the Lambeth and Southwark riots of May 1640 were classified as rebellious, and the invasion of the Court of High Commission (as any attack upon a court of justice) was also a capital crime, apparently only one of the former rioters suffered the ultimate penalty.[31]

Ironically, the attack upon High Commission on the 22 October 1640 followed the court's earlier adjournment from Lambeth to the Convocation House of St Paul's because its persistent persecution of religious dissidents had raised fears for its security. Although the rioters demolished the court, its records were not discovered and a much smaller crowd returned on the 1 November to tear up papers in the Vicar General's office, believing them to be high commission records. The day after the main assault, Archbishop Laud warned his fellow judges in Star Chamber that they would be the next target for popular tumult, because of their prosecution of Prynne, Burton and Bastwick, if exemplary punishments did not follow, yet subsequent legal proceedings at the Guildhall ended in the acquittal of all but one of the suspects.[32] On the 28 November, the records of High Commission over the previous ten years were sent for by the Commons (and one of the court's victims was set free by the Lords), and in the afternoon thousands of Londoners staged an impressive demonstration at the triumphal return of Prynne and Burton from their imprisonment. The demonstration was 'generally esteemed the greatest affront that ever was given to the courts of Justice in England'. Further popular applause greeted Bastwick's entry into London six days later. Clarendon attached particular significance in his account of the origins of open conflict to the impunity with which people demonstrated, preached or published from this point onwards, as government and judiciary lost the will to proceed against offenders and the people became accustomed to such license.[33]

The trial of Strafford and the issue of episcopacy provoked the most serious disorders in 1641, as large crowds descended upon Westminster and Whitehall calling for speedy justice upon the Earl or denouncing bishops. The Commons passed Strafford's attainder after an estimated 10,000 petitioning citizens had pressed for his execution, but a less compliant House of Lords was subjected to much more direct popular pressure. On the 3 and 4 May, thousands of demonstrators (urged on by some London preachers the previous Sunday) crowded about Westminster and members of both Houses were forced to file through the demonstrators in their coaches to take their seats. The only demonstrator to be subsequently arrested was John Lilburne who was charged before the Lords with uttering menacing and treasonable words, but his accusers failed to make the charge stick and he was free to mingle with the enormous crowds at the Earl's execution.[34] Popular pressure seems to have played a significant part in facilitating the passage of Strafford's attainder through the Lords and securing the King's assent. One London citizen was to recall in the following September (when a demonstration outside the House of Lords over the issue of protections was contemplated) 'that my Lord of Strafford had not died if the people had not pressed the Lords in a tumult as they did'.[35]

The anti-episcopal demonstrations outside Parliament and Whitehall which began at the end of November 1641 were among the gravest manifestations of popular disorder yet seen in London. The demonstrations took place on several consecutive days and were more violent and potentially explosive than previously, with the blatant intimidation of bishops and some peers, and violent confrontations with opponents. They eventually led to the questioning of whether Parliament could be regarded as free in the circumstances, and the suicidal protest of the twelve bishops. They also confirmed the King's suspicions that all this popular pressure was being orchestrated by parliamentary leaders and hence helped prompt the attempt on the five members. A well-organised City campaign against bishops began with the petition of the 11 December 1640 which caused considerable embarrassment in the Commons. With popular attention later focussed on Strafford, there were no further anti-episcopal demonstrations until the 29 November 1641 when armed men crowded into the Court of Requests crying down with bishops and popish lords. Further crowds gathered the next day and soon the Christmas holidays released London apprentices to join in the demonstrations. At their height, only two bishops dared to brave the crowds to take their seats in the Lords, and in confrontations in and about Westminster Hall and the Abbey a number of men were wounded, at least one (Sir Richard Wiseman) fatally.[36] Lilburne featured among the wounded but this time he was not paraded before the authorities for there was little in the way of punitive action despite official alarm. Only a handful of prominent offenders were subsequently questioned or taken into custody.[37]

The anti-episcopal campaign achieved its first success with the impeachment of the twelve protesting bishops, and was followed on the 5 February 1642 with their exclusion from the House of Lords. In the interval, the King struck at what he regarded as the source of this continuing tumult and sedition by framing a charge of treason against Lord Kimbolton and the five members. The popular disapproval he experienced when he pursued the five members into the City, together with Walker's notorious pamphlet, shook Charles. He avoided the ultimate humiliation of witnessing the spectacular demonstration which marked the return of the five members to their seats in parliament on the 11 January by leaving the day before.[38] After the King's departure there was a reduction in the kind of popular disorder recently witnessed. The martyred Sir Richard Wiseman was given a hero's funeral on the 19 January, but it bore no comparison with the impressive political demonstration mounted by London Levellers at Robert Lockyer's funeral seven years later.[39] Crowds accompanied the presentation of petitions to parliament complaining of severe economic hardship, or either calling for peace or a more vigorous prosecution of the war,[40] but there was no return to the sort of popular influence upon events seen in 1641–2 until a new political crisis in 1647. In that year, it was a counter-revolutionary crowd that ironically took the earlier popular pressures on Parliament to their logical conclusion and invaded both Houses on the 26 July to dictate their wishes.[41]

The circulation and presentation of petitions was another means of articulating grievances and exerting pressure for change which was revived on a large scale in 1640 after a lengthy absence from the political scene. Most petitions were addressed to one or both Houses of Parliament and boasted signatures (and marks) in their thousands, and sometimes in their tens of thousands,[42] although there was an obvious temptation for promoters of petitions to exaggerate the extent of their support.[43] Signatures were canvassed by sympathetic clergy in their parishes, collected at wardmotes, in company halls, taverns and shops, at gatherings in recreational areas, and even in church on a Sunday morning on one occasion. Threats, coercion and other pressures sometimes supplemented the more usual use of exhortation and persuasion to gain signatures in the early 1640s.[44] A demonstration of mass support could accompany the presentation of a petition to parliament or the organisers might advertise their responsibility and self-restraint by entrusting presentation to a disciplined few.[45] After the outbreak of the Civil War, petitions came increasingly to be regarded as at best an irritant and at worst a breach of parliamentary privilege. The outrageous spectacle of a crowd of women petitioners, headed by Mrs Lilburne, in September 1646 provoked one of Bulstrode Whitelocke's moralising asides to his children about the danger of countenancing 'the beginnings of any unfit thing, though to promote your designs at that time, least the growth of those unfit things, become afterwards a greater prejudice, than it was before an advantage to you'.[46]

The royalist tendency to dismiss the demonstrators and petitioners of

1640–2 as 'the meaner sort of people', dredged up out of the City and its suburbs, distorted reality. Even the Lambeth and Southwark rioters of May 1640 had more complex social and geographical origins than the contemporary description of them as apprentices and 'base people' from those parts and the eastern suburbs. Among the detained suspects were a variety of craftsmen (some of whom, but by no means all, may still have been apprentices) in company with the more humble waterman, sailor or labourer, and although largely from the south bank, they were also drawn from the City, Westminster and St Giles in the Fields.[47] Men of substance and social standing, joined by craftsmen, tradesmen and others of middle rank, clearly played a prominent role in some demonstrations. Yet the social composition and character of demonstrations could change markedly, especially if they were prolonged, and more intimidating crowds drawn from the lower orders of the City and suburbs might assemble.[48] The organisers of some petitions were socially selective in the support they enlisted, excluding base signatories, and the presenters deliberately stressed their respectable social standing and responsibility.[49] However, when the leading issues were bishops, popery or economic hardship lower social elements were more likely to be at the forefront of more threatening and urgent demonstrations.[50] Popular disorder inevitably drew in apprentices, with or without their masters' approval, in the 1640s as earlier in the century, especially during holiday or recreational periods.[51] There were also demonstrations composed wholly or mainly of women, but the role of women will be examined later.

Pym and his associates were accused of orchestrating, or deliberately encouraging, popular interventions in parliamentary affairs in the early 1640s.[52] The first major demonstration before parliament, the presentation of the anti-episcopal petition in December 1640, earned a gentle rebuke from the Commons, but many subsequent petitions and demonstrations were either countenanced or given encouragement by the House. Although the full conspiracy theory of popular pressures cunningly engineered by parliamentary leaders, in alliance with Isaac Penington and John Venn, is non-proven and improbable, the timing of many of the protests, and the pressures they exerted, were certainly not unwelcome to such leaders. By allowing petitioners to interrupt proceedings to present petitions, and moreover permitting spokesmen an extended constitutional liberty to state their case at the bar of the House, the Commons were signalling their consent to mass lobbying.[53] Nathanial Fiennes made one of the most eloquent Commons' defences of mass petitioning on the 8 February 1641 in reply to Lord Digby's condemnation of the recent anti-episcopal petition as a dangerous popular intrusion into parliamentary affairs. Fiennes argued that the number of petitioners and the crowds accompanying it were grounds for taking the petition into serious consideration rather than rejecting it, and warned that a refusal to consider it might have tumultuous consequences.[54] In the tense weeks leading up to the King's departure, the Commons defended the right of petitioning Parliament and condemned those who tried to interrupt it. Legal proceedings were stopped by the House in the case of the Southwark petitioners and the Westminster constable accused of complicity in the riotous rescue of demonstrating apprentices, and a Middlesex JP was committed to the Tower for affronting petitioning citizens. The Commons also gave a warm reception to one of the first crowds of exclusively female petitioners in February 1642.[55] By this stage, however, the Commons' tolerance of demonstrations was on the wane and, as the mood changed, earlier justifications of popular access to Parliament returned to haunt them. London youths petitioning for peace in January 1643 recalled the words of Nathaniel Fiennes and parliament's own declarations, and the Levellers too were to claim the benefit of those liberties proclaimed in the early 1640s. When faced with renewed and unwelcome popular pressure in 1646 and 1647, those Members of Parliament who had previously encouraged popular mobilisation became victims of their own expediency.[56]

As the House of Lords took the lead in trying to prevent tumultuous assemblies at Westminster in the early 1640s, tension inevitably arose between them and the Commons over the latter's failure to give the matter priority. Yet the Lords were not prepared to vote that Parliament was not free in December 1641 when mobs surrounded the Houses. They merely warned the Commons that they might subsequently be accused of acting under duress.[57] The governors of the City of London shared the Lords' concern about popular petitioning and disorder, at least until the political changes of early 1642. It was an established tradition that parliamentary petitions from citizens received the prior approval of the Lord Mayor and aldermen, but all the controversial citizens' petitions, from November 1640 to January 1642, bypassed the City government and were unofficial.[58]

Despite royalist convictions that the demonstrations were all stage-managed, there neither was nor could be any one influence moulding and directing street politics in London. Petitions and demonstrations could be alternately more radical or more conservative than parliamentary leaders like Pym would have wished. Fiery radicals like Lilburne and his separatist brethren were not always amenable to external control and direction, and the initiative lay outside conventional politics in later radical demands for the abolition of tithes or a fundamental shift in political power as envisaged by the Levellers. The fortuitous or spontaneous element in some demonstrations also needs to be recalled in this context.[59]

Whether spontaneous or premeditated, the pressures exerted by crowds at Westminster led to claims that the political arena was being invaded by the masses, dictating their upstart demands, and ultimately to the allegation that Parliament was no longer free. Lord Digby led the attack on mass petitioning. 'What can there be of greater presumption', he declared after the anti-episcopal petition of December 1640, 'than for Petitioners, not only to prescribe to a Parliament, what, and how it shall do, but for a multitude to teach a Parliament, what, and what is not, the government according to God's Word'.[60] A preacher exhorted demonstrators in December 1641 to confine themselves to their God-given trades and callings and not intrude themselves into matters beyond their comprehension, a view that would have been widely shared by the political élite. Conservative sentiment was also aroused by the radical implications of some popular demands. If the campaign against bishops were successful, it was claimed, the way would be open to more general social levelling; or if the later campaign against tithes succeeded, the payment of rents to landlords would be the next target. Earlier conservative prophecies were confirmed by the invasion of Parliament on the 26 July 1647 and the activities of the London Levellers.[61]

Parliamentary attempts to regulate or prevent popular pressure were begun in earnest within a few weeks of the King's departure as conservative citizens copied the lobbying tactics of the radicals. Sir George Benion and his fellow petitioners of the 24 February 1642 were the first of a number of critics of the parliamentary leadership to be denied the freedom to petition, and to face fines and imprisonment.[62] A panic proposal in July 1647 to make petitioning treasonable was eventually dropped, but a longer term desire to place restrictions on the numbers and manner of presenting petitions to Parliament did bear fruit in the ordinance of the 22 May 1648.[63]

All this activity helped to heighten popular political awareness in London and its suburbs. Petitions were read out and explained to potential signatories and the subscriptions of all, including illiterates, were generally welcomed. Passive subscription was sometimes not enough; the signatory had to have the issues explained to him to ensure his firm and active commitment. Thus the gathering of hands served the dual function of furthering political education and rallying active support. Popular participation in, and an awareness of, public affairs was further encouraged by parliament itself when it required subscriptions to the Protestation and other public engagements, and when it sanctioned the printing and circulation of the Grand Remonstrance.[64] And in the midst of the early demonstrators were future popular leaders like John Lilburne.

Freedom of conscience and religious observance was a vital component in the more general freedom of expression and action enjoyed by Londoners in the 1640s. The breakdown of ecclesiastical authority, and the Long Parliament's hostility to Laudian innovations, disturbed the relative peace and order of most parishes in the London area as determined minorities seized the opportunity to indulge their reforming zeal either within or outside of the established church. Three London churches led the revolt against Laudianism a month before the gathering of the Long Parliament and once it was in session hopes of reformation ran high. On the 21 November 1640 some parishioners from Allhallows Barking took the initiative by sawing off the 'popish' wooden figures of angels from their communion rails and brought them before the Commons. The following day, MPs refused to receive the sacrament at the communion table in St Margaret's, Westminster, while it was positioned like an altar and urged the dean to relocate it. Further alterations to the interior of St Margaret's were to be made in subsequent years, including the removal of the screen, the organ and 'superstitious' brasses.[65] Interruption of the Anglican liturgy in some London churches by both men and women on Sunday, the 10 January 1641, and the discovery of a Southwark conventicle on the same day, prompted an order of the Lords condemning such disorders.[66] The Lords continued to take a more conservative line upon changes to the interiors of parish churches and departures from the established liturgy than the Commons, and these differing attitudes soon led to a clash between the Houses. However, the church disturbances which followed the circulation by the Commons' committee for the recess of the controversial order of the 8 September (which sanctioned the removal of altars and all popish imagery) led the reconvened House to shelve it and warn congregations to peacefully await parliamentary reform.[67] The interiors of churches and the structure of worship were gradually changed in subsequent years, largely on the initiative of Parliament, and these changes encountered a wide variety of popular response.

The drama of some early church disorders could give a misleading impression about popular attitudes to changes in the externals of worship in London. Many incidents were protests by a section of parishioners against Laudian ceremonialism and reminders of popery rather than expressions of the dreaded advent of sectarian extremism.[68] Yet whatever their precise nature, they certainly disrupted parish unity as parishioners divided into rival factions.

The well-documented case of Allhallows Barking illustrates the divisive way in which religious differences surfaced in the 1640s. Although one of the poorer intramural parishes, its more substantial inhabitants, as happened in many other London parishes, contributed generously to the renovation and 'beautifying' of their church in the 1630s. In August 1638 the parish obeyed the call to convert its communion table into an altar and required communicants to receive the sacrament kneeling at the altar rails. Finding these changes repugnant, some parishioners petitioned the bishop for their reversal and also the removal of carved images from both the rails and above the new font. In January 1640 the bishop's chancellor, Arthur Ducke, brought the vicar, the vestry and some of the petitioners together to resolve their differences. Most of the vestry approved of the recent changes but eventually a compromise was reached with some 'of the more moderate' objectors, involving the removal of some of the more offensive images. Yet the peace of the parish was shattered in the following November when some militants took it upon themselves to saw off the wooden angels from the altar rails and carry them before the Commons. The vicar, Edward Layfield, a nephew of Laud, was also sent for by the Commons, having been denounced for ceremonialism. The vestry and other principal parishioners did not approve of these actions and defended Layfield who was not finally removed from the living until 1643. The repercussions of parish factionalism has been obscured by the deliberate later removal of pages from the vestry's records. Some of Layfield's defenders were still serving on the vestry in 1643–44 when they complied with parliamentary instructions for the abolition of superstition by taking down painted glass, cutting 'superstitious letters' out of church brasses and painting over the mural of Moses and Aaron. As vestrymen, they were able to vote down a proposal made in 1644 that parish business should be governed not by the traditional select vestry but by the voice of the whole parish. Religious radicalism assumed a different form in 1645 when some parishioners refused to pay tithes on religious grounds to the presbyterian incumbent.[69]

Other churches experienced similar divisions in the early 1640s as a wave of iconoclasm swept through the capital and surrounding country. Altars were converted into communion tables; altar rails were taken down and occasionally chopped up and burnt in the churchyard; church organs were dismantled and removed; popish images or inscriptions on windows, walls or funeral monuments were defaced; and ministers were interrupted, and even assaulted, during church services.[70] Some, and possibly a minority, of these changes were effected by a militant few of lower social status than the parish élite and acting without their authority. The altar rails in St Saviour's, Southwark, for example, were torn down on 7 June 1641 by 'sundry of the meaner sort of parishioners' with no parish officers present. The leading offenders were too poor to meet the costs of re-erecting the rails and were forced to beg the Lords for clemency. The vestrymen and other substantial St Saviour's inhabitants joined with their counterparts in St Olave's, Southwark, and St Magnus the Martyr, London, to denounce and dissociate themselves from parish militants.[71] It was from the ranks of local men of substance like these that presbyterianism was to derive much of its later strength as the only surviving bulwark against religious and social anarchy.

Despite fears that recognised authority in church and state was crumbling,[72] many parishes did not experience the impatient acts of militants but had their church interiors changed in an orderly and gradual fashion on instructions from parish officers.[73] Occasionally the latter acted to head off violence, as in the case of St Olave's, Southwark. Reluctant compliance may have been the case in St Martin in the Fields where the altar rails were carefully removed for storage in the vestry and by 1657 had been returned to the chancel.[74] Church organs were still in position and were being played in at least two London churches for most of 1643, but they were removed before the parliamentary ordinance of May 1644.[75] Conservatism in such matters was not confined to leading parishioners but was also reflected at a popular level, and Cheapside Cross became an appropriate rallying point for religious and political conservatism in the early 1640s.[76]

As the decade progressed, there was a general breakdown of parochial discipline in London and the suburbs. Church attendance became impossible to enforce and communion became a divisive rather than unifying ritual, as communicants were vetted and the numbers taking it tailed off after the middle of the decade.[77] The poor may have been hit by the declining numbers of communicants and a corresponding drop in donations towards poor relief, but collections held upon fast days and other occasions, and the distribution of money acquired from the sale of altar rails and other church furnishings, helped to compensate for this. In at least thirty-eight City parishes the clergy's income from tithes declined as some parishioners refused or neglected to make payment and, by the late 1640s, a large number of parishes were without incumbents.[78] The earlier iconoclasm may have encouraged a growing disrespect for church property. Although thefts of lead from church roofs did occur before 1640, the stealing of church plate, money and other property from St Clement Danes on the 30 May 1648, and from St Martin in the Fields on the 25 September 1649, were exceptionally shocking offences. Soldiers also had few scruples about plundering and wrecking the interiors of St Paul's and St Martin Ludgate.[79] But the biggest blow to parish morale was the existence of apparently flourishing rivals in the form of the sects.

One of the Long Parliament's earliest acts was to send for the records of Laudian persecution and secure the freedom of prisoners of conscience.[80] Persecution in the 1630s had forced religious radicalism underground or into exile, but heterodoxy at a popular level continued to plague the Laudian church in London.[81] Very few radicals took the hazardous steps into separatism; most remained outwardly conforming members of their parish church and even parishes like St Saviour's, Southwark, which acquired a radical reputation, could expect an almost universal conformity before 1640.[82] The virtual ending of the coercion of protestant consciences after 1640 brought a resurgence of religious radicalism. A militant minority did not rest content with a purge of pulpits and church interiors but turned its back upon the state church altogether and opted for separatism. While parliament was alarmed and embarrassed by the new boldness of sectaries, there could be no immediate return to suppression. Self-confessed Southwark conventiclers referred by Charles to the Lords for repression in January 1641 were simply dismissed with a warning of future severity if they remained obdurate.[83] At the same time a group of Whitechapel separatists were bailed by order of the Lords and were subsequently acquitted at a Middlesex gaol delivery.[84] There was some legal harrassment of separatists in the London area in the 1640s, as the records testify, yet the removal of some of the indictments into King's Bench, and the fining of a Westminster constable who proceeded over-zealously against two sectaries, did not encourage a sustained campaign of repression.[85]

Alarm generated by the mushrooming of sects led to exaggerations of their strength. One 1646 report claimed that there were 180 sects active in London and the City protested that there were eleven conventicles in one of its parishes alone. However, one recent estimate of the numerical strength of organised separatism in London arrives at the relatively modest figure of about 1,000 at the beginning of the 1640s and the existence of approximately thirty-six separate churches by 1646.[86] These totals do not take into account the less formal, and difficult to quantify, groupings of sects. Nevertheless, the separatists were a tiny minority of the total population of London; the crucial point is that they were a militant and organised minority, with an influence spreading far and wide. By the late 1640s, Ranters and other products of sectarian extremism were adding to the broad religious diversity of the capital and were preparing the way for the advent of the Quakers in the next decade.[87]

Both the press and pulpit proclaimed the evils of the sects as subverters of church and state and whipped up public hostility.[88] From 1643 the Assembly of Divines gave orthodox clergy a base from which to launch attacks on the sects. Many London clergy joined in the attacks and mobilised their parishioners as the issue of religious toleration divided the City politically and eventually gave control of its government to the Presbyterians. The appearance and influence of Thomas Edwards's *Gangraena* was of paramount importance in discrediting the sects.[89] Part of his case against them was their alledgedly low social origins and social subversion.[90] But the sects were generally not composed of the lowest social elements; they drew their principal strength from artisans, tradesmen and others of middle rank. The General Baptists appear to have recruited members from a lower social level in London, but even their congregations could not be described as plebeian, and the London followers of the Particular Baptists included some wealthy merchants.[91] Nevertheless, the fact remains that a small minority of the London populace rejected the spiritual leadership of their betters and sought guidance either from their own consciences or from co-religionists of equivalent social standing.

Much of our evidence on sectarian beliefs and practices comes from the highly propagandist accounts of their enemies. The association of the sectaries with the violent excesses of sixteenth-century German Anabaptists, or with the leaders of the Peasants' Revolt, conjured up a powerful image of subversion, and sectarian preachers were parodied as rejecting all superior authorities and advocating egalitarianism and community of property, wives and children.[92] Yet propaganda apart, sectarianism undoubtedly exhibited potentially subversive characteristics. Compulsory attendance at a hierarchically-controlled state church was rejected in favour of voluntary gatherings of like-minded believers who conducted congregational affairs on an egalitarian and democratic basis. When individual conscience came into conflict with congregational consensus, the dissident left, or was expelled, to seek spiritual satisfaction elsewhere.[93] Traditional parochial order was undermined by 'mechanic' preachers and disruptive sectaries. Sects, like the Baptists, rivalled the parochial system of poor relief by providing for the material welfare of their members, and the whole system was placed in jeopardy by refusals to pay tithes.[94] The smooth functioning of the basic units of City government, like the ward, was endangered when religious radicals refused to take oaths or perform other religious observances associated with the performance of duties.[95] The very basis of order, the patriarchal authority of father, husband or master, was threatened when women preached and families divided along religious lines, as the call of God took precedence over family or contractual obligations. A notorious woman preacher in London, Mrs Attaway, who was apparently conversant with Milton's tract on divorce, was reported to have deserted her unsanctified husband to share godliness with a married man.[96] Sectarianism was seen in fact as subverting conventional morality; it rejected the austere face of Puritanism with its fasts and strict sabbatarianism and condoned immorality by popularising erroneous beliefs, like Antinomianism, which were more compatible with the desires of the flesh than the stern godly discipline of Calvinism.[97] Added to all of which, there was the strong popular millenarian impulse in sectarianism, and the belief in a state of perfection realisable in this world rather than the next, with God once again conveying his message through humble folk.[98]

The growth of the sects added immeasurably to the range of beliefs and opinions current in London in the 1640s. Convictions once whispered in corners or extracted by church courts were now openly proclaimed. The range of heterodox beliefs was immense, as Edwards's painstaking catalogue demonstrates. Few of the fundamentals of religion escaped re-examination, be it the nature of the Godhead, the infallibility of scripture, the doctrine of salvation, the existence of an afterlife or the Christian moral code.[99] Baptism became an especially controversial issue and led to incidents in which the sacrament was disparaged by advocates of adult baptism.[100] The sects encouraged congregational discussions of religion in which women too occasionally added their voices.[101] The most notorious sectarian congregation in the mid-1640s was that of the General Baptist Thomas Lambe, a soapboiler, which was located in Bell Alley, in the radical neighbourhood of Coleman Street. Lambe's church met openly and admitted all comers, the curious as well as the convinced, and was enormously influential in sectarian circles. Mrs Attaway, for example, began her career in this church. The church drew sizeable crowds, especially of young men and women (like the twenty-year old weaver questioned by the authorities), and its activities had a strong revivalist and participatory element. Sometimes the preacher was chosen by a vote and open debates of points raised both during and after the sermon, either in the full congregation or in smaller groups, were quite usual. Members of other churches came to Bell Alley on Sundays after other devotions to experience its novelty and vitality. This movement of people between churches and sects carried knowledge of sectarian beliefs and practices to a wider public. After the Lord Mayor's failure to silence Lambe, the church moved to Spitalfields and was weakened by internal division.[102]

The sects inevitably became embroiled in politics, especially when toleration of their very existence became a key issue, and their militancy, personal loyalty and regular contacts made them an effective, if not always easily directed, vehicle for radical politics. Some sectaries had participated in the popular demonstrations of the early 1640s, and by the middle of the decade controversial pamphlets were being distributed by them and petitions to parliament were being drawn up and signed in their congregations. Sectaries canvassed support to oust the sitting presbyterian members in the Common Council elections of 1645, and later demonstrated at the Guildhall in favour of religious toleration. By this stage, the Levellers were giving London sects the kind of leadership they so urgently needed in the face of conservative intolerance, and they reciprocated by distributing Leveller literature and giving them both moral and material support. Thomas Lambe, for example, became a central figure in organising support for the Leveller movement. Their association with radical politics lasted until 1649 when they prepared to ignore the social and economic shortcomings of a new regime that granted them toleration.[103]

Anti-sectarian sentiment among the political élite was predictably strong but the sects also encountered violent popular hostility. Conservatives of middle social rank (the sects' own recruiting territory), along with apprentices and the lower orders, harassed and abused the religious dissidents in their midst in the 1640s and demonstrated the kind of deep popular hostility which the Quakers were also to experience in the following decade.[104] As they briefly emerged into the open in 1641, sectarian congregations were reminded of the necessity of keeping a low profile when Thomas Lambe and his fellow conventiclers at Whitechapel and Praise-God Barbone and his fellows in Fleet Street had their meetings broken up by hostile crowds. The apocalyptic preaching of Prophet Hunt about the City and Westminster was given a similar rough reception, and apprentices assaulted and ridiculed members leaving a conventicle in Leadenhall Street in March 1643. At a neighbourhood level, the Golding Lane heel-maker and his wife accused of deriding infant baptism were abused and hounded through the courts by some of their neighbours.[105]

The expression and discussion of political and religious opinions by ordinary men and women were stimulated by the highly-charged atmosphere of London in the decade. Earlier in the century, 'vulgar persons' had been forbidden to engage in discussions 'of matters above their reach and calling', and a feltmaker of St Dunstan in the West had suffered a traitor's death for voicing subversive views about the Spanish match and James I.[106] But in the 1640s Londoners enjoyed an exceptional freedom of speech, and although some who spoke out were censured (depending on changing political moods and sensitivities), those who found themselves before the courts may have been only the tip of the iceberg. Men and women who were traditionally supposed to accept without question the opinions and beliefs handed down by their superiors began to assume the courage and independence to voice their own convictions on current issues.

News and comment about the riots of May 1640 swiftly circulated by word of mouth through the conversations of apprentices and others in shops or as they moved about the capital, and some of them made no secret of where their sympathies lay.[107] Two Southwark tailors discussed the Scots' invasion and the pro-Scottish inclinations of London Puritans in a local alehouse in September 1640. A Thames waterman became so incensed at one of his passenger's insulting remarks about the recently convened Long Parliament and its supporters that he dropped him off before his destination and took no fare.[108] By 1641–2 there were complaints that religion had become a common topic for discussion in every tavern and alehouse, and that the King was also being criticised or spoken of derisively by ordinary folk.[109] Threats against the King were said to have been uttered by Lilburne in May 1641 and by the crowds that passed by Whitehall later.[110] In November 1642, a Stepney currier who had enlisted in Parliament's army expressed in a conversation at Mile End an eagerness to kill the King.[111] A quarrel developed between two neighbours in Whitecross Street in March 1643 in which a bodice-maker said that the King was 'a Traitor and his Crown was the whore of Babylon', and a brickmaker denounced Parliament.[112] A similar altercation in the previous September provoked a Westminster semptress into making derogatory remarks about the Book of Common Prayer.[113] In March 1643, a Lambeth shipwright answered a local woman's query about why 'people should speak so much against the King' when he was the Lord's anointed by allegedly saying 'what anointed is the King more than I or another man: I am as much the Lord's anointed as the King', and these 'levelling' sentiments became a local talking-point. Four women had earlier engaged in a street discussion in Lambeth about the validity of scripture and how salvation was to be achieved, and three illiterate watermen had had a radical discussion over a pot of beer about the Bible and Jesus Christ.[114]

Some of these verbal outbursts and unorthodox conversations resulted in proceedings at sessions or assizes, in King's Bench or before Parliament. Unfortunately, the gap in London sessions records in the decade means that our knowledge is largely confined to the better documented Middlesex suburbs and the south bank. A grand total of 131 men and women of below gentle rank found themselves in trouble for expressing a variety of offensive political or religious opinions in the period 1640–50 inclusive.[115] Forty-six people (or 35 per cent of the total) had uttered remarks about the King or royal family; twenty-six (or 20 per cent) had voiced unorthodox religious opinions; and fifty-nine (45 per cent) had expressed anti-parliament/parliamentarian views. Nearly three-quarters of the cases in the first category were concentrated in the first four years of the decade; remarks about royalty may have been made with greater impunity later. All but one of the cases in the second category were concentrated in the period 1641–5, with 1642 as the peak year with twelve cases. In contrast, people were liable to be proceeded against for making offensive remarks about parliament and its supporters throughout the whole period 1642–50, with the last year witnessing a peak of fourteen cases – reflecting no doubt the political sensitivity of the new regime.

Sentiments antagonistic to the King varied from general abuse of his person and authority to wishing his death. Charles was called a knave, a bastard, a papist, a stuttering fool and a murderer,[116] and his authority was disparaged as early as 1642.[117] The conviction that they were as good as, or even better than, the King was shared by a Stepney man in 1642, a Lambeth shipwright in 1643, a waterman in 1646 and a Southwark tailor in 1648.[118] A shoemaker of St Giles in the Fields declared in September 1642 'That if the King was conquered neither he nor his Children should enjoy the Crown'; a gunsmith of East Smithfield asserted in 1643 that 'there is no King and that he would acknowledge no King'; a Whitechapel cordwainer believed in 1646 'that the King was run away from his parliament, and that he was no King, neither had he a foot of land but what he must win by the sword'; and a Westminster man was accused of saying in 1647 'that the King is not King since he set up his standard'.[119] The royal family were also slandered with claims that the Queen was a whore and the royal offspring all bastards.[120] A wish to kill the King or see him dead was expressed by a Stepney currier in November 1642; by a Westminster sempstress in 1643 who believed that Charles 'was an evil and an unlawful King, and better to be without a King than have him King'; by a spinster of St Dunstan in the West in 1644 who declared 'Is there never a Felton yet living? If I were a man as I am a woman, I would help to pull him to pieces'; and by a lawyer's wife of St Andrew's, Holborn, in 1645 who intended to kill Charles.[121] A linkage between religious and political radicalism is indicated in the case of the above Westminster sempstress and a Stepney man who in 1642 believed he was 'as good a man as the king'; they were both abusers of the Prayer Book as well.

Twelve of the twenty-six instances of offensive religious remarks concerned the Anglican liturgy and a further four the clergy. The Prayer Book was denounced as popish, superstitious and idolatrous; of being like a mass book; all lies and not divine prayer but 'the scraps and scum of hell'. Everyone who 'heard and read it were damned' and the officiating clergy were Baal's and mass priests.[122] A Westminster joiner in 1644 was convinced that orthodox clergy were 'Antichristian Ministers' who taught 'Antichristian doctrine or the doctrine of Devils'.[123] Preaching under a tree was as good as, if not better than, from a church pulpit so far as a stationer and a groom were concerned in 1641 and 1642, and a Limehouse spinster declared in 1642 'that she would rather go to hear a Cart wheel creak and a dog bark' than hear the curate of Stepney preach.[124] Two shoemakers from St Martin in the Fields absented themselves after about 1643 from a parish church which they believed to be no true church.[125] Heresy or blasphemy were involved in the remaining cases. Both a Lambeth waterman and a local women

expressed the view in 1642 that 'if Christ were now upon earth as he was
before he suffered, he would be ashamed of what he had done'. The
woman also told her female listeners that the church was 'nothing but
Lime and stone, and fit for nothing but to make prisons to keep such as
you are in'; that Christ was only a carpenter's son and the Bible 'was but
a dead letter and though her father and mother were led in blindness
thereby she would not be led in that way any longer'.[126] The validity of
scripture was also denied by a Southwark woman in 1644 who called
God a liar and Christ the bastard son of Joseph the carpenter.[127] A
Golding Lane heel-maker and his wife derided the sacraments of
baptism and the eucharist, and especially the former, declaring 'that a
Cat or a Dog may be as well baptised as any Child or Children in their
Infancy'.[128] The doctrine of the Trinity was disputed by a Southwark
tailor in 1645 and in 1648 a woman who professed to being a Jew was
accused of denying that Christ was a prophet.[129] The broader signifi-
cance of these and other heterodox beliefs has been demonstrated in
Christopher Hill's pioneering work on the subject.[130]

   The comparatively large number of anti-parliament/parliamentarian
utterances may owe as much to parliamentary vigilance over potential
enemies as the relative strength of popular conservatism. In a few
instances, radical disillusionment with Parliament may have prompted
the remarks,[131] and some seem acts of bravado.[132] Most of the abuse in
this category was directed at Parliament itself and its members. Parliament was cursed and its members called rogues, roundheaded rogues
and rascals, Brownists or Puritans, rebels or traitors and thieves. They
were plunderers and imprisoners of all honest men in London; they had
murdered the King's good subjects.[133] One man hoped to see all its
members hanged and the City on fire in 1642; a Cow Cross widow in
1644 wished to see them all blown up with gunpowder; a Whitechapel
cutler in 1646 was preparing his sword to kill roundheads in an
imminent rising; a war-disabled cordwainer was ready to venture
another limb in the service of Prince Charles in July 1649; and healths
were drunk to Charles II and to the confusion of Parliament in 1649 and
1650.[134] At least a couple of people insisted that Charles I's seized
correspondence had been forged by Parliament. Sir Thomas Fairfax
was derided by a woman who also felt that parliamentary committees 'sat
to Cozen and Cheat the people'.[135] A Holywell Street butcher had a
similar low estimate of committees in 1648 and threatened to pull down
the house of a Tower Hamlets' committeeman.[136] Parliamentary
soldiers were discouraged or abused by a buttonmaker of St Martin

le Grand and a victualler of Turnmill Street in 1642 and by a vinter and
a labourer's wife, both of St Giles in the Fields, in 1644 and 1648
respectively.[137] Prominent figures were singled out for special abuse,
like Lord Saye, Sir Thomas Fairfax, Cromwell or Colonel Pride.[138]
The King's trial and execution, and the new régime, were condemned
by several men, including a tailor of St Botolph Aldgate who believed
that Charles 'was illegally put to death' and that the present régime was
'Maintained only by the Sword, And that they do seek to infringe the
liberty of the Subjects which they did formerly promise to maintain'.[139]

A comparison of the status or occupation of men accused under the
categories of, firstly, words against the King, secondly, against religion,
and thirdly, against Parliament, makes it quite clear that men of middle
social rank constituted the vast majority of cases in all three categories.[140] The main distinction would appear to be that victuallers, vint-
ners and butchers are only to be found in the third category, where they
account for 21 per cent of the males, perhaps reflecting a particular
grievance against the excise. Thirty-nine cases, or nearly 30 per cent of
the total, involve women – about 35 per cent of those in the second
category, and 30 per cent and 27 per cent of those in the first and third
categories. So far as geographical distribution is concerned, Westminster and the western suburbs account for just under a third of those in
the first and third categories, and about a quarter of the cases in the
second. The most striking differences are that there is only one instance
of verbal abuse of Parliament recorded on the south bank (while 24 per
cent of the cases in the first, and almost 35 per cent in the second
category involve south bank inhabitants), and the first category is similarly out of step with the other two so far as the northern suburbs are
concerned. The eastern suburbs are represented strongly in the first
category but are rather less important in the other two.

With only six exceptions, the accused men and women appeared
before the courts. Most were discharged, found not guilty (in four cases
because the prosecution made no case) or were required to enter
recognisances. Twenty-eight were committed to prison awaiting trial or
after sentence. There are only thirteen cases of recorded convictions
when the usual sentence was a hefty fine (there is only one instance of a
fine of £1 6s 8d, the rest vary between twenty nobles and £200 or 500
marks), and sometimes a short spell in prison. In one extreme example, a
Southwark feltmaker in 1642 was sentenced to a 100 mark fine and six
months imprisonment for denigrating the Prayer Book, and a £200 fine
and imprisonment at the king's pleasure for words against the King.[141]

Three others who had spoken violent words against the King were indicted for treason; one was acquitted and there is no record of further proceedings against the other two. Five cases were investigated upon instructions from the House of Lords and in one case of blasphemy the Commons intervened because they felt that the pillory and six months in Bridewell was an inadequate punishment.[142] The temper of the Commons is indicated in the serious consideration they gave in March 1646 to hanging Paul Best for his heretical views on the Trinity.[143] Some men and women, therefore, who freely voiced their opinions found themselves being proceeded against and, although under 10 per cent subsequently faced harsh penalties, a number had to carry the burden of a recognisance or endure a short period in custody. Many others perhaps expressed unorthodox views more discreetly, or benefitted from lapses in official vigilance, but the extent of dissident views is largely speculative.

The voicing of subversive opinions was symptomatic of a more general loosening of the normal ties of authority, and weakening of habits of social deference, which made some members of the political élite the target of abuse or defiance. Affronts to the peerage began with attacks on particular peers thought to be blocking progress on issues like Strafford's attainder, or arose from personal grudges. Anti-Strafford demonstrators were 'very rude with some of the Lords' and the Earl of Pembroke had to descend from his coach to pacify them with his hat in his hands.[144] Individual peers were verbally abused for reasons which are not always readily apparent, and a song was sung in 1646 by a Clerkenwell glover denigrating the earls of Essex, Warwick, Stamford and other peers.[145]

These attacks were soon broadened to encompass the whole of the aristocracy. A printed account of two fictional speeches about reaching an accommodation with the King attributed to the Earl of Pembroke and Lord Brooke gained widespread popular credence in London towards the end of 1642. Pembroke's alleged speech highlighted the threat to aristocratic lives, honours and fortunes from below. The Lords were now facing the consequences of their earlier appeasing of the people for 'nothing will content them, but no Bishop, no Book of Common Prayer, and shortly it will be no Lords, no Gentlemen, and no Books at all, for we have Preachers already, that can neither write nor read'. Things had reached such a pass that 'We hear every base fellow say in the street as we pass by in our Coaches, That they hope to see us afoot shortly, and to be as good men as the Lords; and I think they will be as good as their words' if peace is not quickly concluded. Lord Brooke's supposed reply compounded those fears for he saw the conflict as one between the godly and the ungodly, and believed that worldly considerations should not stand in the way. Furthermore,

We do not find that among all the Acts of the Creation, the Almighty ever made an Earl, or a Lord . . . and surely if we shall be contented for the setting forward of a good cause, to mingle our selves with the meanest of the people, for the procuring a parity in the Church, to consent to a parity in the State; and for the subduing the pride of Kings for a time, to part with the power of Noble-men, I doubt not, but when the good work in hand shall be finished, we shall be again advanced above our Brethren, according to our several Talents, and govern them according to that Rule which shall most advantage God's cause.[146]

These fictional speeches were effective propaganda, playing upon deep anxieties in the upper ranks of society, but giving such views wide currency may have inadvertently contributed to the decline of social deference .

Diligent servants of the state, like Stephen Spratt, trod upon aristocratic toes in 1643 and, in the ensuing quarrel with Lord Howard of Escrick, Spratt was reported to have widened his attack to include Lord Saye and the House of Lords in general, comparing the latter with Star Chamber, and threatening to draw upon his influence among the sectaries and London citizens against Parliament.[147] A scandalous libel against the peerage, which concluded with the words 'No more lords and yee love me, they smell of the Court', was being dispersed by a Cornhill hosier's apprentice in December 1644. In August 1648, some of the men who had enlisted under Major-General Skippon denounced the aldermen who had petitioned against Skippon being allowed to recruit, hoping 'to see some of those men that went in their gold Chains to wear halters ere Long about their Necks', and added 'all would not be well until they pulled the Lords out of the House by the ears'.[148] Other individual instances of men abusing the peerage or the House of Lords could be added,[149] but it was the Levellers who presented the most powerful case against the power and privileges of the aristocracy and the upper House.[150]

Attacks on bishops, and actions like the defacing of 'superstitious' brasses commemorating local worthies, carried wider implications for social hierarchy. When the Court of High Commission was first interrupted on the 20 October 1640, great offence was taken at the demonstrators' failure to observe social deference by demanding bluntly 'where is Wren . . . without any other title but plain Wren'.[151] The

Bishop of Lincoln was the subject of 'most uncivil speeches' uttered by a Westminster carpenter in 1641 who also wanted all JPs in England hanged.[152]. Anti-episcopal demonstrators in 1641 pelted bishops with stones as they tried to get into the Lords by water; the Bishop of Durham was assaulted by a crowd crying 'down with him'; and other bishops were assaulted or chased. Two bishops who did manage to take their seats in the Lords had to listen to the crowd outside threatening to 'cut the Bishops' corner caps', and wondering aloud at their audacity. When bishops were eventually removed from the House, the bells of St Botolph Bishopsgate rang out in celebration.[153] On the 8 May 1642, when the Bishop of Chichester stepped up into the pulpit of St Olave Jewry in his vestments to preach to a distinguished congregation which included the Lord Mayor and MPs, about a hundred protesters cried out repeatedly 'a Pope' and, having been cleared from the church by the mayor's officers, demonstrated in the street during the sermon, breaking many of the church windows and denouncing those within as being 'at Mass' and calling the Lord Mayor a papist.[154] The latter had been assaulted, and his chain broken and gown torn, earlier in the year 'by a multitude of Rude Citizens and other uncivil women' as he was returning from escorting the King back to Whitehall after his journey into the City in pursuit of the five members.[155] City aldermen and other principal citizens who had failed to contribute voluntarily to the parliamentary cause had their homes searched by order of Parliament; 'by this means', according to Clarendon, 'the poorest and lowest of the people became informers against the richest and most substantial' and frequently plundered their victims. Some of these aldermen later complained that the customary deference to their position was being ignored in their harsh treatment by men of the trained bands.[156] Other prominent individuals were verbally affronted in the streets by social inferiors, and the subjection of apprentices to the wills of their masters was undermined by defiance arising from conflicting loyalties.[157]

Women's subjection to male authority and direction was also loosened when a small minority of London women defied the conventions governing their behaviour. Women came to play a prominent part in some political demonstrations in which they appeared to be acting independently of men, as a kind of female pressure group. They began asserting some political rights, including the right to petition Parliament, and made some tentative claims of sexual equality. There is evidence of female enthusiasm for the parliamentary cause; 'some poor women' donated their 'wedding rings and bodkins' for the army's support and worked with their children on the fortifications about London. But women as a whole appear to have been divided in their attitudes to the conflict, like their male counterparts, for they were almost as likely to voice opposition to Parliament as to the King, and they were particularly prominent in the peace demonstrations of 1643. Furthermore, there is always the suspicion that their political activities were being directed by their menfolk, as was probably the case in many rural disorders in which women were involved. Their petitions may in fact have been penned by men (women were after all still massively illiterate) and men disguised in women's clothes were reported to have been instigating the female peace petitioners of August 1643 from their midst. The political activities of some women reached a peak with their support for the Levellers, but the over-riding impression is that their support was taken for granted by the movement, which never contemplated giving them a share in the franchise, but consigned them to the ranks of the vote-less with servants and alms-takers. In fact women did not openly dispute male superiority; they retained their customary deference to men when engaged in political activities and generally accepted their inferior status.[158] On the surface, the spiritual equality of the sexes inherent in religious radicalism held out greater promise for their emancipation, but women in most cases had to rest content with spiritual equality and no more. Women played their part in some of the early church disturbances; some preached and wrote about religious matters, with Katherine Chidley and Mrs Attaway earning special prominence; and there is evidence of women engaging in radical discussions about religion amongst themselves or participating in congregational debates. Although religious radicalism did not lead to female emancipation, it was still potentially subversive of the patriarchal family unit. A few women followed the dictates of their consciences rather than the spiritual direction of fathers or husbands. The Quakers were to accord women a greater degree of independence, allowing them, for example, to preach and proselytise, than seventeenth-century society as a whole would have allowed them but even they did not offer women equality.[159]

The relative freedom of the decade also encouraged the intrusion of a popular element into City politics, both at the centre and in the wards, precincts and vestries, and led to attempts to establish the government of City guilds and companies upon a more popular basis. Space does not permit more than a brief outline of these developments. The City's electoral body, Common Hall, was opened up to a wider body of opinion than previously and its standing in the constitution was enhanced. ┃The way in which Common Council assumed a new importance in the government of London, eventually challenging the dominance of the oligarchic Court of Aldermen, is already familiar.╽Yet its membership was still drawn from the upper ranks of society, with only a slight downwards movement, and it was left to the Levellers to launch a frontal assault upon the City oligarchy. There were popular stirrings in the wards where the right of freemen to choose their councillors or aldermen, or to participate in the choice of MPs, was again championed by the Levellers.[160] Parish élites in the vestries of the City and surrounding area encountered pressures for a broadening of parochial decision-making, and William Walwyn played a leading part in opening up the vestry of St James Garlickhithe.[161] There were also attempts to overturn the oligarchic control of some City guilds and companies, as the 'generality' sought the right to participate in the running of their company. As the City's governing elite were drawn from the top of these companies, these challenges from below had serious implications for the municipal power structure.[162]

The large measure of freedom enjoyed by the middle and lower ranks of London society in the 1640s eventually made possible the emergence of a political party with a mass appeal which was organised in London on remarkably modern lines.[163] The Levellers were the product of a powerful combination of great political turmoil, freedom of expression and belief, the questioning of traditional authority and popular intervention into the affairs of church and state at all levels. London provided an ideal arena for this brief popular challenge to the dominance of the political élite.

Notes

1   W. Haller, *Liberty and Reformation in the Puritan Revolution*, New York, 1955; V. Pearl, *London and the Outbreak of the Puritan Revolution*, Oxford, 1964; C. Hill, *The World Turned Upside Down: Radical Ideas during the English Revolution*, London, 1972; B. Manning, *The English People and the English Revolution*, London, 1976; M. Tolmie, *The Triumph of the Saints: the Separate Churches of London 1616–1649*, Cambridge, 1977, are the most central works on this subject.

2   For example P.R.O., SP 16/488/57; *A Collection of Several Speeches, Messages, and Answers of the King's Majesty, to both Houses of Parliament*, London, 1642, E. 145/21, pp. 50, 54, 56, 62–3, 76; *Mercurius Impartialis*, 5–12 December 1648, E. 476/3, pp. 1–2, 7.

3   W. M. Clyde, *The Struggle for the Freedom of the Press from Caxton to*

Cromwell, London, 1934, pp. 46, 295–7; F. S. Siebert, *Freedom of the Press in England 1476–1776,* Urbana, 1952, chapters VI and VII; J. Frank, *The beginnings of the English Newspaper 1620–1660,* Cambridge, Mass., 1961, chapter I; B.L., Additional MS. 11,045, ff. 27, 29; Corporation of London Records Office (henceforth C.L.R.O.), Jor. 39, ff. 69–70.

4   Siebert, *Freedom of the Press,* pp. 167, 202; Frank, *English Newspaper,* pp. 20–21, 45–6. Sixty percent of the works collected by George Thomason were published in the 1640s (G. K. Fortescue, *Catalogue of the Pamphlets, Books, Newspaper, and Manuscripts* . . . *collected by George Thomason, 1640–1661,* London, 1908, I, p. xxi).

5   S. Lambert, 'The beginning of printing for the House of Commons, 1640–42', *The Library,* 6th. ser., III, 1981, pp. 43–61; Clarendon, *The History of the Rebellion and Civil Wars in England,* Oxford, 1888, I, pp. 419–20, 428 note; Pauline Gregg, *Free-born John: A Biography of John Lilburne,* London, 1961, p. 133.

6   Siebert, *Freedom of the Press,* pp. 174–7, 179–88; Frank, *English Newspaper,* pp. 42–3, 174–5, 178, 197–81; House of Lords Record Office (henceforth H.L.R.O.), main papers, 12 May 1643 petition of Joseph Hunscot; H. R. Plomer, 'Secret printing during the Civil War', *The Library,* new series, V, 1904, pp. 374–403; *The Humble Petition and Information of Joseph Hunscot Stationer,* E. 340/15, *passim.*

7   Clyde, *The Struggle for Freedom of the Press,* p. 220; Siebert, *Freedom of the Press,* pp. 193–4, 198–9; R. Overton, *A Defence Against All Arbitrary Usurpations,* E. 353/17, p. 26.

8   J. Rushworth, *Historical Collections of Private Passages of State,* London, 1721, IV, p. 540; H.L.R.O., main papers, 4 March 1641 annexed list of unlicensed books and pamphlets; Clyde, *The Struggle for Freedom of the Press,* pp. 100–101.

9   E. Sirluck, ' "To your tents, O Israel": a lost pamphlet', *The Huntington Library Quarterly,* XIX, 1955–56, pp. 301–5; J. Taylor, *The Whole Life and Progress of Henry Walker the Ironmonger,* E. 154/29, *passim;* H.L.R.O., main papers, 30 December 1642 schedule of the names of such prisoners as are and have been committed to the Fleet since the beginning of the parliament; ibid., 25 June 1642 motion of king's counsel concerning one Walker; ibid., 22 March 1648 annexed petition of Henry Walker; *Lords Journals,* IV, pp. 182, 702; V, pp. 160, 647, 651; VI, p. 264; *Commons Journals,* II, p. 349; Frank, *English Newspaper,* pp. 80–81, 244–7.

10   This paragraph is derived from Clyde, *The Struggle for Freedom of the Press,* and Frank, *English Newspaper.*

11   H. E. Rollins, *Cavalier and Puritan: Ballads and Broadsides Illustrating the Period of the Great Rebellion 1640–1660,* New York, 1923, introduction; *Commons Journals,* V, p. 73; C.L.R.O., recognisance 31 May 1649.

12   Rollins, *Cavalier and Puritan,* pp. 20, 24, 46, 132–8, 139–43, 320–24; *Lords Journals,* IV, pp. 374, 377, 382–3; T. Edwards, *Gangraena,* pt. II, E. 338/12, pp. 155–6.

13   D. Cressy, *Literacy and the Social Order: Reading and Writing in Tudor and Stuart England,* Cambridge, 1980, pp. 72, 75–7, 124–5, 128–9, 134–5. In the case of London, the sample from which literary rates are derived is

unfortunately a small one but it accords well with other evidence (Cressy, pp. 72, 198).

14 For example *All the Memorable and Wonder-Striking Parliamentary Mercies Afforded unto our Nation, A. D. 1641 and 1642*, E. 116/49.

15 Frank, *English Newspaper*, pp. 57, 314 note; V. Pearl, 'London's counter-revolution', in G. E. Aylmer (ed.), *The Interregum: The Quest for Settlement 1646–1660*, London, 1972, p. 36; Rollins, *Cavalier and Puritan*, p. 13.

16 Above, p. 113.

17 Frank, *English Newspaper*, pp. 23, 39; Gregg, *Free-born John*, pp. 77, 140, 333; Pearl, *London*, p. 234; Clyde, *The Struggle for Freedom of the Press*, p. 237; Tolmie, *The Triumph of the Saints*, p. 151; *Lords Journals*, V, p. 597; VII, p. 97; *Commons Journals*, V, p. 428; C.L.R.O., Jor. 40, ff. 73, 78; ibid., Common Hall (minute book), II, f. 277; ibid., recognisances 9 June, 1 August and 6 September 1649; Greater London Record Office (henceforth G.L.R.O.), MJ/SR. 1014/101, 112; ibid., 1045/53; H.L.R.O., main papers, 23 January 1647 petition of master and wardens of Company of Stationers; Taylor, *The Whole Life and Progress of Henry Walker; A Petition to the People for a Christian Decision of Cases of Conscience*, E. 240/1; *The Conclusion of Lieut. General Cromwell's Letter to the House of Commons*, 669 f. 10/38; J. Canne, *Lieut. Colonel John Lilburne Tried and Cast*, E. 720/2, p. 109 note; Edwards, *Gangraena*, pt. II, p. 9.

18 Rushworth, *Historical Collections*, III, pp. 1085–6; IV, p. 248; VII, p. 747; B.L., Harley MS. 6424, ff. 69–70, 71; Gregg, *Free-born John*, pp. 80–81; *Cal. S. P. Venetian*, XXV, pp. 148–9, 225, 236–7; Clarendon, *History*, III, p. 138.

19 Victoria Library Westminster (henceforth V.L.W.), St Margaret's church-wardens' accounts, E. 28, E. 30, E. 31; Frank, *English Newspaper*, p. 273; Cressy, *Literacy*, p. 189; C. Hill, *Some Intellectual Consequences of the English Revolution*, London, 1980, pp. 46–9, 51.

20 Haller, *Liberty and Reformation*, pp. 15–6; Pearl, *London*, pp. 195, 220; A. Argent, 'Aspects of the ecclesiastical history of the parishes of the City of London 1640–49', Ph.D. thesis, University of London, 1984, chapters III and IV.

21 Tolmie, *The Triumph of the Saints*, pp. 30–1, 35, 37–8, 48–9; *Commons Journals*, II, p. 168; B.L., Additional MS. 14,828, f. 65; ibid., 6521, f. 182; *A True Relation of a Combustion, Happening, at St Anne's Church by Aldersgate . . . August 8, 1641*, E. 169/6; *His Majesty's Special Command to the Lord Mayor of London for the Sending of Precepts into the City to Suppress the Tumultuous Assemblies*, E. 179/19.

22 Tolmie, *The Triumph of the Saints*, pp. 39, 206 note 45; Rollins, *Cavalier and Puritan*, pp. 146–7; J. Taylor, *A Swarm of Sectaries and Schismatiques*, E. 158/1; id., *An Honest Answer to the Late Published Apology for Private Preaching*, E. 154/7; *A True Relation of a Combustion*, E. 169/6; *The Doleful Lamentation of Cheapside Cross*, E. 134/9, pp. 1–2; Edwards, *Gangraena*, pt. I, the epistle dedicatory.

23 *Commons Journals*, II, p. 168; V, pp. 75, 109; B.L., Sloane MS. 1467, f. 98; Tolmie, *The Triumph of the Saints*, pp. 126–7, 136–7; Edwards, *Gangraena*, pt. I, epistle dedicatory, pp. 94–5.

24 Clarendon, *History*, I, p. 448; II, pp. 319–21; *Cal. S. P. Venetian*, XXVI, p. 198; Pearl, *London*, pp. 195, 231–2, 280; J. E. Farnell, 'The social and

intellectual basis of London's role in the English Civil Wars', *Journal of Modern History*, XLIX, 1977, pp. 654, 656.

25   For example C. Burges, *Another Sermon Preached to the Honourable House of Commons now assembled in Parliament, November the Fifth, 1641*, epistle and pp. 60, 63–4; id., *The Necessity and Benefit of Washing the Heart . . . 30 March 1642*, pp. 46–7; O. Sedgewick, *England's Preservation or, a Sermon Discovering the Only Way to Prevent Destroying Judgements . . . May 25, 1642*, p. 32.

26   S. Ashe, *The Best Refuge for the Most Oppressed . . . 30 March 1642*, pp. 28–9.

27   J. Taylor, *A Swarm of Sectaries and Schismatiques*, E. 158/1, pp. 9–10; id., *An Honest Answer to the Late Published Apology for Private Preaching*, E. 154/7.

28   Tolmie, *The Triumph of the Saints*, pp. 36–7, 67–8, 181–4; *Commons Journals*, VI, pp. 175, 183.

29   K. Lindley, 'Riot prevention and control in early Stuart London', *Transactions of the Royal Historical Society*, 5th. ser., XXXIII, 1983, pp. 109–115. There were also anti-Spanish demonstrations in the early 1620s (*ibid.*, p. 112).

30   Tolmie, *The Triumph of the Saints*, p. 47; Gregg, *Free-born John*, pp. 65–6.

31   Lindley, 'Riot prevention', pp. 115–26.

32   R. Quatermayne, *Quatermayne's Conquest over Canterbury's Court*, London, 1642, pp. 20–39; B.L., Additional MS. 11,045, ff. 127–131; Rushworth, *Historical Collections*, III, p. 1086.

33   B.L. Additional MS. 6521, f. 12; Clarendon, *History*, I, pp. 264, 265 note, 269–70.

34   B.L., Harley MS. 4931, ff. 121–2; ibid., 6424, ff. 58–9; Additional MS. 37,343, f. 226; ibid., 6521, ff. 134–37; H.L.R.O., Braye MS. 18, f. 54; ibid., 2, f, 138; *Lords Journals*, IV, p. 233; Gregg, *Free-born John*, pp. 86–7.

35   Manning, *English people*, pp. 15–18, Clarendon, *History*, I, pp. 334 note, 337–8, 340; B.L., Additional MS. 37,343, f. 226; H.L.R.O., main papers, 24 November 1641 information of Robert Stephens; 27 November 1641 affidavit of Robert Stephens.

36   Manning, English people, pp. 52–70 and chapter IV; Pearl, *London*, pp. 212–3, 224–5.

37   Gregg, *Free-born John*, pp. 88–9; H.L.R.O., Braye MS. 22B, f. 153; G.L.R.O., MJ/SR. 903/55; MJ/GBR. 4/382–4, 386.

38   Manning, *English people*, pp. 95–8, 110; P.R.O., SP 16/488/27; Rushworth, *Historical Collections*, IV, pp. 483–4.

39   *London's Tears, Upon the Never Too Much to be Lamented Death of Our Late Worthy Member of the House of Commons, Sir Richard Wiseman*, 669 f. 4/46; Gregg, *Free-born John*, pp. 277–8.

40   Manning, *English people*, chapter V; Pearl, *London*, pp. 250–75.

41   *Lords Journals*, IX, pp. 376–7; *Commons Journals*, V, pp. 258–9, 277.

42   Pearl, *London*, pp. 173–4, 223; S. R. Smith, 'The social and geographical origins of the London apprentices, 1630–1660', *The Guildhall Miscellany*, IV, 1973, p. 198; Gregg, *Free-born John*, pp. 245, 249.

43   For example *A Petition of Citizens of London. Presented to the Common Council for their Concurrence*, 669 f. 10/57.

44   Pearl, *London*, pp. 230–5; *Lords Journals*, V, p. 248; *Commons Journals*, II,

pp. 885; P.R.O., SP 16/486/30, 32, 45; *The Image of the Malignants' Peace*, E. 244/12.

45 Pearl, *London*, pp. 216, 222–3; Gregg, *Free-born John*, p. 271.

46 B.L., Additional MS. 31,116, ff. 179, 259–60; ibid., 37,344, ff. 65–6; *Commons Journals*, V, pp. 179–80.

47 Rushworth, *Historical Collections*, IV, p. 634; V, pp. 21, 51–2, 562; P.R.O., PC 2/52/493–4, 518, 526–7; ibid., KB 29/289/76, 79, 90, 139. One of the suspects, Humphrey Landon of St Margaret's, Westminster, glazier, was thirty years old when the riots took place (J. Foster (ed.), *London Marriage Licences, 1521–1869*, London, 1887; A. M. Burke (ed.), *Memorials of St Margaret's Church, Westminster: The Parish Registers 1539–1660*, London, 1914, pp. 79, 352).

48 Pearl, *London*, pp. 216–7, 228–9; Clarendon, *History*, I, p. 265 note.

49 P.R.O., SP 16/486/32, 63; C.L.R.O., Jor. 40, f. 184; *The Petition of the Citizens of London to Both Houses of Parliament, Wherein is a Demonstration of the Grievances, together with their Desires for Justice to be Executed Upon the Earl of Strafford, and other Delinquents*, 669 f. 4/13.

50 For example Clarendon, *History*, I, pp. 450–51; *The Humble Petition of 15000 Poor Labouring Men, known by the name of Porters, and the Lowest Members of the City of London*, 669 f. 4/55.

51 S. R. Smith, 'Almost revolutionaries: the London apprentices during the Civil Wars', *The Huntington Library Quarterly*, XLII, 1978–9, pp. 313–28.

52 Rushworth, *Historical Collections*, V, pp. 21–3, 51–2, 110–11.

53 B.L., Additional MS. 11,045, f. 135; Pearl, *London*, pp. 196, 221, 230, 280.

54 *A Speech of Nathaniel Fiennes in answer to the Third Speech of the Lord George Digby, concerning Bishops and the City of London's Petition*, e. 196/32, pp. 1–3.

55 *Commons Journals*, II, pp. 339, 342, 354, 382; *XIIII Orders voted by Parliament*, E. 179/20; G.L.R.O., MJ/GBR. 4/384; Pearl, *London*, pp. 226–7.

56 *Commons Journals*, II, p. 415; *An Humble Declaration of the Apprentices and other Young Men of the City of London, who were Petitioners for Peace*, E. 245/2, p. 7; J. Lilburne, *London's Liberty in Chains Discovered*, E. 359/17, p. 52; *An Outcry of the Youngmen and Apprentices of London*, E. 572/13, p. 4; B.L., Additional MS. 37344, ff. 66, 83.

57 *Lords Journals*, IV, pp. 233, 491–4; *Commons Journals*, II, pp. 327, 329–31, 358; C.L.R.O., Jor. 39, f. 185; Clarendon, *History*, I, pp. 451–3.

58 Pearl, *London*, pp. 113–6.

59 *Ibid.*, pp. 200–201, 212, 236; Tolmie, *The Triumph of the Saints*, p. 48; H.L.R.O., House of Lords manuscript minute books no. 8; ibid., Braye MS. 22B, f. 153.

60 *The Third Speech of the Lord George Digby to the House of Commons concerning Bishops and the City Petition*, E. 196/30, pp. 10–11.

61 T. Warmstry, *Pax Vobis or a Charm for Tumultuous Spirits*, E. 180/24; *A Speech made by Master Waller, Esquire, in the House of Commons concerning Episcopacy*, E. 198/30, pp. 4–5; B.L., Additional MS. 31,116, f. 268; *A Declaration of Some Proceedings of Lt. Col. John Lilburne and his Associates*, E. 427/6, pp. 24–5.

62   R. Ashton, *The City and the Court 1603–1643*, Cambridge, 1979, pp. 216–7; *Commons Journals*, V, pp. 179–80; B.L., Additional MS. 37,344, f. 121.

63   Clarendon, *History*, IV, pp. 240–41; *Lords Journals*, V, pp. 490, 493, 496, 524; Rushworth, *Historical Collections*, VII, p. 1122.

64   Cressy, *Literacy*, pp. 67–70; *Commons Journals*, II, p. 892; *A Declaration of Some Proceedings of Lt. Col. John Lilburne*, pp. 13–14; Clarendon, *History*, I, pp. 419–20, 428 note.

65   B.L., Harleian MS. 4931, f. 63; Additional MS. 11,045, ff. 122–3; ibid., 6521, ff. 8–9; Allhallows Barking by the Tower, vestry minutes 1629–69, insert between ff. 25 and 26; V.L.W., E. 25 Churchwardens' accounts 1644–45.

66   P.R.O., 31/3/72 Baschet's transcripts, f. 407; *Lords Journals*, IV, pp. 133–4.

67   *Commons Journals*, II, pp. 278–81; *Lords Journals*, IV, pp. 392, 395; B.L., Sloane MS. 3317, f. 25.

68   J. P. Boulton, 'The social and economic structure of Southwark in the early seventeenth century, with special reference to the Boroughside district of the parish of St Saviour's, Southwark', Ph. D. thesis, University of Cambridge, 1983, pp. 347–8.

69   Allhallows Barking by the Tower, churchwardens accounts 1628–60, ff. 59–63, 107, 117–8, 148, 150; ibid., vestry minutes, ff. 20, 25–6, 30; G.L.R.O., DL/C/344, ff. 68–9; A. G. Matthews, *Walker Revised*, Oxford, 1948, p. 53; A. Argent, 'Aspects of the ecclesiastical history of . . . London', pp. 159–61.

70   *The Brownists' Synagogue or a Late Discovery of their Conventicles, Assemblies, and Places of Meeting*, E. 172/32, p. 2; T. May, *The History of the Parliament of England*, London, 1812, p. 75.

71   H.L.R.O., main papers, 10 June 1641 petition of certain parishioners of St Olaves and St Saviours, Southwark, and St Magnus, London; ibid., Braye MS. 19, 17 June 1641; *Lords Journals*, IV, p. 318.

72   For example *His Majesty's Special Command to the Lord Mayor of London for the sending Precepts into the City to Suppress the Tumultuous Assemblies*, E. 179/19.

73   For example, St Botolph Bishopsgate (Guildhall, MS. 4524/2, f. 61); St Botolph Billingsgate (ibid., 943/1, f. 57; 942/1, f. 155); St Margaret New Fish Street (ibid., 1175/1, vestry minutes 1 June 1641; 1176/1, churchwardens' accounts 1641–2).

74   H.L.R.O., main papers, 15 June 1641 petition of churchwardens of St Olave's, Southwark; V.L.W., F. 6, inventory 1649/50; ibid., F. 2517, ff. 179, 182.

75   Guildhall, MS. 4524/2, ff. 79–80; ibid., MS. 7882/1, ff. 195–6, 198, 215; B.L., Additional MS. 37343, f. 297.

76   B.L., Sloane MS. 3317, f. 30; *Lords Journals*, V, pp. 230, 239, 247.

77   This observation is derived from my current research into parish records in the London area.

78   A. Argent, 'Aspects of the ecclesiastical history of . . . London', pp. 159–61, 169.

79   V.L.W., B. 1055, f. 6; ibid., F. 6; C.L.R.O., Rep. 59, f. 322; Guildhall, MS. 1313/1, ff. 3–4.

80   Above p. 119.

81   Bodl., Tanner MS. 70, f. 181.

82   J. P. Boulton, 'The social and economic structure of Southwark', chapter VI and p. 357.

83   *Lords Journals*, IV, pp. 133–4; B.L., Harley MS. 6424, f. 6.

84   *Lords Journals*, IV, pp. 135, 138; B.L., Harley MS. 6424, f. 7; G.L.R.O., MJ/SR. 887/22; MJ/GBR. 4/361–2, 365, 371.

85   P.R.O., ASSI 35/84/10, m. 62; KB 29/291, mm. 53, 99; ibid., 292, mm. 5, 21, 45; ibid., 293, m. 5; ibid., 294, m. 5; ibid., 296, mm. 8–9; G.L.R.O., MJ/SR. 972/103–4, 121, 12. 6; MJ/SR. 991/149.

86   Frank, *English Newspaper*, p. 102; C.L.R.O., Jor. 40, f. 160; Tolmie, *The Triumph of the Saints*, pp. 4, 37.

87   Tolmie, *The Triumph of the Saints*, p. 84; B. Reay, *The Quakers and the English Revolution*, London, 1985, pp. 27–9.

88   For example J. Taylor, *The Anatomy of the Separatists, alias Brownists*, E. 238/14; C. Burges, *Another Sermon Preached to the Honourable House of Commons . . . November 5th. 1641*, pp. 60, 64; id., *The Necessity and Benefit of Washing the Heart*, pp. 45–7.

89   Tolmie, *The Triumph of the Saints*, pp. 130–8.

90   Edwards, *Gangraena*, pt. I, epistle dedicatory.

91   The social ranking of the sectaries is based upon the status or occupation of those sectaries appearing in legal records in the early 1640s. For the baptists see J. F. McGregor, 'The baptists: fount of all heresy', in J. F. McGregor and B. Reay (eds.), *Radical religion in the English Revolution*, Oxford, 1984, pp. 36–7.

92   *A Warning for England, Especially for London, in the Famous History of the Frantic Anabaptists*, E. 136/33; J. Taylor, *A Seasonable Lecture, or a Most Learned Oration: Disburthened from Henry Walker, a Most Judicious Quondam Ironmonger*, E. 143/13, p. 4; R. Yarlott, 'The Long Parliament and the fear of popular pressure, 1640–1646', M.A. thesis, University of Leeds, 1963, pp. 20–2.

93   McGregor, 'The baptists', pp. 40–1, 45.

94   Ibid., p. 44; *An Order from Parliament, read in Every Church . . . Also a Seditious Paper delivered to the Minister of Christ Church*, E. 181/1; Edwards, *Gangraena*, pt. II, pp. 173–4.

95   C.L.R.O., Rep. 58, f. 38.

96   McGregor, 'The baptists', pp. 47–8; Edwards, *Gangraena*, pt. I, pp. 89, 106; ibid., pt. II, pp. 10–11.

97   Edwards, *Gangraena*, pt. I, pp. 124, 135; ibid., pt. II, pp. 10, 144–5.

98   Hill, *The World Turned Upside Down*, pp. 27–9, 77; B. Capp, 'The fifth monarchists and popular millenarianism', in J. F. McGregor and B. Reay (eds.), *Radical Religion in the English Revolution*, Oxford, 1984, pp. 165–89.

99   For the range of radical ideas in the period see Hill, *The World Turned Upside Down*, passim.

100   J. Taylor, *An Honest Answer to the Late Published Apology for Private Preaching*, E. 154/7; G.L.R.O., MJ/SR. 952/56–7.

101   Edwards, *Gangraena*, pt. I, p. 85.

102   Ibid., pp. 92–5; M. Tolmie, 'Thomas Lambe, soapboiler, and Thomas Lambe, merchant, general baptists', *The Baptist Quarterly*, XXVII, 1977–8, pp. 6–7.

103   Tolmie, *The Triumph of the Saints*, chapter VII and pp. 138–43, 182–4; id., 'Thomas Lambe', pp. 8–9; Edwards, *Gangraena*, pt. I, pp. 40, 105; ibid., pt. II, pp. 8–9; *Animadversions upon John Lilburne's Two Last Books*, E. 362/24, p. 14; B.L., Additional MS. 31,116, f. 304.

104   Reay, *The Quakers*, chapter IV; the social status of the opponents of the sects is derived from both literary evidence and legal records.

105   *The Brownists' Synagogue*, pp. 5–6; *Lords Journals*, IV, pp. 135, 138; H.L.R.O., main papers, 19 January 1640/41 petition of divers of his majesty's loyal and faithful subjects, prisoners in New Prison; *The Discovery of a Swarm of Separatists, or a Leatherseller's Sermon*, E. 180/25; *A Sermon Preached Last Fast Day in Leadenhall Street*, E. 91/32; G.L.R.O., MJ/SR. 952/56–7; 956/32–3, 34–7, 215; 957/28; 958/94, 124–5; 959/22, 25; 965/35, 37, 184, 186.

106   C.L.R.O., Jor. 31, ff. 264, 341–2; ibid., sessions of oyer and terminer, 17 July 1622.

107   P.R.O., SP 16/453/96–7, 112, 112I; G.L.R.O., MJ/SR. 877/2; ibid., MJ/SBR. 6/114.

108   P.R.O., SP 16/468/89; 470/100; 472/43; *Lords Journals*, IV, pp. 614–5; H.L.R.O., Braye MS. 23C, f. 295.

109   *Religion's Enemies. With a Brief and Ingenious Relation, as by Anabaptists, Brownists, Papists, Familists, Atheists, and Foolists, Saucily Presuming to Toss Religion in a Blanket*, E. 176/7, p. 6; Taylor, *The Anatomy of the Separatists*, p. 1; *A Just Apology for His Majesty; Or, An Answer to a Late Pamphlet Entitled Behold Two Letters*, E. 154/21; *John Taylor's Manifestation and Just Vindication Against Josua Church his Exclamation*, E. 234/8, postscript.

110   Above p. 119; *The Lord George Digby's Apology for Himself*, E. 84/32, p. 11.

111   G.L.R.O., MJ/SR. 919/25.

112   Ibid., MJ/SR. 926/28; 927/3; 972/4.

113   G.L.R.O., WJ/SP/? 1644/7 (the correct date is 1642); MJ/SR. 914/173.

114   H.L.R.O., main papers, 17 March 1642/43 information of Thomas Wells and others; information of George Fuller and others; 20 March 1642/43 information of Robert Bookham and others.

115   The vast majority of cases come from the Middlesex sessions but they can be supplemented with further examples from the assizes, King's Bench and the House of Lords.

116   G.L.R.O., MJ/SR. 916/104; 919/55; 950/11; 951/32; 1001/135.

117   Ibid., 917/139; 906/3.

118   Ibid., 915/71; 1001/135; H.L.R.O., main papers, 17 March 1642/43 information of Thomas Wells and others; P.R.O., ASSI 35/89/7, m. 57.

119   G.L.R.O., MJ/SR. 915/239; 932/12; 983/31; 1006/196.

120   Ibid., 1016/23.

121   Ibid., 919/25; 927/6; 951/32; J. C. Jeaffreson, *Middlesex County Records*, old ser., III, p. 94.

122   P.RO., ASSI 35/84/6, m. 45; ibid., 10, m. 73; ibid., 84/9, m. 78; G.L.R.O., MJ/SR. 915/71; 914/172; 930/104; 895/151. On the other hand, John Wood, the minister at Knightsbridge, was presented at the Westminster sessions on the 30 September 1642 for refusing to use the Prayer Book

(G.L.R.O., MJ/SR. 914/173).
  123 G.L.R.O., MJ/SBB. 51/12.
  124 Ibid., MJ/SR. 895/90; 913/5.
  125 Ibid., 972/103, 104.
  126 H.L.R.O., main papers, 17 March 1642/43 information of George
Fuller and others; 20 March 1642/43 information of Robert Bookham and
others.
  127 B.L., Additional MS. 31,116, f. 214; ibid., 18,779, ff. 34–5.
  128 G.L.R.O., MJ/SR. 952/56–7.
  129 P.R.O., ASSI 35/87/2, m. 49; G.L.R.O., MJ/SBB. 82/10.
  130 Hill, *The World Turned Upside Down, passim.*
  131 For example G.L.R.O., MJ/SR. 1003/47.
  132 For example ibid., 1009/92.
  133 Ibid., MJ/SR. 911/27; 916/102–3; 991/68; 939/34; 977/17;
1015/96; 1016/54; 952/109; 957/43, 52; 946/14; 947/43; WJ/SP/? 1644/7;
H.L.R.O., main papers, 24 January 1643/44 information of Stephen Spratt.
  134 G.L.R.O., MJ/SR. 917/174; 925/98; 983/92; 1032/105; 1029/52;
1027/116; 1046/233.
  135 Ibid., 970/158; 994/36.
  136 Ibid., 1013/72.
  137 Ibid., 917/62; 922/93; 960/185; 1020/57.
  138 Ibid., 939/34; 1016/54; 1054/32.
  139 Ibid., 1050/352.
  140 Twenty-six of the occupations appear on Cressy's ranking of London
and Middlesex trades by illiteracy, 1580–1700 (Cressy, *Literacy*, pp. 134–5).
This small sample reveals broadly similar literacy ratings in all three categories.
  141 P.R.O., ASSI 35/84/6, mm. 45–6.
  142 Ibid., 35/85/4, mm. 1–2; B.L., Additional MS. 31,116, f. 214.
  143 B.L., Additional MS. 31,116, ff. 262–3.
  144 Ibid., 6521, ff. 134–5; ibid., 37343, f. 226.
  145 G.L.R.O., MJ/SR. 894/106; 914/105; 926/121; MJ/SBB. 45/6;
41/4; 48/6; 58/38; H.L.R.O., main papers, 21 August 1643 letter from
Stephen Spratt to Lord Howard of Escrick; 23 December 1643 information of
Henry Brodnax and John Gwinne against Stephen Spratt.
  146 *Two Speeches Made in the House of Peers, on Monday the 19 December, For,
and Against Accommodation. The one by the Earl of Pembroke, the other by the Lord
Brooke*, E. 84/35; *The Malignants' Conventicle: or, a Learned Speech Spoken by M.
Webb, a Citizen, to the rest of his Society*, E. 245/24, p. 4; *Lords Journals*, V, p. 545.
  147 H.L.R.O., main papers, 13 November 1643 note of letter concerning
Stephen Spratt; 23 December 1643 information of Henry Brodnax and John
Gwinne and annexed papers.
  148 Ibid., main papers, [9 December] 1644 copy of a scandalous libel
against the peerage; 11 August 1648 information of Richard Stobart; *Lords
Journals*, VII, pp. 91, 97, 115–6, 142; I. Gentles, 'The struggle for London in the
second Civil War', *The Historical Journal*, XXVI, 1983, pp. 298–9.
  149 For example G.L.R.O., MJ/SR. 996/57; H.L.R.O., main papers,
26 August 1648 petition of William Pendred and annexed papers.
  150 Manning, *English people*, pp. 263–9; H. N. Brailsford, *The Levellers and*

the English Revolution, ed. C. Hill, London, 1961, pp. 98, 129–30.

151   B.L., Additional MS. 11,045, f. 127.

152   G.L.R.O., MJ/SR. 894/45.

153   Clarendon, *History*, I, pp. 463 note, 464, 470–2; J. Vicars, *God in the Mount; or, England's Remembrancer*, E. 112/25, pp. 66–7; H.L.R.O., Braye MS. 23C, ff. 243–5; Guildhall, MS. 4524/2, ff. 63, 72.

154   Taylor, *The Anatomy of the Separatists*, p. 6.

155   *The King's Majesty's Demand of the House of Commons, Concerning those Members who were Accused of High Treason*, E. 131/19.

156   Clarendon, *History*, II, pp. 329–30; C.L.R.O., Rep. 56, ff. 98, 224.

157   For example G.L.R.O., MJ/SR,. 911/15; 1035/81; MJ/SBR. 7/114.

158   Above pp. 121–2, 123, 133–5; Patricia Higgins, 'The reactions of women, with special reference to women petitioners', B. Manning (ed.), in *Politics, Religion and the English Civil War*, London, 1973, pp. 179–222; B.L., Additional MS. 37343, ff. 253, 257; Rushworth, *Historical Collections*, V, p. 357; K. Lindley, *Fenland Riots and the English Revolution*, London, 1982, p. 63; K. Thomas, 'The Levellers and the franchise', in G. E. Aylmer (ed.), *The Interregnum: The Quest for Settlement 1646–1660*, London, 1972, p. 76.

159   Above pp. 117, 125, 130–1; K. Thomas, 'Women and the Civil War sects', T. Aston (ed.), *Crisis In Europe, 1560–1660*, London, 1965, pp. 317–40; McGregor, 'The baptists', pp. 47–8; Reay, *The Quakers*, p. 26.

160   Pearl, *London, passim*; R. Yarlott, 'The Long Parliament and the fear of popular pressure, 1640–1646', chapter III; *London's Liberty in Chains Discovered*, E. 359/17; J. Lilburne, *The Charters of London*, E. 366/12; *London's Ancient Privileges Unveiled, or an Extract Taken out of the Principal Charters of London*, 669 f. 13/23.

161   Argent, 'Aspects of the ecclesiastical history of . . . London', pp. 34–41.

162   G. Unwin, *Industrial Organisation in the Sixteenth and Seventeenth Centuries*, Oxford, 1904, pp. 196–210; C. Blagden, 'The stationers' company in the Civil War period', *The Library*, 5th. ser., XIII, 1958, pp. 1–17; C. O'Riordan, 'The democratic revolution in the company of Thames watermen, 1641–2', *East London Record*, 6, 1983, pp. 17–27; C.L.R.O., Rep. 59, ff. 248–9.

163   Brailsford, *The Levellers*, chapter XV.

Winstanley and freedom

Gerrard Winstanley was born in Wigan in 1609, into a middle-class puritan family of clothiers. He came to London, was apprenticed to a clothier, married and set up in business just before the Civil War. The war, severing communications between London and Lancashire, ruined him; he retired to the Surrey countryside where he herded other men's cows as a hired labourer.

The 1640s were years of religious and political turmoil – the Civil War, leading to the defeat of the King; Levellers in London; and the Army arguing for a republic and a wide extension of the parliamentary franchise. In 1647 the Army seized the King, hitherto a prisoner of Parliament, and in January 1649 he was tried and executed as a traitor to the people of England. An MP for Wigan was one of the regicides. The House of Lords was abolished, and England was proclaimed a Commonwealth. Millenarian expectations ran high: almost anything seemed possible, including the return of King Jesus as successor to King Charles. There was a ferment of political and religious discussion.

But the forties were also years of great economic hardship for the lower classes. Over the century before 1640 wages had halved. The years between 1620 and 1650, Professor Bowden has said, were among the most terrible the English lower classes have ever endured. The economic disruption of the war, leading to unemployment, was accompanied by exceptionally high taxation, billeting and free quartering of soliders, and plunder. On top of all this there was a series of exceptionally bad harvests, famine and disease. The problem of the poor was acute. Rioting crowds seized corn. Men were said to lie starving in the London streets.

In the years 1648–9 a spate of pamphlets was published advocating use of confiscated church, crown and royalist lands to provide for the poor, and even fresh land confiscations; there were those who suggested expropriating the rich and establishing a communist society. Many predicted the second coming of Jesus Christ, and foresaw a thousand-year rule of the saints in which a materialist utopia would be established on earth – egalitarian, just to the poor at the expense of the rich. So Winstanley, who brooded deeply over these matters in his poverty, was not alone. But he was the only thinker we know of to break through to a systematically worked-out theory of communism which could be put into immediate effect. More's *Utopia*, published in 1516, had been in Latin, and More rejected with horror any idea of making it accessible to ordinary people by translating it into English. But Winstanley wrote, at a time of acute social and political crisis, in the vernacular, and appealed to the common people of England to take action to establish a communist society. 'Action is the life of all', he wrote; 'and if thou dost not act thou dost nothing'.[1]

It started, as so much seventeenth-century thinking did, with a vision, in which Winstanley received the messages 'Work together, Eat bread together', 'Let Israel go free: . . . Israel shall neither give nor take hire'. Winstanley decided he must 'go forth and declare it in my action' by organising 'us that are called the common people to manure and work upon the common lands'.[2] This was two months after the execution of Charles I. Winstanley, with a handful of poor men, established a colony on St. George's Hill, near Cobham, to take symbolic ownership of the uncultivated common and waste lands. It lasted a year.

Winstanley wrote a series of pamphlets defending the Digger colony and calling on others to imitate their example. At least ten more colonies were established. In the process Winstanley elaborated a quite original theory of communism. It is not possible to do full justice to the theory as a whole since we are concerned with Winstanley and freedom; but freedom was crucial to his thinking. It had indeed been crucial for the revolutionaries from the start. 'Liberty and property' was the slogan of the moderates; 'back to Anglo-Saxon freedom' the cry of the radicals. The word 'liberty' was hopelessly ambiguous. The close association of liberty and property in orthodox Parliamentary discourse is not fortuitous, for the Latin word '*libertas*', like the French word '*franchise*', came very close to meaning a property right: a 'liberty' is something you can exclude others from. To these Norman words Winstanley preferred the more plebeian Anglo-Saxon 'freedom'. Throwing off the Norman Yoke, as John Hare argued in a pamphlet published in 1647, involved a linguistic as well as a political revolution. There was no agreement on what liberty was, or should be.

'All men have stood for freedom', wrote Winstanley;

> and now the common enemy is gone, you are all like men in a mist, seeking for
> freedom and know not where nor what it is . . . And those of the richer sort of you
> that see it are ashamed and afraid to own it, because it comes clothed in a
> clownish garment . . . Freedom is the man that will turn the world upside down,
> therefore no wonder he hath enemies.[3]

He summed up in *The Law of Freedom* (1652): 'The great searching of
heart in these days is to find out where true freedom lies, that the
commonwealth of England might be established in peace'.[4] (A few
years earlier Edward Hyde, in exile, had observed from a more conservative viewpoint that 'though the name of liberty be pleasant to all kinds
of people, yet all men do not understand the same thing by it'.)[5]

Winstanley listed four current versions of freedom; and the order in
which he discusses them is perhaps significant:

1 'Free use of trading, and to have all patents, licences [i.e. monopolies] and
   restrictions removed;' freedom for business men;
2 Freedom of conscience, no constraints 'from or to any form of worship'; the
   sort of freedom the sects called for;
3 'It is true freedom to have community with all women, and to have liberty to
   satisfy their lusts' – Ranter libertinism;
4 absolute freedom of property, for landlords and their eldest sons – the
   freedom the gentry most wanted.

Curiously, there is no mention of constitutional liberty. None of these,
Winstanley thought, are 'the true foundation freedom which settles a
commonwealth in peace'.[6]

So Winstanley was aware that his concept of freedom differed from
that of most Parliamentarians. He insisted on economic freedom for the
poor as well as the rich, on social as well as religious freedom. 'If thou
consent to freedom to the rich in the City, and givest freedom to the
freeholders in the country and to priests and lawyers and lords of
manors . . . and yet allowest the poor no freedom, thou art there a
declared hypocrite'. All men had a 'creation birth-right' of access to
cultivate the land.[7] In his final pamphlet, published in 1652 after the
defeat of the Diggers, Winstanley was quite specific: 'True freedom lies
where a man receives his nourishment and preservation, and that is in
the use of the earth . . . A man had better to have no body than to have no
food for it . . . True commonwealth's freedom lies in the free enjoyment
of the earth'.[8] Living in a preponderantly agrarian society, Winstanley
uses 'the land', 'the earth', to signify property in general; but he knew

from his own experience in Wigan and London that England was already becoming an industrial country, and he had interesting things to say about a state monopoly of foreign trade and the abolition of commercial secrets.

In 1646 the Leveller John Lilburne had asserted that 'the poorest that lives hath as true a right to give a vote as well as the richest and greatest'.[9] The Levellers were agitating for a wide extension of the parliamentary franchise. Next year there were debates at Putney in the Army Council between generals, elected representatives of junior officers and of the rank and file, as well as some London Levellers – a remarkable occasion. Discussing the parliamentary franchise, Colonel Rainborough echoed Lilburne in memorable words: – 'the poorest he that is in England has a life to live as the greatest he, and therefore ... the poorest man in England is not at all bound in a strict sense to that government that he hath not had a voice to put himself under'. This led to a long debate with Commissary-General Ireton, who argued that 'liberty cannot be provided for in a general sense if property be preserved'. If the right to a vote derived from 'the right of nature', then 'by the same right of nature' a man 'hath the same right in any goods he sees, ... to take and use them for his sustenance'. Natural right leads to communism: 'constitution founds property'.[10]

This argument nonplussed the Levellers at Putney, because most of them wanted to retain the institution of private property. William Walwyn was believed to be a theoretical communist, and the boundary line between Levellers and True Levellers (Diggers) was never clearly drawn. But Lilburne and other Levellers leaders repudiated the communism of the Diggers.[11] Many of them were prepared to exclude servants and paupers from the franchise. Winstanley, on the other hand, insisted uncompromisingly that 'the common people' are 'part of the nation'; 'without exception, all sorts of people in the land are to have freedom', not just 'the gentry and clergy'.[12]

Winstanley alone grasped Ireton's theoretical nettle. He agreed that a natural right to accumulate property was incompatible with liberty. 'There cannot be a universal liberty till this universal community be established.'[13] 'I would have an eye to property', Ireton had insisted.[14] Winstanley preferred liberty. For him the introduction of private property – and he speaks especially of property in land – had been the Fall of Man. 'In the beginning of time the great Creator Reason made the earth to be a common treasury'; and all men were equal, none ruling over another. But covetousness overcame Reason and equality together.

'When self-love began to arise in the earth, then man began to fall.'[15] 'When mankind began to quarrel about the earth and some would have all and shut out others, forcing them to be servants: this was man's fall.'[16] 'Murdering property' was founded on theft; and the state was set up to protect the property of the plunderers: 'You hold that cursed thing by the power of the sword'. Property is the devil, and to support it is 'rebellion and high treason against the King of Righteousness'.[17] Buying and selling, hiring wage labour, the laws regulating the market, are all part of the Fall.

So long as private property survives, 'so long the creation lies under bondage'. The government that maintains private property is 'the government of . . . self-seeking Antichrist', 'the government of high-waymen'.[18] Exploitation, not labour, is the curse of fallen man. Property and wage labour, Winstanley thought, must be abolished before all can enjoy freedom.

The Levellers and many in the Army argued that Parliament's victory in the Civil War over the Norman Yoke of King and landlords ought to lead to the establishment of political democracy. Winstanley held that it must lead to a restoration of economic equality. 'Everyone upon the recovery of the [Norman] conquest ought to return into freedom again without respecting persons . . . Surely all sorts, both gentry in their enclosures, commonalty in their commons, ought to have their freedom, not compelling one to work for another?' 'The laws that were made in the days of the kings . . . give freedom' only 'to the gentry and clergy; all the rest are left servants and bondmen to those task-masters'. 'If the common people have no more freedom in England but only to live among their elder brothers [landlords] and work for them for hire, what freedom then can they have in England more than we can have in Turkey or France?'[19]

This would necessitate wholesale change. 'All laws that are not grounded upon equity and reason, not giving a universal freedom to all but respecting persons, ought . . . to be cut off with the King's head'.[20] What Winstanley called 'kingly power' had survived the King: 'that top bough is lopped off the tree of tyranny, and kingly power in that one particular is cast out. But alas, oppression is a great tree still, and keeps off the sun of freedom from the poor commons still'.[21] 'Everyone talks of freedom, but there are but few that act for freedom, and the actors for freedom are oppressed by the talkers and verbal professors of freedom.'[22]

Winstanley thus insisted that formal political liberty was inadequate unless accompanied by economic freedom, by equality. When J. C. Davis says that 'to Winstanley the only freedom that mattered was freedom from economic insecurity', he is, I think, quite wrong.[23] Winstanley said, indeed, that 'free enjoyment' of the earth 'is true freedom';[24] and that heaven is a 'comfortable livelihood in the earth'. 'There cannot be a universal liberty till this community be established.'[25] But freedom for Winstanley meant intellectual as well as economic freedom, meant the rule of Reason, the beginning of civilised life for all. 'When men are sure of food and raiment, their reason will be ripe, and ready to dive into the secrets of the creation.'[26] He foresaw a commonwealth in which science would flourish. Hitherto 'fear of want and care to pay rent to task-masters hath hindered many rare inventions'. In a free commonwealth, men would be encouraged to 'employ their reason and industry'; inventions would benefit all, not just the inventor. Kingly power had 'crushed the spirit of knowledge'; now it could 'rise up in its beauty and fullness'.[27] His belief in the possibilities of democratically controlled science is one of the most attractive features of Winstanley's thought.

In his final pamphlet, Winstanley declared that 'all the inward bondages of the mind, as covetousness, pride, hypocrisy, envy, sorrows, fears, desperation and madness, are all occasioned by the outward bondage that one sort of people lay upon another'.[28] 'No true freedom can be established for England's peace ... but such a one as hath respect to the poor as well as the rich.' But economic freedom is the beginning, not the end. 'Freedom', he declared, 'is Christ in you and among you'.[29]

For Winstanley, Christ was not a person. The Biblical stories are allegories, not history. 'Whether there was any such outward things or no', he remarked nonchalantly, 'it matters not much'.[30] In a pamphlet written in his pre-communist phase, Winstanley explained that he preferred to use the word Reason rather than God, because he had been 'held in darkness' by the word God.[31] Reason is 'the great Creator', not a personal God beyond the skies but the law of the universe which will ultimately prevail among all men and women. For Winstanley, the Second Coming is 'the rising up of Christ in sons and daughters' – Christ, the spirit of Reason entering the hearts of all men and women, 'comes to set all free'. Freedom 'is Christ in you'.[32]

And what will Reason tell us? 'Is thy neighbour hungry and naked today, do thou feed him and clothe him; it may be thy case to-morrow, and then he will be ready to help thee.'[33] Reason is co-operation, and the rising of Reason in all men and women will lead to recognition of the necessity of a communist society. The ethos of existing society was the negation of co-operation, of sharing. Here Winstanley drew on his own rudimentary version of the labour theory of value:

No man can be rich, but he must be rich either by his own labours, or by the labours of other men helping him. If a man have no help from his neighbours, he shall never gather an estate of hundreds and thousands a year. If other men help him to work, then are those riches his neighbours' as well as his; for they be the fruit of other men's labours as well as his own . . . Rich men receive all they have from the labourer's hand, and what they give, they give away other men's labours, not their own.[34]

Men and women will be truly free when Reason 'knits every creature together into a oneness, making every creature to be an upholder of his fellow, and so everyone is an assistant to preserve the whole'.[35] 'To live in the enjoyment of Christ . . . will bring in true community and destroy murdering property.'[36] 'True freedom . . . lies in the community in spirit and community in the earthly treasury; and this is Christ . . . spread abroad in the creation'.[37] 'This commonwealth's freedom will unite the hearts of Englishmen together in love, so that if a foreign enemy endeavour to come in we shall all with joint consent rise up to defend our inheritance, and shall be true to one another. Whereas now the poor . . . say . . . "We can as well live under a foreign enemy working for day wages as under our own brethren, with whom we ought to have equal freedom" '.[38]

Every man subject to Reason's law becomes a Son of God. His ruler is within, whether it is called conscience, or love, or Reason, or Christ. After the Second Coming, when Reason has risen in sons and daughters, 'the ministration of Christ in one single person is to be silent and draw back' before the righteousness and wisdom in every person.[39] Religion will wither away.

But kingly power proved stronger than the Christ within. After the destruction of his communist colony in 1650, a less optimistic Winstanley asked why 'Most people are so ignorant of their freedom, and so few fit to be chosen commonwealth's officers?' His answer was that 'the old kingly clergy . . . are continually distilling their blind principles into the people and do thereby nurse up ignorance in them'.[40] He had a virulent anti-clericalism worthy of Milton. It made Winstanley almost anticipate Marx's 'opium of the people'.

'While men are gazing up to heaven, imagining after a happiness or fearing a hell after they are dead, their eyes are put out, that they see not what is their

birthrights, and what is to be done by them here on earth while they are living . . .
And indeed the subtle clergy do know that if they can but charm the people . . . to
look after riches, heaven and glory when they are dead, that then they shall easily
be the inheritors of the earth and have the deceived people to be their servants.
This . . . was not the doctrine of Christ'.[41]

'The upshot of all your universities and public preachers . . . is only to
hinder Christ from rising', 'a cloak of policy' to cheat the poor of 'the
freedom of the earth'. Only when the clergy have been deprived of their
privileged position will each of us be free to 'read in your own book, your
heart'.[42]
The 'murdering God of this world', 'the author of the creatures'
misery', who defends property and ensures that the clergy get their
tithes, is covetousness. Any external God must be rejected: the Diggers
would 'neither come to church, nor serve their God'. The true God is
within, and each man has 'his God'.[43]
Winstanley originally evisaged the transition to a communist society
in ingeniously simple and peaceful terms. The example of the Digger
community inspired ten or more similar communities in central and
southern England. Winstanley believed that 'the work of digging' is
'freedom or the appearance of Christ in the earth'.[44] 'For the voice is
gone out, freedom, freedom, freedom'.[45] The rising of Christ in men
and women would be irresistible, starting from the lowest classes. 'The
people shall all fall off from you, and you shall fall on a sudden like a
great tree that is undermined at the root.' The poor would take over and
begin to cultivate the commons and wastes everywhere.[46] Then a
universal withdrawal of wage labour would be organised. The gentry
would find themselves possessed of large estates which they were unable
to cultivate. In time, they too would be influenced by the rising of Christ
in them, would see that the only rational course was for them to throw
the lands they could not farm themselves into the common stock and
share in the advantages of a communist society. Winstanley even envisaged facilitating the transition by giving them specially favourable
compensatory terms.
It was deliciously simple; but it failed to allow for the continued
existence of 'kingly power' even after the abolition of kingship. Landlords, lawyers, clergy, all stood together to preserve the *status quo* and
their privileged position. So, by the time he published *The Law of
Freedom* in 1652, the experience of harassment, persecution, and finally
violent suppression, had finally convinced Winstanley that Christ would
be prevented from rising by lords of manors, priests, lawyers, and their

state. *The Law of Freedom* was dedicated to Oliver Cromwell: 'you have power . . . to act for common freedom if you will: I have no power'.[47] Whether or not Winstanley really hoped that Cromwell would help to set up a communist state in England, he was right in thinking that it could not be done without the support of the revolutionary Army. And Oliver had not yet adopted the conservative posture he found appropriate after 1653.

Previously Winstanley had attacked all forms of state authority and punishment. 'What need have we of imprisoning, whipping or hanging laws to bring one another into bondage?' To execute a murderer is to commit another murder.[48] But now the title of his pamphlet, *The Law of Freedom: Or, True Magistracy Restored,* shows a new recognition that the state will have to be used if kingly power is to be overcome. Winstanley looks forward to a transitional period in which 'it is the work of a Parliament to break the tyrants' bonds, to abolish all their oppressing laws, and to give orders, encouragements and directions unto the poor oppressed people of the land'. Then 'the spirit of universal righteousness dwelling in mankind' and 'now rising up' would be able to take over.[49] 'In time . . . this commonwealth's government . . . will be the restorer of long lost freedom to the creation.' But till then, landlords, priests and lawyers must be curbed; so must be the 'rudeness of the people' from which the Diggers had suffered. Christ, 'the true and faithful Leveller', 'the spirit and power of universal love' 'or the law written in the heart',[50] would not rise in all men and women as quickly as Winstanley had hoped. Meanwhile the law of the commonwealth must 'preserve peace and freedom'.[51] The battle had still to be fought, education and political education carried on (a subject on which Winstanley is very interesting). Choices had to be made. 'There is but bondage and freedom', he wrote, 'particular interest or common interest'.[52]

For some especially grave offences, the death penalty would have to be retained as a deterrent during the transitional period: and it is interesting to see what these offences were. They were murder, 'buying and selling' (which 'killed Christ' and hindered his resurrection), taking money as a lawyer ('the power of lawyers is the only power that hinders Christ from rising') or as a priest; and rape.[53]

But Winstanley was well aware that 'freedom gotten by the sword is an established bondage to some part or other of the creation'.[54] 'Tyranny is tyranny . . . in a poor man lifted up by his valour as in a rich man lifted up by his lands.'[55] Experience had taught Winstanley that a standing army separate from the people could swiftly lose its political ideals. Instead he wanted government by a really representative Parliament and magistrates, elected annually and responsible to 'their masters, the people, who chose them'. The ultimate check was that the people retained arms in their hands and had a right of insurrection.[56] Winstanley rejected in advance the theory of forcing men to be free, of dictatorship in the interests of democracy, which has defaced some later communist practice.

Winstanley's ideas were unprecedented. What is astonishing is the sophistication of his analysis, the distance he covered in the years from 1649 to 1652. At Putney, Rainborough and the Levellers could find no answer to Ireton's 'Liberty cannot be provided for in a general sense if property be preserved'. Basing political democracy on natural rights would leave no logical argument against a natural right to equality of property: the right to property derived from substantive laws, not natural rights. This was conventional wisdom by Ireton's day. Thomas Hedley had said in the Parliament of 1610 that property existed not by the law of nature but by municipal law.[57] But then, how did the state which passed these substantive laws get its authority?

Forty years later, Locke thought he had solved the problem. A right to property arises in the state of nature, anterior to the state. 'As much land as a man tills, plants, improves and can use the product of, so much is his property. He by his labour does, as it were, enclose it from the common.'[58] All men by mutual agreement then set up a state to guarantee their property: all men were property-owners. Locke's theory is all very well as an explanation of the *origins* of property, avoiding the danger of giving all men a natural right to it. But how had gross inequalities of property developed? Could they be justified? Locke attributed them to the invention of money, which allowed some men to amass more property than they needed to sustain life; and the state protected them in their unequal ownership in the interests of law and order, of social peace. But what about those with no property at all? Locke seems always to have been uneasy about this part of his argument, insisting that the poor had a *right* to subsistence in time of dearth and to maintenance in old age. What kind of right?[59]

Unlike the Levellers, Winstanley was able to answer this position, adumbrated by Ireton before being worked out by Locke. Money, buying and selling land, led to inequality. That was for Winstanley the Fall of Man. 'Thereby . . . man was brought into bondage and became a greater slave to such of his own kind than the beasts of the field were to him . . . The earth . . . was hedged into enclosures by the teachers and rulers, and the others were made servants and slaves.' Property ever since has been held 'by the power of the sword'; even if the present owners 'did not kill or thieve', yet their ancestors had done so.[60] This state of affairs can be reversed only by abolishing buying and selling which, Winstanley agreed with Locke, was the source of inequality. 'This will destroy all government and all our ministry', Winstanley imagined someone objecting; and he replied 'it is very true'.[61] It meant a total overthrow of kingly power and a reconstruction of society and the state on the basis of communal property. There was no other solution. It was a difficult programme, which could be put into effect only when Christ – the power of Reason – had risen in all men and women. Then there would be a decent society.

Winstanley seems to have had an equally effective answer to Hobbes. *Leviathan* was not published until 1651, but in 1650 Winstanley seems to be answering Hobbist arguments. He was hardly likely to have read Hobbes in Latin, but Hobbism was in the air; the economic and political situation gave rise to Hobbist theories, in others as well as in Hobbes.[62] Hobbes based the state on an original contract which all men had entered into to escape from the state of nature. In his state the competitive drives of individualistic men all roughly equal in physical strength, and enjoying equal individual rights, inevitably produced anarchy until they agreed to elevate a sovereign with, in the last resort, absolute authority. Winstanley agreed with much of Hobbes's analysis, but drew different conclusions. If you abolish competitive individualist property relations, you abolish the problem. Property was not created by sinful human nature but vice versa; so only the abolition of property could get rid of the coercive state and the preachers of sin, both of which had come into existence to protect property. Winstanley saw that Hobbes's system was based on challengeable psychological assumptions: 'This same power in man that causes divisions and war is called by some the state of nature, which every man brings into the world with him'.[63] Winstanley rejected the competitive spirit which Hobbes pushed back from his own society into the state of nature as something universal. Winstanley had a rival psychology. 'Look upon the child that is new-born, or till he grows up to some few years; he is innocent, harmless, humble, patient, gentle, easy to be entreated, not envious.' He is corrupted by the competitive world in which he grows up.[64] But Reason governs the universe; when Reason rules in man he lives 'in community with . . . the spirit of the globe'. Man stands in need of others, and others stand in need of him.

He 'dares not trespass against his fellow-creature, but will do as he would be done unto'.[65]

This strikes us as a fairly obvious criticism of the competitive psychology on which Hobbes's philosophy was based. But in the seventeenth century Hobbes seemed more difficult to refute on that plane. For his psychology was that of the almost universally accepted Calvinism, and was reinforced by the pressures of early capitalist society. Only someone who had emancipated himself from the ethos of that society (and from Calvinism) could attack Hobbes at what then seemed his strongest point.

One further point on Winstanley's refutation of Hobbes: 'Winstanley', says Dr Eccleshall, 'rejected, more fully and explicitly than any previous writer, the assumption that human nature was a fixed datum of which the established political system was the natural and invariable counterpart. Human nature . . . was an historical artefact', and was 'historically modifiable' as social relationships changed.[66] In his recognition that you *can* change human nature, Winstanley, unlike Hobbes and Locke, was in the modern world.

In the context of what mattered in the seventeenth century, a word on Filmer and patriarchialism seems necessary. His argument, that the authority of kings derives by direct descent from Adam and is therefore absolute over all subjects, seems puerile to modern readers; yet Locke felt it necessary to answer him seriously, and historians have pointed out what strong roots patriarchialism had in that society where (not to mention the Bible) the household was also the work-place (family farms, family businesses) and the father was responsible for the conduct and discipline of his apprentices and servants, no less than of his children. The father of a family indeed wielded over his dependants all the powers of the state except that of life and death. He could flog, fine and imprison his dependants. (Pepys locked up one of his maids in a cellar for the night). He was also responsible for their education, technical training, religious and moral behaviour. In the countryside, where the vast mass of the population lived, with no police force, no state educational system or social services, the authority of the head of the household could be highly beneficial as well as on occasion tyrannical. Recall too the deference still shown to fathers. In this society, where symbols mattered, Quaker sons who kept their hats on and thou'd their fathers had a painful time of it. The commandment, Honour thy father and thy mother, was regularly used in sermons and treatises discussing political obligation. As late as 1700, Mary Astell argued from the example of

1688 that if monarchial tyranny in the state was wrong, male tyranny in the family must be wrong too.[67]

The household plays an important part in the community which Winstanley sketched in *The Law of Freedom*. But he totally rejected the political conclusions which Filmer drew from the authority of heads of households. Authority for Winstanley is based on the social functions which the father performs and acceptance of them by his dependants. The only justification of authority is 'common preservation . . . a principle in everyone to seek the good of others as himself without respecting persons'. For a magistrate to put self-interest above the common interest 'is the root of the tree of tyranny', which 'is the cause of all wars and troubles'. 'A true commonwealth's officer is to be . . . chosen . . . by them who are in necessity and judge him fit for that work', just as 'a father in a family is a commonwealth's officer because the necessity of young children chose him by joint consent'. The chain of authority goes upwards from the family to the parish or town, each of which is governed by elected officers, to MPs – all to be chosen annually. The implied contract is 'Do you see our laws observed for our preservation and peace, and we will assist and protect you'. And these words 'assist' and 'protect' imply the rising up of the people by force of arms to defend their laws and officers against 'any invasion, rebellion or resistance', or any who 'are fallen from true magistracy'[68] – for example, by trying to restore private property. So the paternalism of the society, which Filmer used to justify absolute monarchy, becomes for Winstanley an argument for communities in his ideal state to defend their rights.

Only one of his contemporaries seems to have entered directly into controversy with Winstanley. This was Anthony Ascham. In 1648 he published *A Discourse Wherein is examined What is particularly lawfull during the Confusions and Revolutions of Government*. In the following year, after the execution of Charles I, an expanded version appeared under the title *Of the Confusions and Revolutions of Governments*. This included a new chapter called 'The Originall of Property'. 'Some authors of this age', Ascham said, 'by a new art of levelling, think nothing can be rightly mended or reformed unless the whole piece ravel out to the very end, and that all intermediate greatness betwixt kings and them should be crumbled even to dust'. Such men say 'the law enslaves one sort of people to another. The clergy and gentry have got their freedom, but the common people are still servants to work for the other'. 'I wonder not so much at this sort of arguing', Ascham continued patronisingly, 'as to find that they who have such sort of arguments in their mouths should have spades in their hands'.[69] The reference to the Diggers could hardly be more explicit.

Ascham's arguments against Winstanley are rather disappointing. He was critical of what he took to be the Digger's primitivism. In Hobbist vein he argued that the state of nature would have been a state of perpetual war. It was inequality that 'perfectly bred dominion, and that [bred] property'. Men are bound by the contract which got them out of this state of nature and legitimised private property. Significantly perhaps, in view of Locke's later argument, Ascham followed his chapter on property with another inserted chapter 'Of the Nature of Money'. Property, Ascham thought, had good as well as evil consequences: 'that some faultlessly lead indigent lives in a state is no argument of tyranny in property, but of the ill use of it'. The rich 'are unhappier than the poor', who do not suffer from diseases like gout and the stone.[70] It is possible that he wrote this chapter in rather a hurry!

My claims for Winstanley are being pitched high, setting him up against in some respects the greatest political thinkers to emerge from the fertile soil of the English Revolution – the Levellers, Hobbes, Filmer, Ascham, Locke. One remains – James Harrington. Both Winstanley and Harrington recognised the economic basis of society and of political change. Russell Smith speculated seventy years ago that Harrington might even have been influenced by Winstanley. It is an interesting coincidence that Richard Goodgroom, who signed one of the Digger manifestoes in 1649, wrote a tract (probably in 1654) which incorporates many of the ideas elaborated in Harrington's *Oceana* two years later.[71]

Harrington argued that the land transfers of the century before 1640 necessitated a commonwealth – by which he meant a state ruled by property-owners, who alone constitute 'the people'. 'Robbers or Levellers', servants and paupers, cannot be free and so are excluded from the franchise, and representation in Harrington's ideal state would be tilted to favour the well-to-do. Harrington himself disliked anything like the oligarchy which complete freedom for capitalist development was to produce in eighteenth-century England. He thought to safeguard against oligarchy by two devices: an agrarian law – no one to inherit more than £2000 per annum – and secret ballot to prevent the domination of elections by money.

Harrington dedicated *Oceana* to Oliver Cromwell in 1656, when it seemed as little likely that the Lord Protector would establish an 'equal commonwealth' as it was likely in 1652, when Winstanley dedicated *The*

Law of Freedom to him, that he would establish a communist society. In this sense, both writers were utopians. Harringtonianism was very influential in the later seventeenth and eighteenth centuries, when England was (in Harringtonian terms) not a monarchy but a commonwealth headed by a prince. Harrington was interpreted as arguing that the men of property *ought* to rule, thus justifying the Whig oligarchy; and his prediction that a commonwealth would be far more effective than absolute monarchy 'for increase', for aggressive colonial expansion, proved well founded.[72]

Complete freedom for private property was incompatible with Harrington's 'equal commonwealth' – as Winstanley could have told him. Winstanley rejected Harrington's starting point no less than he did that of Hobbes, from whom Harrington no doubt derived it. For Harrington, reason taught self-interest, not co-operation. (Primary allegiance is due to ourselves, Ascham thought).[73] Whether Winstanley's system would have proved any more workable than Harrington's is debatable; unlike Cromwell, Winstanley was never tested by having to exercise power;[74] but at least he had faced head on the intellectual problems which made Harrington's 'equal commonwealth' utopian.

Winstanley is arguably the most intellectually respectable and consistent of the great political theorists who emerged from the English Revolution. (Milton cannot be included in this context, since he was not an original political thinker). Central to Winstanley's vision was his argument that 'there cannot be a universal liberty till this universal community be established'.[75] True freedom and true equality can be guaranteed only when 'community . . . called Christ or universal love' rises unimpeded in sons and daughters and casts out 'property, called the devil or covetousness'.[76]

Winstanley failed; but his writings justify the words he prefixed to one of his Digger pamphlets:

When these clay bodies are in grave, and children stand in place,
This shows we stood for truth and peace and freedom in our days.[77]

Notes

1   G. Winstanley, *The Law of Freedom and Other Writings,* Cambridge, 1983, pp. 127–8. See G. E. Aylmer, 'The religion of Gerrard Winstanley' in J. F. McGregor and B. Reay (eds.), *Radical Religion in the English Revolution,* Oxford, 1984; C. Hill, 'The Religion of Gerrard Winstanley', *Past and Present Supplement 5,* 1978; K. V. Thomas (ed.), 'A Declaration . . . [from] Iver, *Past and Present,* 42, 1969; D. W. Petegorsky, *Left-Wing Democracy in the English Civil*

War, London, 1940.

2   G. H. Sabine (ed.), *The Works of Gerrard Winstanley*, New York, 1941, pp. 190, 194, 199.

3   Winstanley, *The Law of Freedom*, p. 128.

4   *Ibid.*, p. 294.

5   Edward Hyde's Commonplace Book, 1646–7, quoted by F. Raab, *The English Face of Machiavelli. A Changing Interpretation, 1500–1700*, London, 1964, p. 148.

6   Winstanley, *The Law of Freedom*, p. 294.

7   *Ibid.*, pp. 129, 306.

8   *Ibid.*, p. 295.

9   Lilburne, *The Charters of London*, 1646, quoted in D. M. Wolfe (ed.), *Leveller Manifestoes of the Puritan Revolution*, New York, 1944, p. 14.

10   A. S. P. Woodhouse (ed.), *Puritanism and Liberty*, London, 1938, pp. 53, 58, 69, 73. (2nd. ed., London, 1950, reprinted 1973.)

11   See my *The World Turned Upside Down*, Harmondsworth, 1975, p. 119.

12   Winstanley, *The Law of Freedom*, pp. 182, 116.

13   Sabine, *op. cit.*, p. 199.

14   Woohouse, *op. cit.*, p. 57.

15   Winstanley, *op. cit.*, pp. 77–8, 193.

16   Sabine, *op. cit.*, p. 424.

17   Winstanley, *op. cit.*, pp. 85, 99, 120–1, 141, 222, 266–8; Sabine, *op. cit.*, p. 201.

18   Winstanley, *op. cit.*, pp. 244, 306–7.

19   Sabine, *op. cit.*, pp. 287–8.

20   *Ibid.*, p. 288.

21   Winstanley, *op. cit.*, p. 166.

22   *Ibid.*, p. 129.

23   J. C. Davis, 'Gerrard Winstanley and the restoration of true magistracy', *Past and Present*, 70, 1976, pp. 78, 92.

24   Winstanley, *op. cit.*, p. 296.

25   Sabine, *op. cit.*, p. 199.

26   Winstanley, *op. cit.*, pp. 365–6.

27   *Ibid.*, pp. 355–6.

28   *Ibid.*, p. 296.

29   *Ibid.*, pp. 128–9.

30   *Ibid.*, p. 232.

31   Sabine, *op. cit.*, p. 105.

32   Winstanley, *op. cit.*, pp. 216, 128; Sabine, *op. cit.*, pp. 114–15, 162, 204–5, 225.

33   Winstanley, *The Saints Paradice*, 1648?, p. 123.

34   Winstanley, *Law of Freedom*, p. 287.

35   Sabine, *op. cit.*, p. 105.

36   Winstanley, *op. cit.*, p. 222.

37   *Ibid.*, p. 129.

38   Sabine, *op. cit.*, p. 414.

39   Winstanley, *op. cit.*, pp. 222, 227; Sabine, *op. cit.*, p. 162.

40   Winstanley, *op. cit.*, p. 324.

41 *Ibid.*, pp. 353–4.
42 Sabine, *op. cit.*, pp. 238–42, 213–14.
43 Winstanley, *op. cit.*, pp. 138, 144, 196–8, 225–6, 271–2, 307–8, 310, 379; Sabine *op. cit.*, pp. 197, 434.
44 Thomas, *op. cit.*, pp. 57–60; Sabine, *op. cit.*, p. 437.
45 Winstanley, *op. cit.*, p. 217.
46 *Ibid.*, p. 203.
47 *Ibid.*, p. 285.
48 Sabine, *op. cit.*, p. 193, 283; cf. p. 197, and Winstanley, *op. cit.*, p. 192.
49 Winstanley, *op. cit.*, pp. 340, 312.
50 *Ibid.*, pp. 199, 203–4, 312.
51 *Ibid.*, p. 222.
52 *Ibid.*, p. 342.
53 *Ibid.*, pp. 171, 366, 383, 388; Sabine, *op. cit.*, p. 238.
54 Winstanley, *op. cit.*, p. 190.
55 Sabine, *op. cit.*, p. 198.
56 Winstanley, *op. cit.*, pp. 318–20.
57 E. R. Forster (ed.), *Proceedings in Parliament, 1610*, New Haven, Conn., 1966, II, pp. 189, 194–6.
58 Locke, *Two Treatises*, ed. P. Laslett, Cambridge, 1967, Second Treatise, p. 325.
59 Locke's views are usefully summarised in J. Dunn, *Locke*, Oxford, 1984, especially pp. 29–41. They were perhaps not altogether original. Aquinas described appropriation as a dictate of natural reason and denied that uncorrupted reason dictated communal ownership (Beryl Smalley, '*Quaestiones* of Simon of Henton' in R. W. Hunt, W. A. Pantin, and R. W. Southern (eds.), *Studies in Medieval History Presented to F. M. Powicke*, Oxford, 1948, p. 219.).
60 Winstanley, *op. cit.*, pp. 77–8, 99.
61 *Ibid.*, p. 243.
62 Cf. *The World Turned Upside Down*, appendix I; Q. Skinner, 'Conquest and Consent: Thomas Hobbes and the Engagement Controversy', in G. E. Aylmer (ed.), *The Interregnum: The Quest for Settlement, 1646–1660*, London, 1972.
63 Winstanley, *op. cit.*, p. 268. cf. p. 309.
64 *Ibid.*, p. 269.
65 Sabine, *op. cit.*, pp. 109–12; Winstanley, *The Saints Paradice*, p. 123.
66 R. Eccleshall, *Order and Reason in Politics: Theories of Absolute and Limited Monarchy in Early Modern England*, Oxford, 1978, pp. 174–6.
67 Mary Astell, *Some Reflections upon Marriage*, 1706, preface. The work was first published in 1700. For Filmer, see Laslett's Introduction to *Patriarcha and other Political Works of Sir Robert Filmer*, Oxford, 1949.
68 Winstanley, *op. cit.*, pp. 314–20.
69 Ascham, *Of the Confusions*, pp. 18–19.
70 *Ibid.*, pp. 20–5. Ascham was assassinated in 1650 by royalist exiles when he was acting as agent for the parliamentary Commonwealth in Madrid.
71 H. F. R. Smith, *Harrington and his Oceana*, Cambridge, 1914. For Goodgroom see J. G. A. Pocock (ed.), *Political Works of James Harrington*, Cambridge, 1977, pp. 11–12, 58.

72   See my *The Experience of Defeat: Milton and Some Contemporaries*, London, 1984, ch. 10, section 5.
73   Ascham, *Of the Confusions*, pp. 106–7.
74   See Roger Howell on Cromwell, pp. 25–44, above.
75   Sabine, *op. cit.*, p. 199.
76   Winstanley, *op. cit.*, p. 268.
77   *Ibid.*, p. 125.

Notes on contributors

Warren L. Chernaik

Warren L. Chernaik is Senior Lecturer in English at Queen Mary College, University of London, and has taught at a number of universities in Great Britain and America. He is the author of *The Poet's Time. Politics and Religion in the Work of Andrew Marvell*, Cambridge, 1983, and *The Poetry of Limitation: A Study of Edmund Waller*, New Haven and London, 1968. His current project, 'Sexual Freedom and its Discontents: From Rochester to Richardson', is due for completion (optimistically) in 1986.

Thomas N. Corns

Dr Thomas N. Corns was educated at Brasenose and University Colleges, Oxford, and the Maximiliananeum Foundation, Munich. He is the author of *The Development of Milton's Prose Style*, Oxford, 1982, and (with B. H. Rudall) of *Computers and Literature: A Practical Guide*, (1985), as well as articles and papers, mainly on the literature of the English Civil War. He is the Reviews Editor of *Prose Studies* and the Honorary Secretary of the Association for Literary and Linguistic Computing. Since 1975 he has been a lecturer in the Department of English of the University College of North Wales, Bangor.

Christopher Hill

Christopher Hill was Master of Balliol College, Oxford from 1965 to 1978 and subsequently Visiting Professor at the Open University (1978–1980). His many publications on seventeenth-century England include *The Economic Problems of the Church*, Oxford, 1956; *Society and Puritanism in Pre-Revolutionary England*, London, 1964; *The World Turned Upside Down*, London, 1972; *Milton and the English Revolution*, London, 1977; and *The Experience of Defeat. Milton and Some Contempo-*

raries, London, 1984.

Roger Howell Jr

Roger Howell, Jr is Professor of History at Bowdoin College, Brunswick, Maine. A graduate of Bowdoin College and of Oxford University, where he was a Rhodes Scholar, he was a Junior Research Fellow at St John's College, Oxford before joining the Bowdoin faculty in 1964. From 1969–1978 he was President of Bowdoin College. He is the author of seven books and numerous articles, mostly on seventeenth-century England.

William Lamont

Professor of History, and Dean of the School of Cultural and Community Studies, in the University of Sussex. His published works include *Marginal Prynne*, London, 1963; *Godly Rule*, London, 1969; *Richard Baxter and the Millennium*, Brighton, 1979; (with C. Hill and B. Reay) *The World of the Muggletonians*, London, 1983.

Keith Lindley

Keith Lindley is Senior Lecturer in History at the University of Ulster at Coleraine. He was an undergraduate at the University of Manchester, where he also obtained the degrees of MA and PhD. He was previously Assistant Lecturer in History at Magee University College, Derry, and Lecturer in History at the New University of Ulster. His publications include *Fenland Riots and the English Revolution*, London, 1982 as well as a number of articles, and he is currently writing a book on popular movements and disturbances in London during the English Revolution.

R. C. Richardson

Dr Richardson is a graduate of Leicester and Manchester Universities and since 1977 has held the post of Head of the History/Archaeology Department at King Alfred's College, Winchester. In 1982 he was Visiting Professor at the University of Southern Maine. His publications include *Puritanism in North-West England*, Manchester, 1972; *The Debate on the English Revolution*, London, 1977; and (with T. B. James) *The Urban Experience. English, Scottish and Welsh Towns 1450–1700,*

Manchester, 1983. He is co-editor of the journal *Literature and History*.

G. M. Ridden

Geoffrey Ridden is Principal Lecturer in English at King Alfred's College, Winchester, and Course Director of the B.A. Honours course in English with Associated Subjects. He is a graduate of the University of Leeds, where he also obtained the degree of M.Phil. He has held teaching Posts at the University of Ghana, the University of Durham, Westfield College, London, and University College, London; he has also been Visiting Professor at the University of Wisconsin, Eau-Claire. His publications include *Studying Milton*, 1985, as well as a number of articles and book reviews.

Selected bibliography

Introduction

R. Ashton, *The English Civil War. Conservatism and Revolution 1603–1649*, London, 1978.

G. E. Aylmer (ed.), *The Interregnum. The Quest for Settlement 1646–1660*, London, 1972.

G. E. Aylmer (ed.), *The Levellers in the English Revolution*, London, 1975.

A. E. Barker, *Milton and the Puritan Dilemma*, Toronto, 1942.

C. Blitzer (ed.), *The Commonwealth of England. Documents of the Civil Wars, the Commonwealth and Protectorate*, New York, 1963.

M. Butler, *Theatre and Crisis 1632–1642*, Cambridge, 1984.

J. T. Cliffe, *The Puritan Gentry. The Great Puritan Families of Early Stuart England*, London, 1984.

G. R. Cragg, *Freedom and Authority. A Study of English Thought in the Early Seventeenth Century*, Philadelphia, 1975.

S. R. Gardiner, *History of England 1603–42*, new ed., 10 vols., London, 1894.

C. Geisst, *The Political Thought of John Milton*, London, 1984.

C. Hill, *The Experience of Defeat. Milton and Some Contemporaries*, London, 1984.

C. Hill, *Milton and the English Revolution*, London, 1977.

C. Hill, *Puritanism and Revolution*, London, 1958.

C. Hill, *The World Turned Upside Down*, London, 1972.

C. Hill, *Writing and Revolution in Seventeenth-Century England (Collected Essays vol. I)*, Brighton, 1985.

W. Lamont and Sybil Oldfield (eds.), *Politics, Religion and Literature in the Seventeenth Century*, London, 1975.

P. Malekin, *Liberty and Love*, London, 1981.

B. Manning, *The English People and the English Revolution*, London, 1976.

J. S. Morrill (ed.), *Reactions to the English Civil War 1642–1649*, London, 1982.

G. Parry, *Seventeenth-Century Poetry: the Social Context*, London, 1985.

C. A. Patrides and R. B. Waddington (eds.), *The Age of Milton. Backgrounds to Seventeenth-Century Literature*, Manchester, 1980.

Mary Radzinowicz, *Toward Samson Agonistes*, Princeton, 1978.

R. C. Richardson, *The Debate on the English Revolution*, London, 1977.

G. M. Ridden, *Studying Milton*, London, 1985.

Isabel Rivers, *The Poetry of Conservatism*, Cambridge, 1973.

A. Sinfield, *Literature in Protestant England 1560–1660*, London, 1983.

K. W. Stavely, *The Politics of Milton's Prose Style*, New Haven, Conn., 1975.

D. Underdown, *Pride's Purge. Politics in the English Revolution*, Oxford, 1971.

A. S. P. Woodhouse (ed.), *Puritanism and Liberty*, 2nd ed., London, 1950, reprinted 1973.

Oliver Cromwell and English liberty

Writings and speeches of Cromwell
T. Carlyle, *The Letters and Speeches of Oliver Cromwell*, ed. S. C. Lomas, 3 vols., London, 1904.
W. C. Abbott (ed.), *Writings and Speeches of Oliver Cromwell*, 4 vols., Cambridge, Mass., 1937–1947.

Bibliographical sources
W. C. Abbott, *A Bibliography of Oliver Cromwell*, Cambridge, Mass., 1929.
P. H. Hardacre, 'Writings on Oliver Cromwell since 1929', in E. C. Furber (ed.), *Changing Views on British History*, Cambridge, Mass., 1966.
D. Underdown, 'New ways and old in early Stuart history', in R. Schlatter (ed.), *Recent Views on British History: Essays on Historical Writing Since 1966*, New Brunswick, 1984.

General works
M. Ashley (ed.), *Cromwell*, (*Great Lives Observed*), Englewood Cliffs, 1969.
M. Ashley, *The Greatness of Oliver Cromwell*, London, 1957.
E. Barker, *Oliver Cromwell and the English People*, London, 1937.
C. H. Firth, *Oliver Cromwell*, London, 1900.
C. H. Firth, *The Last Years of the Protectorate 1656–1658*, 2 vols., London, 1909.
Antonia Fraser, *Cromwell, Our Chief of Men*, London, 1973.
S. R. Gardiner, *Cromwell's Place in History*, London, 1897.
S. R. Gardiner, *History of the Great Civil War 1642–1649*, 4 vols., London, 1893.
S. R. Gardiner, *The History of the Commonwealth and Protectorate*, 4 vols., London, 1903.
C. Hill, *Oliver Cromwell 1658–1958*, London, 1958.
C. Hill, *God's Englishman: Oliver Cromwell and the English Revolution*, London, 1970.
R. Howell, *Cromwell*, London, 1977.
R. S. Paul, *The Lord Protector*, London, 1955.
I. Roots, *The Great Rebellion 1642–1660*, London, 1966.
I. Roots (ed.), *Cromwell: A Profile*, New York, 1973.
C. Veronica Wedgwood, *Oliver Cromwell*, London, 1973.
B. Worden, *The Rump Parliament 1648–1653*, Cambridge, 1974.

Christian liberty in Marvell and Milton

A. Barker, *Milton and the Puritan Dilemma*, Toronto, 1942.
W. L. Chernaik, *The Poet's Time. Politics and Religion in the Work of Andrew Marvell*, Cambridge, 1983.
T. N. Corns, 'Milton's quest for respectability', *Modern Language Review*, LXXVII, 1982.

D. Danielson, *Milton's Good God. A Study in Literary Theodicy*, Cambridge, 1982.

J. Dunn, *The Political Thought of John Locke*, Cambridge, 1969.

Barbara Everett, 'The shooting of the bears', in R. L. Brett (ed.), *Andrew Marvell. Essays on the Tercentenary of his Death*, Oxford, 1979.

Zera S. Fink, *The Classical Republicans*, Evanston, 1945.

M. Fixler, *Milton and the Kingdoms of God*, London, 1964.

W. Haller (ed.), *Tracts on Liberty in the Puritan Revolution*, 3 vols., New York, 1934.

A. W. Harrison, *Arminianism*, London, 1937.

C. Hill, *God's Englishman: Oliver Cromwell and the English Revolution*, Harmondsworth, 1972.

C. Hill, *Milton and the English Revolution*, London, 1977.

C. Hill, *The World Turned Upside Down*, Harmondsworth, 1975.

J. S. Hill, *John Milton. Poet, Priest and Prophet*, London, 1979.

J. Illo, 'The misreading of Milton', in Lee Baxendall (ed.), *Radical Perspectives in the Arts*, Harmondsworth, 1972.

M. Kelley, *This Great Argument*, Princeton, 1941.

M. Kelley (ed.), *Milton. Complete Prose Works*, VIi, New Haven, 1973, editor's introduction.

T. Kranidas, *The Fierce Equation. A Study of Milton's Decorum*, The Hague, 1965.

T. Kranidas, 'Milton's *Of Reformation*: the politics of vision', *English Literary History*, XLIX, 1982.

Barbara Lewalski, 'Milton: political beliefs and polemical methods, 1659–60', *Publications of the Modern Language Association of America*, LXXIV, 1959.

J. Mazzeo, *Renaissance and Seventeenth-Century Studies*, New York and London, 1964.

A. Milner, *John Milton and the English Revolution*, London, 1981.

Annabel M. Patterson, *Marvell and the Civic Crown*, Princeton, New Jersey, 1978.

J. G. A. Pocock, *The Machiavellian Moment*, Princeton, New Jersey, 1975.

J. G. A. Pocock and R. Ashcraft, *John Locke*, Los Angeles, 1980.

Isobel Rivers, *The Poetry of Conservatism, 1608–1745*, London, 1975.

B. Sharratt, 'The appropriation of Milton', *Essays and Studies*, 1982.

E. Sirluck, 'Milton's political thought: the first phase', *Modern Philology*, LXI, 1964.

E. Sirluck (ed.), *Milton. Complete Prose Works*, II, New Haven, 1959, editor's introduction.

Q. Skinner, *The Foundations of Modern Political Thought*, 2 vols., Cambridge, 1978.

Q. Skinner, 'The ideological context of Hobbes's political thought', *Historical Journal*, IX, 1966.

K. W. Stavely, *The Politics of Milton's Prose Style*, New Haven, Conn., 1975.

J. Tully, *A Discourse on Property. John Locke and his Adversaries*, Cambridge, 1980.

J. M. Wallace, *Destiny His Choice. The Loyalism of Andrew Marvell*, Cambridge, 1968.

A. S. P. Woodhouse (ed.), *Puritanism and Liberty*, 2nd ed., London, 1950, reprinted 1973.

Pamphleteering

P. Collinson, *The Religion of Protestants*, Oxford, 1982.

A. Fletcher, *The Outbreak of the English Civil War*, London, 1981.

W. Haller, *The Rise of Puritanism*, New York, 1938.

W. Haller, *Liberty and Reformation in the Puritan Revolution*, New York, 1955.

W. Haller and G. Davies (eds.), *The Leveller Tracts 1647–1653*, New York, 1944.

C. Hibbard, *Charles I and the Popish Plot*, Chapel Hill, North Carolina, 1983.

C. Hill, *Milton and the English Revolution*, London, 1977.

C. Hill, *The World Turned Upside Down*, London, 1972.

W. K. Jordan, *The Development of Religious Toleration in England*, III: from *The Convention of the Long Parliament to the Restoration 1640–1660*, London, 1938.

W. Makey, *The Church of the Covenant 1637–1651*, Edinburgh, 1979.

B. Manning (ed.), *Politics, Religion and the English Civil War*, London, 1973.

C. B. Macpherson, *The Political Theory of Possessive Individualism*, Oxford, 1962.

J. F. McGregor and B. Reay (eds.), *Radical Religion in the English Revolution*, Oxford, 1984.

J. S. Morrill (ed.), *Reactions to the English Civil War*, London, 1982.

C. Russell (ed.), *The Origins of the English Civil War*, London, 1973.

A. Sharp (ed.), *Political Ideas of the English Civil War*, London, 1983.

M. Tolmie, *The Triumph of the Saints*, Cambridge, 1977.

D. Underdown, *Pride's Purge*, Oxford, 1971.

D. D. Wallace, Jnr., *Puritans and Predestination: Grace in English Protestant Theology 1525–1695*, Chapel Hill, North Carolina, 1982.

M. Walzer, *The Revolution of the Saints*, London, 1966.

A. S. P. Woodhouse (ed.), *Puritanism and Liberty*, 2nd ed., London, 1950, reprinted 1973.

The freedom of reader-response

H. N. Brailsford, *The Levellers and the English Revolution*, ed. C. Hill, London, 1961.

T. N. Corns, 'Obscenity, slang, and indecorum in Milton's English prose', *Prose Studies*, III, 1980.

T. N. Corns, *The Development of Milton's Prose Style*, Oxford, 1982.

T. N. Corns, W. A. Speck, and J. A. Downie, 'Archetypal mystification: polemic and reality in English political literature, 1640–1750', *Eighteenth-Century Life*, VII, 1982.

J. Egan, *The Inward Teacher: Milton's Rhetoric of Christian Liberty*, Seventeenth-Century News Editions and Studies, University Park, Pennsylvania, 1980.

S. E. Fish (ed.), *Seventeenth-Century Prose: Modern Essays in Criticism*, New York, 1971.

S. E. Fish, *Self-Consuming Artifacts*, Berkeley, Los Angeles and London, 1972.

J. M. French, *The Life Records of John Milton*, New Brunswick, 1949–58.

Pauline Gregg, *Free-born John. A Biography of John Lilburne*, London, 1961.

C. Hill, *Milton and the English Revolution*, London, 1977.

T. Kranidas, ' "Decorum" and the style of Milton's Antiprelatical Tracts', *Studies in Philology*, LXII, 1965, reprinted in S. E. Fish (ed.), *Seventeenth-*

Century Prose. Modern Essays in Criticism, New York, 1971.

M. Lieb, 'Milton's *Of Reformation* and the dynamics of controversy', in M. Lieb and J. T. Shawcross (eds.), *Achievements of the Left Hand. Essays on the Prose of John Milton*, Amherst, Mass., 1974.

D. Masson, *The Life of John Milton*, 6 vols., London, 1859–94.

A. Milner, *John Milton and the English Revolution*, London, 1981.

D. Norbrook, *Poetry and Politics in the English Renaissance*, London, 1985.

K. W. Stavely, *The Politics of Milton's Prose Style*, New Haven, Conn., 1975.

Joan Webber, *The Eloquent 'I'. Style and Self in Seventeenth-Century Prose*, Madison, Wisconsin, 1968

London and popular freedom

H. N. Brailsford, *The Levellers and the English Revolution*, ed. C. Hill, London, 1961.

D. Cressy, *Literacy and the Social Order: Reading and Writing in Tudor and Stuart England*, Cambridge, 1980.

J. E. Farnell, 'The social and intellectual basis of London's role in the English Civil Wars', *Journal of Modern History*, XLIX, 1977.

J. Frank, *The Beginnings of the English Newspaper 1620–1660*, Cambridge, Mass., 1961.

I. Gentles, 'The struggle for London in the second Civil War', *The Historical Journal*, XXVI, 1983.

Pauline Gregg, *Free-born John: A Biography of John Lilburne*, London, 1961.

W. Haller, *Liberty and Reformation in the Puritan Revolution*, New York, 1955.

Patricia Higgins, 'The reactions of women, with special reference to women petitioners', in B. Manning (ed.), *Politics, Religion and the English Civil War*, London 1973.

C. Hill, *The World Turned Upside Down: Radical Ideas During the English Revolution*, London, 1972.

K. Lindley, 'Riot prevention and control in early Stuart London', *Transactions of the Royal Historical Society*, 5th. ser., XXXIII, 1983.

J. F. McGregor and B. Reay (eds.), *Radical Religion in the English Revolution*, Oxford, 1984.

B. Manning, *The English People and the English Revolution*, London, 1976.

C. O'Riordan, 'The democratic revolution in the company of Thames watermen, 1641–2', *East London Record*, 6, 1983.

Valerie Pearl, *London and the Outbreak of the Puritan Revolution*, Oxford, 1964.

Valerie Pearl, 'London's counter-revolution', in G. E. Aylmer (ed.), *The Interregnum: The Quest for Settlement 1646–1660*, London, 1972.

Valerie Pearl, 'Change and stability in seventeenth-century London', *The London Journal*, V, 1979.

H. E. Rollins, *Cavalier and Puritan: Ballads and Broadsides Illustrating the Period of the Great Rebellion 1640–1660*, New York, 1923.

F. S. Siebert, *Freedom of the Press in England 1476–1776*, Urbana, Ill., 1952.

S. R. Smith, 'Almost revolutionaries: the London apprentices during the Civil Wars', *The Huntington Library Quarterly*, XLII, 1978–9.

K. Thomas, 'Women and the Civil War sects', in T. Aston (ed.), *Crisis in Europe,*

1560–1660, London, 1965.

M. Tolmie, 'Thomas Lambe, soapboiler, and Thomas Lambe, merchant, general baptists', *The Baptist Quarterly*, XXVII, 1977–8.

M. Tolmie, *The Triumph of the Saints: The Separate Churches of London 1616–1649*, Cambridge, 1977.

Winstanley and freedom

J. Alsop, 'Gerrard Winstanley's later life', *Past and Present*, 82, 1979.

G. E. Aylmer, *'Englands Spirit Unfoulded, or an Incouragement to take the Engagement:* a newly discovered pamphlet by Gerrard Winstanley', *Past and Present*, 40, 1968.

G. E. Aylmer, 'The religion of Gerrard Winstanley' in J. F. McGregor and B. Reay (eds.), *Radical Religion in the English Revolution*, Oxford, 1984.

C. H. George, 'Gerrard Winstanley: a critical retrospect' in C. R. Cole and M. E. Moody (eds.), *The Dissenting Tradition: Essays for Leland Carlson*, Athens, Ohio, 1975.

P. H. Hardacre, 'Gerrard Winstanley in 1650', *Huntington Library Quarterly*, XXII, 1958–59.

T. W. Hayes, *Winstanley the Digger: A Literary Analysis of Radical Ideas in the English Revolution*, Cambridge, Mass., 1979.

C. Hill, 'The religion of Gerrard Winstanley', *Past and Present Supplement* 5, 1978.

C. Hill, *The World Turned Upside Down*, London, 1972.

O. Lutaud, *Winstanley: Socialisme et Christianisme sous Cromwell*, Paris, 1976.

D. W. Petegorsky, *Left-Wing Democracy in the English Civil War*, London, 1940.

G. H. Sabine (ed.), *The Works of Gerrard Winstanley*, New York, 1941.

D. C. Taylor, *Gerrard Winstanley in Elmbridge*, Elmbridge, Surrey, 1982.

K. Thomas, 'Another Digger broadside', *Past and Present*, 42, 1969.

K. Thomas, 'The date of Gerrard Winstanley's *Fire in the Bush*', *Past and Present*, 42, 1969.

G. Winstanley, *The Law of Freedom and Other Writings*, Cambridge, 1983.

P. Zagorin, *A History of Political Thought in the English Revolution*, London, 1954.

Index